The

BUDGET
TRAVEL

Handbook

The
BUDGET
TRAVEL
Handbook

Pat Yale

Horizon Books

British Library Cataloguing in Publication Data
Yale, Pat (Patricia), 1954-
  The budget travel handbook.
  1. Inexpensive travel
  I. Title
  910.4

  ISBN 1 85461 001 5

Typeset by PDQ Typesetting, Stoke-on-Trent
Printed and bound in Great Britain by
The Guernsey Press Co. Ltd., Guernsey, Channel Islands.

Contents

Introduction

THE THRILLS AND SPILLS OF BUDGET TRAVELLING

There is certainly nothing new in people's desire to see the world; however, travelling was once the preserve of the wealthy and has only recently become part of everyday life for ordinary people. Indeed, as aircraft have improved and charter planes have proliferated, it has come to seem as if the annual two weeks in the sun is everybody's birthright.

People's travelling habits have definitely changed. More families take a second winter sun or skiing holiday, with the odd short break at home or abroad as well. Travellers are casting their eyes further afield, with countries like China and Peru, which were once as remote as the moon, now as firmly stamped on the tourist globe as Israel and Turkey.

The travel market is booming as never before, but not all its clients are flush with money. Budget travellers come in many shapes and sizes — for example, the unemployed head of a household, people with children and those in poorly paid work or on student grants may be strapped for cash, however short their time away from home. Others start out with more money but want to economise so that they can stay away longer. In between fall the bulk of holidaymakers whose funds may be sufficient for their needs but who still like to feel they're getting good value for money. This book is aimed at all those people who, for whatever reason, wish to see the world as economically as possible, although its main emphasis is on the needs of long-haul independent holidaymakers.

Lack of funds is not necessarily a barrier to travelling, provided you choose your time and destination carefully. In fact having to stick to a limited budget can have positive advantages since it forces you into closer contact with local people than if you're flying first class and staying in luxury hotels. There's a special pleasure to be had in trying out local transport, sampling local dishes and getting to grips with the plumbing in modest hotels. You are more likely to be invited into people's homes, offered lifts and taken along to weddings, and you may well discover bargain souvenirs when shopping away from the main tourist crowd.

However, budget travelling also has its drawbacks and those with least to spend often need to take the most care that they're not putting their health at risk by eating and sleeping in unhygienic surroundings. They also need to be on guard against muggers and thieves who frequently concentrate their attentions on just those run down parts of town where bargain accommodation is available.

Some of the cheapest and most interesting places to visit in the world are also places where the local population is desperately poor, wages are low and decent jobs pitifully scarce. In such circumstances, successful budget travelling places certain obligations on visitors. For example, in 1984 I visited Farafra which lies in the New Valley of the Western Desert, well away from Egypt's main tourist trail. It had one small hostel which charged visitors a pound a night and two shops which kept unpredictable hours and stocked only a limited range of goods. Life proceeded at a snail's pace and age-old traditions of hospitality, disrupted elsewhere by the advent of mass tourism, flourished. Strangers were welcomed with open arms.

There I bumped into an English holidaymaker who planned to survive in Egypt for as long as possible on £10.00 a week. In an effort to do this he would hide from the hotelier when he called for his rent each evening. Every day he would wander around the village, making sure he was invited to dine at least twice with local families. As soon as I arrived he urged me to join him, but Farafra could hardly survive as a quiet haven from the crowds of the Nile Valley if all its visitors were so grasping.

In other words, the fact that your budget is tight does not absolve you from responsibility towards local people into whose communities you stray as a guest. In many countries revenues from tourism form a vital part of the national income and visitors are as welcome as their contribution to the national economy. The cherished distinction which budget travellers like to make between themselves and package tourists goes unrecognised by local people, particularly outside Europe and the West. All they see are visitors with money to travel overseas while they may not even be able to feed and clothe their children decently. In such circumstances it is unforgivable to take while offering nothing in return.

Budget travelling brings wonderful opportunities to meet people and experience ways of living that may be totally different from those that you are used to. In a book this length it would be impossible to give detailed advice on how to travel cheaply in every individual country; that is the job of guidebooks and those most suitable for shoestring travellers are indicated in the text. This book suggests where and when to travel if you have limited funds, with the emphasis on those parts of the world which are either close at hand, cheap to reach or economical to stay in. It also recommends ways to make your travel budget stretch as far as possible when doing your shopping and how to turn your experiences into money on your return. There are even hints on how to cope in notoriously expensive countries like Japan and pointers to situations in which cost-cutting may result in false economy.

Since there is no convenient shorthand term for all those areas with a similar standard of living to our own, the phrases 'Europe' and 'the West' should be taken to refer to Western Europe, North America, Australia, New Zealand and Japan. Prices quoted are for cheaper categories of transport; economy class on planes, second class, or lower, on trains. Where this is not the case the text will say so. Including prices is always difficult because of continued inflation around the world, so where prices are given in the text they should not be taken as absolute but as an indication of the scale of cost involved. This is vital if you are to choose the best destination for your particular budget and if your plans are to take into account all the 'extras' which the brochures tend to skim over. I have also included lists of all sorts of hazards and benefits for budget travellers, but again these cannot be comprehensive given the number of countries in the world. The lists are there for guidance and I have pointed out where you should go for the latest information on your chosen destination.

Throughout the text the airlines' three letter currency codes (FFR for French Francs, IRL for Irish pounds and so on) have been used as a convenient shorthand. For those not familiar with this convention they are all decoded in Appendix 3. Where prices are quoted in currencies other than sterling, I have put the approximate sterling equivalent as of June 1989 in brackets. Obviously, to calculate the precise equivalent you would need to find out the latest exchange rate for that currency.

In preparing this book I have been very grateful for all the information provided by the National Tourist Offices in London and by Press Officers too numerous to name individually. I was also ably assisted by the staff of Thomas Cook in Broadmead and Queens Rd, Bristol, including two of my old students, Emma Davis and Anna Jones. To them, many thanks. I am also very grateful to Maggie Crimmins for proof-reading the text for me, and to Kathy McDermott of Bristol Central Reference Library for checking the endless addresses. Thanks are also due to my parents for being so understanding over my urge to quit steady employment whenever a faraway country beckoned. Then there are all those people with whom I've travelled and without whose support and companionship I would not have survived. If any of them pick up this book they will know who they are, but in particular I would like to mention Mark who set me off on my wanderings in the first place and Lesley who has shared many of them with me.

A word of caution
The travel world is vast and ever-changing. Borders open and close, prices go on rising, health and visa requirements alter constantly. Whilst every care has been taken in the preparation of this book you should always check and double-check everything with airlines, consulates,

tourist offices, and so on, before committing yourself. Neither the author nor the publishers can accept legal responsibility for errors, however caused, which appear in this book.

Pat Yale

1

How to Plan Your Trip Cheaply

There are plenty of sources of free information to help you decide where to go for your holiday. These include:

- Public libraries.
- Specialised libraries.
- General travel agents.
- Specialist travel agencies and travel organisations.
- Tourist offices.
- Travel magazines.
- Seminars and film shows.

PUBLIC LIBRARIES

Most towns have at least one **central** and several **branch** libraries. Books are shelved according to the **Dewey decimal system** of classification and the numbers on page 14 are particularly useful to travellers.

Remember that some larger books may appear on separate shelves, although they will still be classified according to the same system.

Most central libraries also have a **reference section** where you can consult books but not take them away. Again the Dewey classification numbers should be your guide. The reference library may have different opening hours to the main library.

If your library does not stock the book you want, you may be able to obtain it from another library through the **Inter-Library Loan Scheme**. To request a book you fill out a form and pay a small administration fee (usually about 30p). The library will let you know when it has found a copy of the book. Be prepared for a wait; it can take months to get hold of particularly popular books.

You can often borrow maps including Ordnance Survey maps of the UK from a library as well.

Most libraries stay open at least one night a week for the benefit of people who are at work all day. They also open on Saturdays, but frequently close for extended bank holidays.

SPECIALISED LIBRARIES

If you are planning to travel off the beaten track, a local library may not be able to supply all the information you need. However there are other possibilities:

Where to find useful books – the Dewey decimal system

Regions

Africa	916
North America	917
South America	918
Arabia	915
Asia	915
Australia	919
Great Britain	914
Europe	914

Types of transport

Air transport	387.7
Bus transport	388.3
Train transport	385
Road transport	388
Hovercraft	629.3
Railways	625
Stations	725
Canals	797.1
Ports	387.1

Health and care

Medicine	610
Health and contraception	613
Travel safety	614.86

Working holidays

VSO	338.91
Working abroad	331.1
and	331.34

Accommodation

Camping	796.54
Caravans	796.79
Hotels	647.94
Kibbutzim	301.34

Outdoors

Backpacking	796.54
Equipment	685.53
Cameras	771.3
Hiking and walking	796.51
Mountaineering	796.42
Orienteering	796.42
Game reserves	639.95

Geography and reference

Cartography	526.8
Physical geography	910.02
Atlases	912
Encyclopaedias	032

Types of holiday

Exploration	910.9
Holidays	394.26
Recreation	790.1
Tourism and travel	910.4
Voyages	910.4

- **The Royal Geographical Society**, 1 Kensington Gore, London SW7 2AR (Tel: (01) 589 5466) has a **Map Room** which is open to the public from Monday to Friday from 1000 to 1700. This is useful if you need to consult maps of remote regions, although their main library is only open to Fellows of the Society.

- **The Expedition Advisory Centre (EAC)** shares the Royal Geographical Society's address and is open during the same hours. The Centre was set up to help people planning scientific or youth projects abroad. It provides access to previous **expedition reports** and other unpublished material, as well as offering a mail order book service. If you send £3.00 to the Information Officer giving details of your plans, the EAC can provide **notes for expeditions** to single countries. These include useful address lists, references, lists of guidebooks and details of other recent expeditions to the same area.

- If you book your trip through **Trailfinders**, 42-48 Earls Court Road, London W8 6EJ, you will be able to use their basement library full of books and pamphlets. There are even desks so you can make notes on the spot.

- The London Office of **Campus Travel**, London Student Travel, 52 Grosvenor Gardens, London SW1W 0AG (Tel: (01) 387 3611) also has a **travel library**, where books can be borrowed for £1.00.

GENERAL TRAVEL AGENTS

Many budget travellers avoid high street travel agencies, thinking that they only offer information about costly flights and package holidays. In fact agencies like Thomas Cook can provide details of rail and shipping services worldwide. They have information about discount air, coach and train services although they may make a service charge to book some of these for you. They also keep details of visa costs and information on current health regulations worldwide. In fact, one call to a good agent can save a considerable sum in postage and phone costs, especially if you live outside London.

Bear in mind that travel agents are often busy. If they have time they may help with a complex enquiry, but you should expect to pay a service charge for lengthy quotations; usually this charge will be offset against the cost of any booking made. Travel agents may be prepared to let you consult some of their books, especially during mid-morning or mid-afternoon when they are least busy. Useful manuals to consult include:

- *ABC Guide to International Travel*: This lists the addresses of **overseas embassies** in the UK and has an alphabetical sequence of countries giving information about **visas**, **inoculations**, **currency regulations**, **voltages**, **banking hours**, and so on. It is published quarterly, so be careful with visa and health information. Check with the appropriate embassy if in the slightest doubt.

- *ABC Passenger Shipping Guide*: A monthly publication, this lists schedules and fares for **ferries**, **shipping services** and **cargo ships** throughout the world. It also gives the addresses of all the shipping lines in the UK.

- *ABC World Airways Guide*: A monthly publication, this lists all **scheduled flights** throughout the world, together with information about airports, minimum connecting times, baggage allowances, and so on. A second volume contains **airline addresses**. There is also an ABC guide showing the main airline flight paths throughout the world which could be useful for route planning.

- *ABC Worldwide Hotel Guide*: This gives the **prices** and **phone numbers** of hotels all over the world. It also indicates which **reservation offices** they use and lists all their phone numbers.

- *St James Press Holiday Guides*: One Guide is published for the summer season and one for the winter. They list all the **holidays** on offer in tour operators' brochures, together with lead-in prices and details of hotels used. Information in the main section is listed alphabetically by country, but there is also a section at the back which lists holidays according to themes—for example, safaris, winter sports, and so on. You can use this manual to check whether other operators are offering a holiday at the same hotel and then compare their prices. There is also a UK edition which includes information on camping, caravanning, self-catering and short break holidays.

- *St James Press Travel Directory*: A yearly publication, this lists the addresses of all ABTA **travel agents** and **tour operators** together with the addresses of all airlines, shipping companies, car hire firms, and so on, in the UK.

- *Thomas Cook European Timetable*: This contains timetables for principal **train journeys** throughout Europe and **shipping services** in the North Sea, Baltic and Mediterranean. It is invaluable for anyone travelling on an Inter-Rail card. The timetable also contains information on visa requirements, currency regulations, temperatures, and so on, and a list of Thomas Cook and Wagons-Lit offices in Europe which is useful if you lose your travellers cheques. It is published monthly and is on sale in all Thomas Cook shops for £4.95. Details of summer services appear in the June to September issues, with advance timetables from February to May. Winter services appear from October to May, with advance timetables in August and September.

- *Thomas Cook Overseas Timetable*: This contains **timetables** for main train journeys throughout the world. It is published six times a year and is on sale at Thomas Cook shops for £5.95.

- *Thomas Cook Railpass Guide*: This contains details of all railpasses in Europe, Australia, Canada, India, Japan, Malaysia, New Zealand, South Africa and the USA. It costs £1.65 and is available from Thomas Cook in Peterborough; it can be sent to you for £1.90 (see address at the end of this list).

- *Agents' Hotel Gazetteer*: Although travel agencies have very little information about budget price hotels, they do keep the *Hotel Gazetteer* which lists the hotels used by the main tour operators and gives an unbiased description of their position in relation to main roads, and so on. It is published in four main volumes, covering main European resorts, major European cities, Alpine resorts and North American resorts. The publishers are CHG Travel Publications.

- *Official Hotel and Resort Guide (OHRG)*: Published in four regularly updated volumes, this American manual lists all the world's **major hotels**, their facilities, prices and booking procedures. It is useful if you have decided to book a 'value for money' hotel in somewhere like India. The OHRG is produced by News Group Publications.

- *TTG Travel Trade Directory*: This contains the addresses of **ABTA tour operators**, **trade press papers**, **tourist offices** and so on.

- *ABTA/ANTOR World Travel Guide*: A glossy volume with detailed information on every country in the world, including where to go, what paperwork is required, and so on.

If your travel agency doesn't have any of these books you could try a reference library. Failing that, their **publishers' addresses** are:

ABC Travel Guides Ltd
World Timetable Centre
Church Street
Dunstable
Bedfordshire LU5 4HB

St James Press Guides
5-11 Worship Street
London EC2A 2AY

Thomas Cook Ltd
Timetable Publishing Office
PO Box 36
Thorpe Wood
Peterborough PE3 6SB

CHG Travel Publications
Waterside House
West Common
Gerrards Cross
Bucks SL9 7QS

TTG Travel Trade Directory
Morgan-Grampian Book
  Publishing
40 Beresford Street
London SE18 6BQ

News Group Publications
One Park Avenue
New York
NY 10016

Travel agencies really come into their own when you want to book cheap package holidays. They can call on computer data banks of information and extra manuals like the *Hotel Gazetteer* as well as on a wide selection of brochures. **Lunn Poly**, in particular, specialises in package holidays and should be able to help with any enquiry.

For information on **cheap flights** high street travel agencies are still a good place to start, and in some cases their offers will match those of anyone else. However, for rock-bottom prices you usually need to track down a non-IATA agency or **bucket shop** and the majority of these are in London. (See '**How to Reach Your Destination Without Busting Your Budget**')

SPECIALIST TRAVEL AGENCIES AND TRAVEL ORGANISATIONS

Trailfinders

This is a specialist travel agency of particular interest to people who want to venture outside Europe. Unlike bucket shops, Trailfinders is licensed by IATA and ABTA. This means that its flight offers, however cheap, are not usually rock-bottom. However, Trailfinders tickets are covered by IATA protection and can be bought without any special precautions. Trailfinders is at 42-48 Earls Court Road, London W8 6EJ, and has the following phone numbers and opening hours:

Transatlantic and European Flights: (01) 937 5400	Monday to Saturday: 0900-1800 Sunday (telesales only): 1000-1400
Long-haul Flights and Adventure Travel: (01) 938 3366	Monday to Friday 0900-2100 Saturday: 0900-1800 Sunday (telesales only): 1000-1600
American Express Foreign Exchange: (01) 938 3444	Monday to Friday 0900-1300 and 1400-1700 Saturday: 1000-1300 and 1400-1600
Information Centre and Travellers' Library: (01) 938 3444	Monday to Saturday: 0900-1800
Medical Advice and Immunisation Centre: (01) 938 3999	Monday to Friday: 1000-1300 and 1330-1630

It is best to phone first since you really only need to visit if you intend to arrange a complex itinerary. Try and avoid calling between 0900-1000 and 1230-1400 when their lines tend to be congested. It also saves time and money to ring the appropriate departmental number and to quote your booking reference immediately if you have already made a reservation.

Like Thomas Cook, Trailfinders is a one-stop travel shop where you can buy travel insurance, travellers cheques, and foreign currency (from an American Express sub-branch), and get your inoculations and advice on health overseas. Trailfinders also has a mail order service for travel books and maps (22% charge for postage and packing) and will post up to three travel brochures to you without charge.

STA Travel
This is another specialist travel agency which also belongs to IATA and ABTA and has four main offices:

74 Old Brompton Road,
London SW7 3LQ
Tel: (01) 581 1022
Telesales for long-haul flights.

25 Queens Road,
Bristol BS8 1QE
Tel: (0272) 294399

117 Euston Road,
London NW1 2SX
Tel: (01) 581 8233
Telesales for Europe.

38 Sidney Street,
Cambridge CB2 3HX
Tel: (0223) 66966

There are also STA Travel sub-offices at the University of London Union, Queen Mary College, Kings College, London School of Economics, Imperial College, Goldsmiths College, Ealing College, Middlesex Polytechnic, Brunel University and the University of Kent. Transworld Travel, 19 High Street, Oxford OX1 4AH (Tel: (0865) 240547), also sells STA Travel products.

STA offers a programme of cheap flights around the world and can also provide information on tours and accommodation. Again you do not need to queue to make an enquiry; there is a postal enquiries service which you can use by writing to STA FREEPOST, London SW7 3BR. Their brochures contain a standard enquiry form, but if you do not use this, remember to let them know if you are a student or under 26 or 35 in case discounts are available.

STA Travel also publishes a *Travellers' Handbook* summarising its services which can be picked up in any STA Travel shop. It also produces leaflets on different areas of the world, describing what STA Travel offers. The shops also sell a limited range of guidebooks and a good insurance policy for long-stay travellers.

There are also STA Travel offices overseas. Any of the UK offices will provide you with their addresses and details of the services they offer.

Campus Travel

This is a chain of agencies specialising in travel for students and young people and with a range of cheap air fares on offer. They also sell **Eurotrain tickets**. There are Campus Travel offices in Bristol, Dundee, Glasgow, Liverpool, London, Manchester, Oxford and Cambridge and sub-branches in many YHA Adventure Shops. Their head office is at 52 Grosvenor Gardens, London SW1W 0AG (Tel: (01) 387 3611).

There are Campus Travel offices overseas in Brussels, Paris, Athens, Dublin and New York.

Wexas International

This is a club-cum-travel agency for independent travellers. It publishes a *Discoverers* brochure of journeys to more unusual destinations which have often been put together by well-known specialist tour operators such as Guerba Expeditions for Africa, Hann Overland, and so on. If you make enquiries about any of these trips you will be sent a dossier of more detailed information to help you decide if they are what you want. Wexas also screens regular **film shows** in London where a rep is available to answer questions, and publishes its own **cheap flights programme**. Annual membership of Wexas costs £30.67. For this you receive regular information on special offers, three copies of *The Traveller* and the chance to buy *The Travellers' Handbook* at a reduced price. Wexas is at 45 Brompton Road, Knightsbridge, London SW3 1DE (Tel: (01) 589 3315).

Odyssey Consultants

This is not quite a travel agency but gives advice to independent travellers. Budget travellers might think its minimum £20.00 consultancy fee too steep and the £40.00 per hour service charge out of the question. However the latter fee is, to some extent, negotiable and if you are pressed for research time and have specific complex questions, it might just be worthwhile. Odyssey provide potential clients with a lengthy questionnaire which acts as a useful checklist for planning. They also produce a newsletter full of up-to-date snippets of information. Their current address is Suite 55, Chesham House, 150 Regent Street, London W1R 5FA (Tel: (01) 352 6951/439 6288).

Travellers' Interests

This is a tour operator specialising in trips to the Red Sea and Egypt. It intends to set up a club to facilitate the exchange of information for independent, long-haul travellers. Unfortunately when this book went to press plans were still rather hazy. If all goes well Travellers' Interests will also offer mail-holding services, and will help its members find publishing outlets for articles about their travels. If you are interested, phone (01) 310 0932 for an update on the situation.

Tourist offices and embassies

Most countries with a tourist trade have a tourist office in London and these are a valuable source of information when planning a trip. In particular they are good at offering suggestions for routes and places to visit.

However, most tourist offices are better at providing data on upmarket hotels than they are on the budget end of the market. Postal enquiries tend to attract standard information packs; if you want to find out about a specific question, then a visit may be necessary, in which case be warned that the United States Travel and Tourism Administration is not open to personal callers at all.

Tourist Offices provide some information on visas and work permits but for more details about the costs and conditions attached to different types of visa you should consult the relevant embassy or consulate, again usually in London (see **Appendix 1** for addresses of tourist offices and embassies). Many tourist offices, including those of Singapore, Jamaica and the individual states of Canada, provide excellent free maps.

World Travel Market

If you live in London and want to obtain information from a number of different tourist offices, pay a visit to the **World Travel Market** which takes place at Olympia early in December every year. Although some days are only open to members of the travel trade, the public is welcome at the weekend. Most tourist offices and many tour operators, airlines and major travel agencies have stands there, so it is a wonderful source of information.

TRAVEL MAGAZINES

Newspaper and magazine articles can often inspire you to visit a particular destination, but for more detailed coverage the following travel publications are useful:

TNT

TNT is published weekly and distributed free through bins outside Central London underground stations. Each issue contains features on travel destinations, with facts and figures on how to reach them. These are usually very up-to-date and are useful if you plan to visit the places featured. There are also several pages of *Travel Talk*—tit-bits of assorted information, some of it culled from travelling readers. Information on visa requirements is mainly aimed at Australians and New Zealanders. Major currency exchange rates are listed and TNT carries adverts for cheap air fare outlets. Quarterly subscriptions cost £9.00, yearly subscriptions £22.00. Contact TNT at 52 Earls Court Road, London W8 6EJ (Tel: (01) 937 3985).

Trailfinder

Trailfinder is published three times a year by the Trailfinders travel agency and is distributed free through bins outside Central London underground stations. Each issue contains features on non-European travel destinations, sometimes focusing on one particular area like New Zealand. *Trailfinder* is useful for finding the cheapest IATA air fares and contains suggestions for stopover routes around the world. It also contains a mail order form for books and maps stocked by the agency. Within the UK and Ireland subscriptions cost £6.00 for four issues. Write to: Trailfinders Ltd, 42-48 Earls Court Road, London W8 6EJ. (Tel: (01) 938 3366).

The Traveller

The Traveller is published three times a year and is issued free to WEXAS members. Each edition contains four feature articles on countries likely to be of interest to independent travellers, complete with **maps** and information on **visas**, and so on. There is also a *Travel Alert* feature on a potential hazard like excess baggage charges, and a *Travel Trend* feature on a topic of general interest like the effects of airline privatisation. In addition the *In Focus* pages provide a round-up of news and information while the *Gear Up* section surveys the latest equipment details. There are also several book reviews and two pages of readers' letters. If you contribute useful information which is published in the *Global Round-Up* page—for example, about a particularly tricky border crossing—you will receive free copies of *The Traveller* for a year.

Business Traveller

Business Traveller is published monthly and covers topics of interest to frequent travellers. Its emphasis is on high class accommodation and value for money flights and every month there is an *International Air Fares and Hotel Guide* supplement at the back. This gives an excellent indication of air fares not just from the UK but from most major European cities and is a good place to find the addresses and phone numbers of cheap ticket outlets. The back of the magazine also lists exchange rates against the US dollar and the dates of worldwide public holidays. The readers' letters pages often contain hints about travel problems but the feature articles are usually geared towards the needs of expense account rather than budget travellers. *Business Traveller* costs £1.50 monthly or £20.00 for an annual subscription. Its address is Perry

Publications Ltd, 49 Old Bond Street, London W1X 3AF (Tel: (01) 629 4688).

Executive Traveller
Executive Traveller is published monthly and is also aimed at frequent travellers. The *Skymarket* supplement at the back is a useful source of addresses and phone numbers for cheap air fare outlets, although this time only the cheapest published scheduled air fares are listed. This is also a good place to look for the phone numbers of airlines, passport offices, vaccination centres, railway stations, hotel booking centres, and so on. Exchange rates against sterling are listed as well. Once again the feature articles are likely to be of most interest to business travellers, although if you want to find out about airports and airlines some of them may be useful. *Executive Traveller* costs £1.50 a month or £18.00 for an annual subscription. Its address is Quadrant Subscription Services, Oakfield House, Perrymount Road, Haywards Heath, Sussex RH16 3DH (Tel: (0444) 440421).

On The Move
A bimonthly magazine costing 90p an issue, *On The Move* contains information about public transport especially within the UK although there are occasional features about other countries too. It is often on sale in YHA Shops and is published by Transit Publications Ltd, South Bank Business Centre, 13 Park House, 140 Battersea Park Road, London SW11 4NB (Tel: (01) 622 4185).

Holiday Which?
Published quarterly by the Consumers Association as a supplement to the general *Which?* magazine, *Holiday Which?* contains detailed surveys of popular holiday destinations and reports on topics as varied as choosing a guidebook, claiming a refund on a package holiday and day trips to France. With its firm emphasis on value for money, this is a particularly useful publication for budget travellers. To find out about subscribing to *Which?* write to The Consumers Association, PO Box 44, Hertford SG14 1SH. *Which?* subscribers can obtain back-issues of the holiday supplement for £3.00 each.

Good Holiday Magazine
A glossy quarterly, costing £1.95 an issue and containing features on many popular holiday destinations, together with advertising for tour operating companies. Although it includes short fact packs about the countries covered, its main use is inspirational rather than informative. *Good Holiday* is published by Hill Publications, 1/2 Dawes Court, 93 High Street, Esher, Surrey KT10 9QD (Tel: (0372) 63301).

The Adventurers

The UK edition of a well-established Spanish magazine, *The Adventurers* is a monthly publication on sale in newsagents for £1.50 an issue. It specialises in lengthy features on expedition-style visits to long-haul destinations with travel guidelines to support them. It also features some of the information which used to be included in the *Lonely Planet Updates*, now no longer running, intended to provide the most up-to-date amendments to the Lonely Planet series of guidebooks. Its *Bush Telegraph* pages are useful for the addresses and phone numbers of travel companies, and include a personal column for people looking for travel companions. *The Adventurers* is edited by Kate Needham and is published from 12 Telford Yard, London E1 9BQ (Tel: (01) 480 6801).

At the budget end of the market travel magazines open and close with rapidity so keep an eye out in your newsagent. The latest venture is *The Independent Traveller*, a quarterly magazine costing £1.20 and available on subscription from 2nd Floor, 1 The Pavement, London SW4 0HY. Since most of the material is supplied by regular travellers it could prove useful if it survives.

Saturday and Sunday newspapers are particularly useful for travel articles and advertisements and most magazines devote a least a column to holiday destinations, especially immediately after Christmas.

In winter there is a glut of seasonal publications on skiing which are also worth looking at. There are also useful special interest publications for walkers, climbers, cyclists, campers and so on. YHA Shops usually stock a good selection of these, including *High, The Great Outdoors, Making Tracks* and *Cycletouring*.

The Globe is the bimonthly magazine of The Globetrotters, a club for independently-minded travellers, and also contains updates on recent changes. Through its *Mutual Aid* column subscribers can obtain specific information from seasoned travellers. It costs £7.00 to join Globetrotters for a year; in return you receive a list of members who might provide hospitality en route, a handbook and notice of meetings. Contact Globetrotters through BCM/Roving, London WC1N 3XX.

For information on guidebooks see **Kitting Yourself Out For Your Trip**.

SEMINARS AND FILM SHOWS

An alternative way to find out information is to attend a seminar run by the Expedition Advisory Centre. These focus on such topics as 'Planning a Small Expedition', and 'Advice for Independent Travellers', and are held at the Royal Geographical Society. Ask the EAC for details; if you send an SAE and indicate the sort of training courses that interest you they will also advise you of other courses available.

You could also attend one of the **film shows** organised by the specialist overland tour operators. Check local listings magazines for dates and venues, but STA Travel and WEXAS regularly arrange such sessions and have details. Meetings of the Globetrotters Club, which are held on the second Saturday of each month at the Friends Meeting House, 52 St Martins Lane, London WC2N 4AP, provide an excellent opportunity to exchange information with other travellers.

Many budget travellers set out with very little advance planning, assuming that most cheap accommodation has to be booked on the spot anyway. However it is worth bearing in mind that some travel perks are only available to passengers who have thought ahead. These include Visit Norway airpasses, Swiss Holiday Cards, Deutsche Bundesbahn Tourist Cards, Italian kilometric rail tickets and Ansett Pioneer Adventure Passports. For more details of these and other examples see **How To Reach Your Destination Without Busting Your Budget** and **Travelling Around Without Busting Your Budget**.

SHOULD YOU TRAVEL ALONE?

One decision you will have to make beforehand is whether to travel alone or with someone else. Even if you usually enjoy your own company and relish the greater opportunity to meet local people and go exactly where you want, bear in mind the following:

- Solo travellers often end up paying more for their accommodation than couples because of a shortage of single rooms and the supplementary charges frequently levied on those that do exist.

- Women may also need to pay more to stay in safer areas if alone, and will almost certainly have to abandon thoughts of hitching everywhere.

Finding a companion

If you want to travel in company you may be lucky enough to know someone whose globetrotting instincts match your own. But if not, there are several ways to find someone to join you. Whenever possible it is wise to meet and get to know potential travelling companions before setting out. Many a good friendship has floundered under the stress of trying to agree an itinerary, and you only have to read Christina Dodwell's *Travels With Fortune* to realise that erstwhile companions have actually been known to vanish when the going gets rough—which could be disastrous if you find yourself stuck in the middle of nowhere.

- Place a personal advertisement in *TNT* (see above) which is widely read by travellers. This will cost at least £7.00.

- Advertise in *The YHA Magazine*, also read by people with an interest in travelling, whether at home or abroad. This will cost at least £6.00 but box number facilities are available if you are not happy about having your home telephone number published. The YHA also refuses to accept advertisements that specify the sex or appearance of 'desired' companions for added security. Write to Classified Advertising, YHA Magazine, Trevelyan House, 8 St Stephens Hill, St Albans, Herts AL1 2DY.

- If you're a member of The Globetrotters Club you can advertise for a companion in their *Mutual Aid* columns. Readers of this magazine are likely to be experienced travellers.

- Place a personal advertisement in the *Bush Telegraph* pages of *The Adventurers*. Up to forty words are published free and should be sent to 12, Telford Yard, London E1 9BQ (Tel: (01) 480 6801) at least six weeks before the desired publication date.

- Finally, if you're prepared to invest £20.00 in an introduction fee for a year, *Travelmate* of 6 Hayes Avenue, Bournemouth, BH7 7AD (Tel: (0292) 33398), might put you in touch with your perfect companion. Their application form allows you to specify which areas of the world you propose to visit and you can also say whether you prefer a male or female companion and what age they should be. If you are away from home the time abroad will be credited against your annual subscription, provided you let Travelmate know in advance.

If you still do not have a travelling companion before you leave, don't despair—people on their own usually bump into other lone travellers along the way. This is particuarly true on popular overland routes with obvious resting spots en route. **Youth hostels** worldwide are always good places to pick up companions, but if you are passing through Bangkok, Koh Samui, Cairo, Nairobi, Delhi or Istanbul you would be very unlikely not to find someone else going your way. Waiting until you are actually on the road has the added advantage that, by the time you do pair up with someone, you have a much clearer idea of your needs and abilities. You also have the chance to get to know the other person as they are when they are away from home before committing yourself to a partnership.

LEARNING THE LANGUAGE

Another decision that definitely needs to be made beforehand is whether or not to try and learn one or more languages for your trip. English speakers are fortunate since their language is widely spoken in many parts of the world. However, those travelling to the Maghreb or West

Africa would be well advised to pick up some French beforehand, and those going to South or Central America should consider learning Spanish; not only will it make travelling around easier but you will also be able to communicate with local people and, hopefully, get more out of your trip.

Language courses

There are many ways to learn a language even if you did not study it at school. Every year most Local Education Authorities run **evening classes** in French, German, Spanish and Italian. Depending on the make-up of the local population and on local needs other languages may also be available. If the particular one you want is not apparently on offer, ask anyway; if a group of about twelve people can be assembled a course may be organised. Most LEA courses start in September and run through the academic year. However, if you fail to enrol at the start of the year or make your travel plans at a later date, some authorities also run summer term crash courses aimed at helping you get by in shops and on buses even if you cannot make deep and meaningful conversation. A typical fifteen-week LEA beginners' course costs about £30.00 with reductions for students, the unemployed, pensioners and others on state benefits.

The **BBC** also runs regular language courses, often starting in October. While the programmes themselves are free, you usually need to buy an accompanying book and cassette to reap the full benefits.

If you think you have the self-discipline you could try **teaching yourself** instead. You can pick up courses in most languages in the *Teach Yourself* (Hodder and Stoughton, average cost £5.00) or *Made Simple* (Heinemann, average cost £5.00) series, but remember that you may find it difficult to understand the pronunciation without anyone to help you. It is probably more sensible to invest in one of the combined book and cassette courses produced by companies like Berlitz and Hugo's, which cover a wide range of languages, not all of them European. These cost more initially (between £11.00 and £30.00), but you may get more out of them in the long run. Unless you need a particularly good grasp of the language you can probably manage without paying for the more expensive courses run by companies like Linguaphone.

Private tutors

Another possibility is to find a **private tutor**, particularly if the language you want to learn is not one of the standard ones. Local language schools may be able to put you in touch with students interested in teaching their own language for extra cash, and it's worth examining the noticeboards in universities and polytechnics to see if anyone is offering tuition. You could also try *Yellow Pages* under 'Tutoring' for local colleges offering private tuition. However, although this method may well be quick, it is unlikely to be very cheap.

Phrase books
Finally, even if you fail to make much headway with the language before leaving home, invest in a **phrase book** to take with you. Berlitz publishes a wide range of these, while Lonely Planet produces books for places like Thailand which are particularly popular with independent travellers. Berlitz phrasebooks cost about £2.00 each, while Lonely Planet's are about £1.95. Collins also publishes a series of handy pocket **dictionaries** for about £3.00 each.

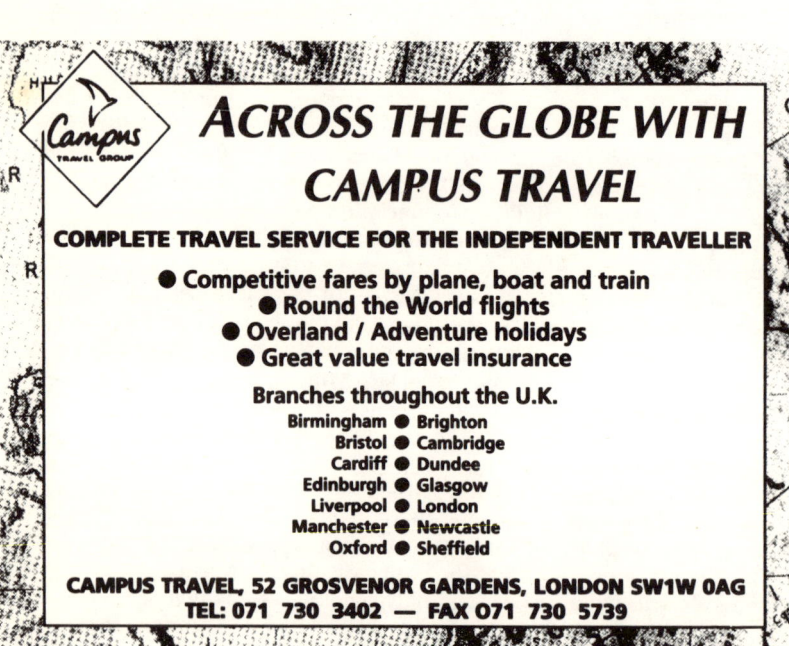

2

Bargain Travel Spots

Your choice of destination can make all the difference in the world to your budget. Cheap places to visit normally fall into one of three broad categories:

1. Those that are cheap to get to from the UK because:
   (a) They can be reached without flying, like The Netherlands or France.
   (b) Cheap flights are readily available, as they are to Thailand.

2. Those that have a lower cost of living than the UK. This means ruling out relatively close places like Scandinavia but including more distant ones like Egypt and India.

3. Those where work is available to visitors, for example Israel or Australia.

In general countries in the **southern hemisphere** tend to be cheaper for travellers than those in the north. This should not be taken as absolute; some African countries like Zambia turn out to have a surprisingly high cost of living.

Europe

Since Europe is nearest to the UK you might expect holidays there to be cheap. Competition between the ferry companies means that it costs very little to reach France, Belgium or The Netherlands. However the cost of living is fairly high even in former 'budget paradises' such as Spain and Italy. These are still cheaper than West Germany and Scandinavia, but prices are comparable to those at home. Ireland turns out to be astonishingly expensive. European Turkey and Eastern Europe probably offer the best bargains for budget travellers nowadays. In general, the further south and east you go in Europe, the lower your daily expenses, although the initial cost of reaching these areas may be higher. Conversely, northern and western Europe have the highest cost of living although they may be less expensive to reach. Prices in Scandinavia are nothing less than exorbitant.

Africa
It's still possible to reach Africa fairly cheaply if you enter via Morocco, Tunisia, Egypt or Kenya. However political problems have closed several of the main overland routes or made them difficult for most independent travellers. Flights paid for within Africa tend to be very expensive and food prices can also be high. On the other hand public transport and accommodation are usually bargains. Deciding whether or not to use black markets can also affect your costs, especially in Egypt, Sudan, Uganda, Tanzania, Malawi, Zambia, Zimbabwe and Zaire.

Asia
Political problems have also put paid to several of the main overland routes across Asia as far as independent travellers are concerned. However, you can easily find bucket shop flights to most popular centres and costs, once you reach your destination, are usually low. An obvious exception is Japan where the cost of living is beyond the reach of most budget travellers.

Australasia
Visitors to Australia or New Zealand are virtually forced to fly to their destination and while, mile for mile, the fares are reasonable, they still represent large amounts of cash to part with at one time. Once you reach your destination, however, money stretches further than in Europe. It is worth bearing in mind that some of the islands near Australia like Papua New Guinea are much more expensive than their Third World image might suggest.

North America
Fares to North America and Canada also represent large, unavoidable investments of cash, although standby and APEX fares are also very good value on a mile for mile basis. Once you arrive, food costs are lower than in the UK, but you will need a lot of money for accommodation unless you are prepared to camp. Public transport is also fairly expensive.

South America
Fares to South America have finally started to come down and places like Mexico and Peru now represent very good value for budget travellers since food, accommodation and public transport, even internal flights, are remarkably cheap.

Compulsory currency exchange
More and more governments are realising the economic benefits of tourism. Where they were once happy to let backpackers come and go,

spending as little as they chose, nowadays they are often determined to wring money out of them by forcing them to change a fixed amount of money for every day of their stay. Normally, none of the money can be re-exchanged, and even when it can be the exchange rate will be so unfavourable that there is a strong incentive to spend it all. Countries with **compulsory currency exchange** include the following (see **Appendix 4** for a complete key to the Currency Codes as used here):

Country	Exchange amount
Algeria	ALD1,000
Poland	UKL10 per day
Romania	USD10 per day (or equivalent in hard currency)
Czechoslovakia	UKL10.30 per day
Burma (Myanmar)	USD100
Nicaragua	USD60 on arrival

Sometimes the amount that must be exchanged is realistic, considering the country's cost of living. However, sometimes, as in the case of Algeria, it is so *un*realistic that a visit is tricky for those on a budget. In many cases compulsory exchange regulations negate the benefits of thriving black markets, so always check carefully before setting out; it can come as a nasty shock to find that you have to change most of your money at unfavourable legal rates just to get into the country, when you have calculated your costs on black market exchange rates. The entry regulations for Burma (now also known as Myanmar) do not stop people using the black markets, but they do mean that the money obtained is less useful than it would be without the rules.

Governments are also alert to the efforts budget travellers make to get away with paying as little as possible for their holidays. At the moment, for example, the Greek authorities are very concerned about flight-only holidaymakers. Regulations can change with very little notice, so don't get caught out.

BUDGET TRAVELLERS' GUIDE TO THE WORLD

Rock-bottom budgets
Morocco
Turkey

If you can afford the air fare
Bangladesh	Kenya	Philippines
Burma (Myanmar)	Malaysia	Sri Lanka
China	Mexico	Thailand

The budget traveller's

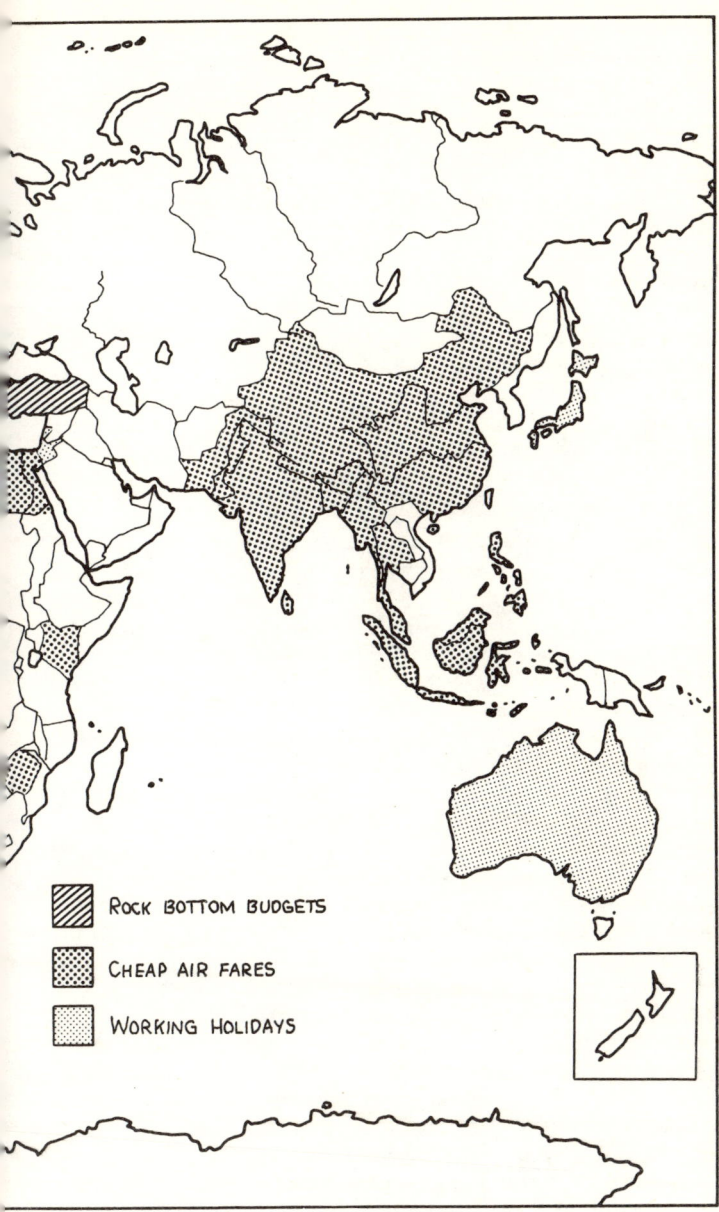

ROCK BOTTOM BUDGETS

CHEAP AIR FARES

WORKING HOLIDAYS

guide to the world

Egypt	Nepal	Tunisia
India	Pakistan	Zimbabwe
Indonesia	Peru	

If you are prepared to work
Japan (teaching English)
Australia (young people's working visa)
Iceland (fisheries)
France (grape picking)
The Alps (ski resort work)
Greece (bar work)
Hong Kong (at least until 1997)
USA (summer camp schemes)
Israel (kibbutz/moshav)
Norway (farming)
See **Working Your Keep** for more details.

WHERE TO FIND A CHEAPER SKIING HOLIDAY

Nowadays many people can afford to have a winter as well as a summer holiday. In the past skiing was the hobby of the wealthy and only expensive resorts like Davos and Klosters flourished. However, all that has changed as the tour operators have rushed into package skiing and made it just another holiday.

The cheapest destinations

The cheapest skiing is likely to be in the Spanish Pyrenees or Sierra Nevada, or in Andorra, the little duty-free country tucked up in the Pyrenees. However, there's very little accommodation there so you may have to stay in Spain and make day trips to the slopes.

The next cheapest resorts are mainly in Italy, especially if you drive there and take advantage of a 'Settimane Bianco' (white week), an arrangement made for independent travellers by the local authorities. This allows visitors between November and April a package deal on accommodation, lift passes and ski hire for very competitive prices. The Italian Tourist Office (see **Appendix 1** for address) has more details.

If you drive to France and opt for self-catering or staying in one of the purpose-built resorts like La Plagne where the slopes are not far from the accommodation, you can also keep your costs to a minimum.

If you decide to venture further afield however, prices start to soar. Package deals to Austria generally offer good value for money although everything you buy outside the package, even a cup of coffee, will cost you a fortune. German resorts are relatively uncrowded but more expensive and Swiss prices are exorbitant. If you do want to ski there your best bet could be to buy a flight-only deal to Zurich or

Geneva and then make daily visits to the slopes while staying away from the actual resorts.

Skiing in Scandinavia is for the wealthy only but do take a look at the less developed winter sports destinations like Bulgaria or Yugoslavia or even those in Cyprus or Morocco for a bargain. Finally, do not forget good old Aviemore in Scotland; if you stay in Inverness and commute to the slopes this can be a very cheap alternative to going overseas.

General advice

South-facing, lower slopes are usually cheaper, especially at the start and end of the season, but be warned that when snow is in short supply these are the places which have the least of it and which will keep it for the shortest time. Picking a **self-catering holiday** should also help keep your costs down, but bear in mind that in small, isolated resorts a solitary supermarket can have a monopoly on food prices.

Whatever you do, avoid the resorts popularised by royalty or film stars. Colorado may be fine for Jack Nicholson but it will cost *you* an arm and a leg to follow him there.

3

When to Find a Bargain

Since prices in one country can vary considerably from season to season, choosing the right time for your visit can be almost as important as choosing the right place.

Europe

If you are planning a holiday in Europe forget about travelling during weeks that coincide with school holidays. Avoid trips during Christmas and the New Year, over Easter, or during July, August and early September. If you must travel at any of these times, resign yourself to peak season prices immediately.

Conversely, it makes sense to travel in periods just before and after these seasonal peaks. The middle of December and mid-January are prime times for rock-bottom prices with mass market tour operators like Thomson, Cosmos and Intasun.

Beyond Europe

There are other times to avoid if you want a cheap deal especially if your destination is outside Europe. Expect high prices in the Caribbean throughout the months that coincide with winter in the northern hemisphere as the islands cash in on the rush to escape the cold. Fares to Australia and New Zealand also come into their own during the European winter when the sun shines brightly in the southern hemisphere.

If you are planning a trip to Australia and New Zealand, Canada, the USA or South Africa, you need to be aware of the *seasons* the airlines use to calculate their fares. Low season fares (YL) are cheapest, followed, in order of expense, by off-peak (YJ), shoulder (YO) and peak (YH) fares.

Approximate seasonal dates for flights east to Australia and New Zealand

Peak Season	September, 10-23 December
Shoulder Season	January, August, October, November, 1-9 December
Off-Peak	February, July, 24-31 December
Low Season	March to June

Approximate seasonal dates for flights west to North America
(different airlines use slightly varying dates)

Peak Season	June to September, mid-December
Shoulder Season	April, May, October
Low Season	January to March, November, early and late December

Approximate seasonal dates for flights to South Africa

Peak Season	April, July to October
Low Season	January to March, May to June, November to December

If your journey falls close to one of the swap-over dates, you may save pounds by travelling a day earlier or later.

Festivals and special holidays
Many countries also have seasonal peaks associated with **carnivals**, or **festivals**. At such times rooms can be hard to find and astronomically priced. Some of the major events and the dates when they take place are shown below.

Place	*Event*	*Date*
Rio de Janeiro, Brazil	Mardi Gras Carnival	February
New Orleans, USA	Mardi Gras Carnival	February
Trinidad	Mardi Gras Carnival	February
The Netherlands	Bulb season	April
Jerusalem, Israel	Easter ceremonies	April (moving date)
Seville, Spain	Fiesta	April (last week)
Cannes, France	Film Festival	May
Nice, France	Jazz Festival	July
Calgary, Canada	Rodeo	July
Pamplona, Spain	Running of the Bulls	July (second week)
Salzburg, Austria	Music Festival	July and August
Venice, Italy	International Film Festival	August
Edinburgh, UK	Festival	August
Munich, West Germany	Beer Festival	October
Bethlehem, Israel	Christmas festivities	December

Apart from these annual festivals, there are also periodic major sporting events which have the same effects on pricing and room availability. The **Summer and Winter Olympics** are both held at four yearly intervals and it would be folly to expect bargain prices in hotels in the cities hosting the games. The **World Cup** is also held four yearly and, once again, puts paid to the likelihood of cheap accommodation at its venue. The ten yearly **Passion Play** staged in the Bavarian village of Oberammergau (next date 1991) is very different, but once again, if economy is your main consideration, you would be well-advised not to coincide your visit with it.

Seasonal package deals

Package tour operators also offer seasonal prices. Special deals are often available at times of year when their programmes switch from summer to winter flight patterns, and vice versa (March/April and October/November). Often this means that planes will not be in the right places to match the usual 7 or 14-night holiday arrangements, so anyone prepared to travel for perhaps 11 nights may be able to get a special deal.

You can also save money on package holidays by choosing flights that leave early in the morning or late at night, particularly if you are travelling to a popular destination like Majorca in the high season when there will be plenty of flights leaving every day. Mid-week flights tend to be cheaper than weekend ones.

If you know someone who works in the travel trade, get them to keep an eye open for **new air routes**, or similar new ventures. Sometimes when these start up there are special promotional offers, as when Laker first began flying to Miami. But remember that you need to move fast to take advantage of any offers made by mass market operators, especially if they are well-publicised.

If you choose to travel out of season to save money, remember that there are often good reasons why prices are lower at certain times of the year. For example, charges for holidays in India in July and August may seem low, but before you snap them up remember that these are the monsoon months, and that in return for the cheaper fare you may be forgoing the benefit of brilliant sun. Of course, you may learn more about India by being there during the monsoon than you would have done during the peak tourist season. The monsoon affects different areas at different times and may even affect different sides of the same country at different times. For example, East and West Sri Lanka are hit by the monsoon at different times.

When the monsoon occurs

Thailand	June–September
Philippines	June–January
Malaysia	November–February
Mauritius	December–March
Seychelles	December–March
Maldives	November-March

India	June–October (depending on area)
Sri Lanka	April–June (south and west coasts)
	September–December (north and east coasts)
Nepal	July–September

Remember that the months immediately preceding the monsoon are often either intensely hot and dry (Central India) or hot and unpleasantly humid (Philippines). Other climatic conditions to take into account include:

- The hurricane season in the Caribbean (August–October).
- The humid season in Florida (July–August).

It is up to you to decide if the discomforts are worth enduring for the sake of a cheaper deal.

Ramadan

In the same way, if you choose to travel in an Islamic country during **Ramadan**, the month of fasting, you may have problems because cafés are closed during the day. In return, you may see a more interesting side of the country than most package tourists and prices are likely to be lower than at other times of year. The date of Ramadan depends on the lunar calendar and moves from year to year, so always check when it will be before you visit a Muslim country. A pocket diary may indicate the start of Ramadan, otherwise the Saudi Arabian embassy will be able to help (see **Appendix 1** for the address).

Savings at your destination

You may be able to save even more out of season once you have reached your destination. With hotel rooms empty, you might find it easier to barter prices down than in high season when people will be queuing up to pay if you are not prepared to. Sometimes local transport is also cheaper out of season. For example National Express coach services in Britain cost less from October to April than during the summer months.

When to go skiing

Prices at the ski resorts hit their peak over Christmas and the New Year and during the weeks of February half-term. They are also high in January and February when most resorts will have their best snow falls. So to find a bargain, think about going either in December or in March and April, the start and end of the season.

Bear in mind, though, that in a bad year for snow these are also the times when it will be thinnest on the ground. Some tour operators offer **snow guarantees**; if there is no snow at your resort they agree to transport you to one where there is or to compensate you for the disappointment. If you travel at either end of the season, it makes sense to pick an operator with such a policy.

A note on exchange rates
When deciding where to go, try to find out something about worldwide currency exchange rate fluctuations. At present few exchange rates are fixed and some can vary wildly even on a daily basis. While the exchange rate for the pound to the peseta has rarely deviated from roughly 200 pesetas to the pound, the exchange rate for the US dollar has dropped from a high of over two dollars to the pound to a low of one and a half dollars to the pound in the last decade.

When the pound was fetching over two dollars the United States was like a giant bargain basement—but when the exchange rate was only one and a half dollars, even bus fares seemed expensive. So anyone planning to visit the States should watch the exchange rates carefully, and try and time their visit for a period when the dollar is comparatively weak.

Since the dollar is such an important currency in world terms, its strength can affect prices in other countries too. For example in Nicaragua many hotel bills will have to be settled in dollars rather than cordobas, so if the dollar is strong visitors will end up paying more for their accommodation than when it is weak.

4

Cutting the Cost of the Paperwork

Before you can set off on your travels, there are a number of formalities to go through. Perhaps the most important is equipping yourself with the cheapest and most appropriate passport and visas.

PASSPORTS

For the vast majority of British travellers, **a full ten year British passport**, available from Passport Offices for £15.00, is the best value for money. This document has 30 pages which is adequate for most people's purposes. However, for £30.00 frequent travellers can buy a **jumbo passport** with 94 pages. This is particularly useful if your trip will take you to a number of different African countries. Often Immigration officials require an entire page for their stamp and will turn you away if there is not enough room. In such circumstances a standard passport fills up very quickly. Buying a jumbo version saves the hassle of trying to replace it while abroad.

Joint passports

A joint passport allows a husband and wife to travel on one passport. It may sound like a bargain at £22.50—however, only the person in whose name the passport is actually issued can use it when travelling without the other holder. This limits its usefulness if both holders travel frequently and not always together. These passports will be phased out as the new EC passports are introduced.

British Visitors Passport

If you only make occasional trips to Western Europe you could manage with a **British Visitors Passport (BVP)** valid for one year and available from Post Offices (except on Saturdays) at a cost of £7.50. This is accepted for holidays or unpaid business trips of up to three months in Andorra, Austria, France, West Germany, Gibraltar, Greece, Italy, Liechtenstein, Malta, Monaco, Portugal, San Marino, Spain, Switzerland, Tunisia, Turkey, Belgium, Luxembourg, The Netherlands, Denmark, Finland, Norway, Sweden, Bermuda and Canada. More and more countries are accepting this passport for short holidays in peak periods when the Passport Office is snowed under with applications, so always check before rushing out to buy a full passport.

If your travelling will be limited to short trips to France, Belgium and The Netherlands you could get by without paying anything for a passport. Instead you could use the **excursion cards/documents** issued at the ferry ports.

Passports	Validity	Cost
British Visitors	1 year	£7.50
Standard	10 years	£15.00
Jumbo	10 years	£30.00
Joint	10 years	£22.50
Joint Jumbo	10 years	£45.00
Child (up to age 15)	5 years (renewable)	£15.00
Excursion Document	60 hours (France)	£2.00
Excursion Card	60 hours (Belgium and The Netherlands)	Free

Children's passports

Passports issued to **children** under the age of 16 are initially valid for five years. If the child is still under 16 when the time comes to renew it, a new passport will be issued for a further five years at no extra charge. Children under 16 can travel on their parents' passports provided their names have been added to them. Passport Offices charge £4.00 to add a child's name to a parent's documentation.

When to apply

Apply for a passport at least a month before you need it, especially if you want to travel over Christmas or between April and August; phone calls and visits to the Passport Office to try and speed up your application can soon wipe out the benefits of buying the cheapest type. If you want your passport returned by **registered post** you should include a cheque for £1.25 to cover the cost. However this is not essential, and may slow the processing of your application. Taking your application to the Passport Office rather than posting it does not necessarily guarantee a faster service.

Even if your passport is still valid, remember that some countries require its expiry date to be some months after you intend to leave the country. For example, travellers intending to visit Botswana should ensure that their documentation still has six month's life left in it, while the Australian Embassy requires a passport to be valid for three months beyond the planned date of return to the UK.

In ten years a person's appearance can alter dramatically. You can have a new photograph added to your passport for a cost of £3.00

Passport Offices in the UK

Areas Covered

London Passport Office
Clive House
70 Petty France
London SW1H 9HD
Tel: (01) 279 3434

Greater London, Middlesex.

Liverpool Passport Office
5th Floor
India Buildings
Water Street
Liverpool L2 0QZ
Tel (051) 237 3010

Cheshire, Cleveland, Clwyd, Cumbria, Derbyshire, Durham, Greater Manchester, Gwynedd, Humberside, Lancashire, Merseyside, Northumberland, North Yorkshire, South Yorkshire, Staffordshire, Tyne and Wear, West Yorkshire.

Newport Passport Office
Olympia House
Upper Dock Street
Newport
Gwent NPT 1XA
Tel (0633) 244500

Avon, Berkshire, Cornwall, Devon, Dorset, Dyfed, East Sussex, Gloucestershire, Gwent, Hampshire, Hereford and Worcester, Isle of Wight, Mid Glamorgan, Oxfordshire, Powys, Shropshire, Somerset, South Glamorgan, Surrey (except London boroughs), West Glamorgan, West Sussex, Wiltshire.

Peterborough Passport Office
55 Westfield Road
Peterborough
Cambs PE3 6TG
Tel (0733) 895555

Bedfordshire, Buckinghamshire, Cambridgeshire, Essex (except London boroughs), Hertfordshire (except London boroughs), Kent (except London boroughs), Leicestershire, Norfolk, Northamptonshire Nottinghamshire, Suffolk, Warwickshire, West Midlands.

Glasgow Passport Office
3 Northgate
96 Milton Street
Cowcaddens
Glasgow G4 0BT
Tel: (041) 322 0271

All Scottish addresses.

Belfast Passport Office
Hampton House
47-53 High Street
Belfast BT1 2QS
Tel: (0232) 232371

All Northern Irish addresses.

Normal hours of business: Monday to Friday 0900 to 1630.

which could be money well spent since Immigration officials are free to refuse entry to anyone about whom they are the slightest bit suspicious.

Replacing your passport

If you lose your passport while travelling, **British embassies** abroad can issue you with a new one. However they need to be entirely satisfied that the original will not reappear. You will have to pay the standard cost for a new passport and may be charged an administration fee as well. In many parts of the world stolen passports are worth a lot of money, so treat yours with great care, keeping it safely with airline tickets and your money.

Political restrictions

While no-one would want to pay for **two passports** unnecessarily, there are some occasions when it may be essential. If you want to visit both Israel and some of the Arab countries, for example, you are likely to have problems. An Israeli entrance stamp in your passport makes you *persona non grata* at all Arab borders other than Egypt's. Immigration officials are also canny; even if you do not have the Israeli stamp but do have an Egyption one showing that you entered through Sinai, other Arab countries will turn you away. They are equally suspicious of new passports conveniently issued in Cairo. You can ask to have the Israeli stamp put on a separate piece of paper if your stay will be a short one. However, the Passport Office will allow you to carry a second passport to circumvent these difficulties.

Similar problems apply to travellers wishing to travel to South Africa and other African countries; once the South African stamp hits your passport, expect to be refused entry almost everywhere else on the continent except Malawi. Once again, you can buy a second passport to get out of the problem, but make sure you dispose of the one with the offending stamp in it carefully; Immigration officials will make your life hell if they find it. They are wise to people with new passports issued in neighbouring countries like Botswana, so make sure your story is water-tight.

A second passport is also useful to people planning to visit both Taiwan and China, or Greece and Northern Cyprus. The Algerians purportedly turn away people with Malawian stamps too, but check this before going to the expense of another purchase. Honduran border officials also frown on passports containing stamps from Communist countries.

VISAS

Passports are not the only formality to cost money before you leave the UK. Most East European and non-European countries will want you to have a **visa** granting you permission to enter the country.

Visas come in many shapes and forms. These include:

- **tourist visas** which allow you to enter the country once, usually for a period of up to three months
- **business visas** which allow you to enter another country to work
- **re-entry visas** which allow you to go back into a country you have already left
- **exit visas** which allow you to leave a country
- **transit visas** which allow you to cross a country to reach another one (usually only valid for a matter of days or hours)
- **multiple entry visas** which allow you to come and go into a country more than once in a set number of months
- **tourist cards** which are not technically visas but are sometimes required instead, for example for entry to Mexico (these are still issued by embassies or consulates but are usually free).

Requirements for each country are listed in the *ABC Guide to International Travel*.

Visa costs

The cost of a visa can depend on:

- the country for which a visa is sought
- the nationality of the applicant
- the type of visa required—tourist, transit, business, and so on (in general more paperwork is required for business visas but they are sometimes processed more quickly than tourist visas, for example in Sudan)
- the geographical location of the consulate where the application is made.

Although some visas are free, others can be surprisingly expensive and people planning a long trip will need to include the price in their budget. Below are rough costs of visas for UK citizens travelling along popular overland routes:

1. **England to India**
   Bulgaria (£20.00 transit visa), Iran (£13.00), Pakistan (£25.00), India (£23.00). **Total**: £81.00.

2. **Far East to Australia**
   Thailand (£8.00), Burma (£3.00), Malaysia/Singapore/Indonesia, Australia (all free). **Total**: £11.00.

3. **USA to Argentina**
   Guatemala (£10.00), Argentina (varied cost), others free. **Total**: £10.00 + .

4. **Egypt to South Africa**
   Egypt (£17.00), Sudan (£6.25), Uganda (£10.00), others free. **Total**: £33.25.

5. **Tunisia to Zaire**
   Algeria (£7.00), Niger (approximately £4.00), Mali (approximately £2.00), Burkina Faso (£10.00), Ghana (£20.00), Togo (£3.52), Benin (£10.00), Nigeria (£20.00), Cameroon (varies), Central African Republic (approximately £5.00), Zaire (varies). **Total**: £81.52, plus Cameroon costs = roughly £90.00.

Before you arrive at an embassy to pay for a visa, always check what **forms of payment** are acceptable. The Nepalese embassy, for example, does not accept cheques, while the Sudanese want only postal order payment.

Additional visa costs

Some countries attach strings to their visas making them even more expensive. For example Algerian visas are only valid after the exchange of ALD1,000. Until recently students were exempted from this regulation, but they too must now fall into line with everybody else. Most East European countries also insist that you change a fixed sum for every day of your stay in return for a visa. Occasionally there are ways round this. One method is to enrol on a language course and pay for it in hard currency, thus freeing yourself from the obligation to change any more marks. Poland requires you to change £10.00 for every day of your stay, while Czechoslovakia stipulates £10.30.

Many non-European countries will only grant you a visa if you have an onward or return air ticket or sufficient funds to support yourself during your stay. What counts as 'sufficient funds' varies from country to country and may depend on the local cost of living or on how keen they are to encourage budget travellers. Countries requiring you to have an onward ticket include:

Benin, Burkina Faso, Burundi, Cape Verde Islands, Ethiopia, Fiji, French Colonies, Indonesia, Israel, Kenya, Madagascar, Malawi, Malaysia, New Caledonia, New Zealand, Nicaragua, Niger, Singapore, South Africa, Uganda, USA (will accept evidence of good reason to leave at the end of temporary stay—namely a job, house or college place), Windward Islands, Zambia, Zimbabwe.

If you are required to show a large lump sum of money to support yourself during your stay (Zimbabwean officials like to see USD1,000 or its equivalent) you can sometimes make a small sum look larger by interleaving travellers cheques owned by a wealthier companion with your own; at borders signatures are rarely scrutinised with the same enthusiasm as the actual sums involved. Unfortunately the Australian embassy wants to see a bank statement with evidence of regular savings before it will issue a working holiday visa without delays.

In countries with flourishing currency black markets like Uganda you can sometimes obtain visas at very competitive prices.

Miscellaneous Charges Order

Some officials will accept evidence of onward travel by some means other than air, for example proof of a rail booking. If you anticipate problems, one way round them is to buy a **Miscellaneous Charges Order (MCO)**, which is an airline document rather like a blank cheque for air services. You can show this as proof that you could fly out if you needed to, knowing that you can cash it in on your return home. However, you will need enough money to buy the MCO in the first place. (You could charge it to Access or Visa and just pay minimum payments until you return and cash it in). Try not to buy an MCO in a country with an unstable currency; it may only be refundable in the place of issue and in the currency of that country.

Health requirements

There may even be compulsory health requirements to fulfil before your visa becomes valid. For example, men wishing to spend more than three months in the USSR or Saudi Arabia will be expected to produce a certificate stating that they are HIV negative before it will be issued. Such demands may well become commonplace as AIDS hysteria spreads.

Applying for a visa

Applying for visas can take even longer than obtaining a passport, and most embassies are only open for limited periods each day. If you are going to send your passport through the post for its stamp, it may be worth sending it by **recorded delivery** which means someone will have to sign for receipt of it. The average passport weighs between 60 and 100 grams and costs about 55p to send recorded delivery.

Visa courier services

If you anticipate problems in getting your visas, there are companies specialising in obtaining them. For a charge their couriers will ferry your passport back and forth to the embassies for you. Hourly paid employees may think the price worth paying to avoid having to take time off work.

Visa services

Rapid Visa Service
15 Hogarth Road
Earls Court
London SW5 0QH
Tel: (01) 373 3026

Thomas Cook
45 Berkeley Street
London W1A 1EB
Tel: (01) 499 4000 (£10.00 per
visa except to VIP clients)

Visa Shop Ltd
44 Chandos Place
London WC2N 4HS
Tel: (01) 379 0419/0376 (basic
charge £7.50)

Visaservice
2 Northdown Street
Kings Cross
London N1 9BG
Tel: (01) 833 2709 (£10.00 per
passport and £3.00 delivery
fee)

Thames Consular Services Ltd
363 Chiswick High Road
London W4 4HS
Tel: (01) 995 2492

Travcour (UK)
270 Vauxhall Bridge Road
London SW1
Tel: (01) 834 7356 (specialises in
obtaining African visas)

Choosing the right visa

Always make sure you buy the most economical visa for your circumstances. Do not assume that buying a multiple entry one will be best. For example, if you're going to Thailand with a week-long side trip into Burma you may be able to arrange your visit so that the first entry to Thailand is for less than fifteen days and therefore free. If you are travelling as part of a group, find out whether a **collective visa** would be more economical. And if you're going on a cruise and will only be going ashore for short excursions, check whether you need any visas at all.

Most visas allow you to stay somewhere without further formality for three months. However, sometimes permission is only granted for the exact period you plan to stay.

- Egyptian visas are given for a month, with a two week 'overstay' normally overlooked. After that you must pay for a new visa.
- Tanzania will only give overland arrivals a one week visa, just long enough for them to get to Dar es Salaam and pay again to have it extended.
- Burma (Myanmar) never lets anyone have a visa for more than a week.
- Thailand will let British citizens in for two weeks without a visa.

Normally it makes sense to ask for a visa for the longest period possible. However, be careful in Eastern European countries where you are required to change a fixed amount of hard currency for every day of the visa's validity. Do not rely on changing any surplus back afterwards; you will lose half its value immediately.

Visa requirements frequently change, so make sure you have the most up-to-date information. Travel agents can usually help, but to be absolutely certain contact the embassy or consulate concerned (addresses given in **Appendix 1**). For example, all visitors to the USA, even those in transit to Canada or South America and not planning to leave the airport, used to need visas. However as of summer 1988 the American Embassy announced that it would waive this requirement for British holidaymakers. Then it emerged that this would only be the case if the airline carrying them to the States had taken out an indemnity agreement, which British Airways was slow to do. The situation remains extremely unclear. For the foreseeable future, check with your agent before assuming you will be admitted to the USA without a visa. (Incidentally 'multiple entry' US visas stamped into expired UK passports remain valid if you attach the old passport to your current one.)

Most visas are only valid for a set length of time from their date of issue, so it is unwise to apply for them too far in advance of your trip. Be realistic about your travel plans. If you are off on a long trip across Africa, Asia or South America, lots of things could happen to upset your schedule, in which case you may find your visas expiring before you reach the appropriate borders. Then you have to reapply and pay again when you are nearer your destination, which obviously bumps up your costs. Since some visas are very expensive, this can make a lot of difference to your budget.

Letters of introduction

If you apply for a visa in any country other than your place of residence, you may also be asked for a **letter of introduction** from your embassy before your application is processed. This is frequently the case in Africa—for example, for Sudan and Ethiopia. Most embassies are happy to oblige but their administration fee of roughly £5.00 automatically increases the cost of the visa.

Passport photos

If you have to buy a visa while abroad, either because it is cheaper or because one issued in the UK will have expired before you reach the country, remember that you will need a supply of **passport-sized photographs** to accompany application forms. If you are travelling to the Far East it may be worth buying these when you are away since they will be cheaper and of better quality than those available in booths at home. However, if you are travelling to Africa, India or South

America, it is sensible to buy the photos at home rather than rely on rare facilities at your destination.

Find out which visas are most expensive and how long they take to obtain in a neighbouring country when you are sure of your arrival date. Of course, travelling in a group makes this harder since you will have to stick to a pre-planned itinerary as far as possible.

Registering with the police

Most countries also require you to register your arrival with the police. In Europe this is usually a formality carried out by the hotelier when you arrive. However, in places like Egypt and Sudan you are responsible for taking your passport to the police and getting it stamped. In these countries you will also be expected to do this whenever you travel off the beaten track, for example into the oases of Egypt's Western Desert. These stamps are usually free.

HOW TO AVOID BORDER HASSLES

There is something about crossing borders which makes the most innocent people sweat; and the further away and more exotic the surroundings, the more alarming borders can be. However, the following guidelines may help your passage:

- *Dress as smartly as you can.* Men might consider carrying a tie just for borders and bear in mind that long trousers are usually taken more seriously than shorts. Remember that what's fine at home is not necessarily so abroad where many authorities still live in terror of 'hippies'. If you are a man and your hair is long(ish), get it cut before arriving in Tangier. If you are a woman, be sure to have a knee-length skirt on when arriving in Malawi.

- *Make sure all your paperwork is in order.* Have your passport with necessary visa and your vaccination certificate to hand. Be ready to produce your return air ticket and travellers cheques if asked.

- *Keep calm and do as you are told.* The bureaucracy may seem interminable but there is nothing you can do about it and losing your temper tends to slow the process down. If you are asked to write details of your travellers cheques on a scrappy piece of paper—as has been known in Wadi Halfa, Sudan—just do it. If officials want to record the make of your camera in your passport, let them. If Customs insist on a body search, now is not the moment to invoke the Statute of Human Rights. When asked if you are carrying drugs or weapons, resist the urge to crack witticisms.

- *Find out about local idiosyncracies and be prepared for them.* Do not try and take Bibles or pornography into the USSR. Leave *Africa On*

A Shoestring behind before going to Malawi, where the authorities do not appreciate the comments it makes about their leader.

- *Do not tell lies if there is the slightest danger of getting caught out.* Read Shiva Naipaul's *North Of South* for a gruelling description of what happened to someone who told Tanzanian officials he had not been to South Africa when his suitcase contained a passport proving he had actually worked there.

- *Find out in advance where a bribe (see below) may be necessary.* If so, have it ready, to avoid having your bags turned out and an appropriate 'gift' selected.

Bribes

Even if your passport is up-to-date and with no incriminating stamps, a current photograph, plenty of empty pages and the necessary visa, you may still have problems at borders, particularly in the poorer and more remote parts of the world. Usually these can be resolved with a 'present'. However much you may disapprove of bribery, the fact is that you may have to deal with a corrupt system at some point—so you need to work out how to keep the cost to a minimum.

Perhaps the best way is to think of items apart from cash which you can use to ease your way across tricky borders. Ask around to find out what is scarce in one country and cheap in another. Even basic items like bars of perfumed soap, biros, glossy magazines and so on can do the trick. A good idea is to pack things like this which you expect to part with near the top of your bag. Then when a Customs official opens it with luck the request for a 'present' will come as soon as he sees what you've put there. In the same way make sure that items that you would hate to part with, such as your personal stereo, are packed right at the bottom.

5

Carrying Money the Cheap Way

Nowadays there are so many ways of taking money abroad that the most important consideration for the budget traveller may well be finding the cheapest means.

TRAVELLERS CHEQUES

Travellers cheques have always been a popular method of carrying money overseas, because if you lose them, you can refund them, usually on the spot, provided that the owner has kept a list of the cheque numbers purchased and those already cashed at the time of loss. You may even find that sterling travellers cheques fetch a better exchange rate overseas than sterling cash.

There are, however, still one or two drawbacks to bear in mind:

1. A number of different banks and companies issue their own cheques. It may be tempting to opt for those sold by your local bank, but if you will be travelling anywhere remotely off the beaten track, try and find a **Thomas Cook** or **American Express** outlet since their cheques are the most widely recognised. They also have the most offices and partners overseas which means you are likely to be able to get a refund more quickly than if you have a British high street bank's cheques.

2. Bear in mind the charges made for issuing the cheques. Most companies charge 1% of the cost, but watch out for hefty **minimum charges**; for example Thomas Cook charge a minimum £2.50. When you cash sterling travellers cheques abroad anywhere apart from a branch of the issuing company, you will usually also be charged at least another 1% commission.

Travellers cheques in overseas currencies

Travellers cheques are also available in currencies other than sterling. You will be charged more (perhaps 1¾%) for buying these cheques but should not be charged commission when you come to cash them abroad. Cheques are available in the following currencies:

American dollars   Portuguese escudos (Visa)
Canadian dollars   Italian lire (not easily refundable)
Australian dollars   French francs

Hong Kong dollars	Swiss francs
German marks	Japanese yen
Dutch guilders	European currency units (stable
Spanish pesetas	exchange rate).

If you intend to visit the United States, you need to take **dollar cheques** which are accepted as cash in hotels, restaurants, garages, and so on. It also makes sense to take the cheques of an American bank (American Express, Citicorp, Visa, and so on) since these are most readily accepted.

Sterling travellers cheques are also difficult to exchange in Latin America and parts of the Middle East and Far East. Watch political developments though—for a while no Iranian banks would touch dollar cheques.

Cashing travellers cheques

Should you be proposing to use black markets overseas, remember that travellers cheques are not always acceptable. In the few places where they are (for example, Egypt), there is a suspiciously high incidence of 'lost' cheques. If you really do lose yours, you may have to wait longer than usual for a refund while the bank checks your story.

Buy cheques in a mixture of denominations, including some small and large ones. The large cheques will come in handy for paying for things like expensive air fares, while the small ones can be used when you are about to leave a country. If you are forced to change £50.00 just before leaving somewhere, you will almost certainly lose money on re-exchange rates, particularly in those countries like Bulgaria where you will be given a very poor rate.

In most places you can cash travellers cheques at overseas branches of the issuing company without paying any more commission, but always check how much you will be charged to cash your money. Sometimes there is a percentage charge, sometimes a charge per cheque, in which case it can be expensive to have your money in small denominations. This will happen if you cash your cheques in German Post Offices, for example, and when you change money in Thailand, although there the amount charged is small enough not to worry about. Before you change money in hotels or shops always check the rates, which can be very poor.

Where to buy travellers cheques

- **Thomas Cook** cheques can be bought at branches of Midland Bank, AT Mays, the Post Office, and the Alliance and Leicester and Anglia Building Societies as well as in the travel agencies. Refunds are available through Thomas Cook and Wagons-Lit offices worldwide and through branches of Hertz. Alternatively, refunds can be authorised through the Peterborough Head Office (Tel: (44733) 502995). Read the details on the Sales Advice form for exact information for your destination. A 24-hour refund service is available in Europe, the USA, Canada, Mexico, Bermuda, the Bahamas and the Caribbean.

- **American Express** cheques can be bought at branches of Lloyds Bank, AT Mays and the Woolwich, Bristol and West, Britannia, National Provincial, Cheltenham and Gloucester, Halifax and Abbey National Building Societies, as well as in travel agencies. Refund information is available when you buy your cheques. Generally, refunding will be through a branch of American Express, Avis or an affiliated company.

- **Visa** cheques are on sale at Barclays Bank and the TSB.

- **Citicorp** cheques are on sale at the Co-Op bank.

- **Building societies** generally charge 1% commission on travellers cheque sales. However, many of them do not have a minimum charge, so they can be cheaper than using a bank. If you have a building society account, watch out for special offers for account-holders as well.

CASH

For sheer convenience it's hard to beat straight cash, and everyone should make sure they buy a small quantity of local currency to avoid the risk of arriving somewhere after the banks have shut with no money to pay the fare into town.

Buying foreign currency

You can buy foreign currency from the foreign exchange sections of high street banks, from specialist foreign exchange agents, especially in London, or from major travel agents like Thomas Cook, American Express and AT Mays. Normally they will charge you 1% of the transaction cost in commission, but again watch out for hefty minimum charges.

Most foreign exchange outlets have constant supplies of popular currencies like francs, pesetas, and so on. However do not expect them to have Hong Kong dollars just waiting to be picked up. If you are travelling anywhere unusual, telephone first to make your order which can often be stocked overnight. Remember that you will only be able to buy £50.00 of cash with a cheque. For larger sums you will usually need to bring a building society cheque, bank draft or cash. If you pay by credit card you will be charged interest immediately without the usual seven week leeway. If you do pay by cheque, remember that most companies will want ten days to clear your cheque before they will release your funds.

Carrying cash

Even if you do not like the idea of carrying the bulk of your funds as cash, it is often worth taking one sizeable cash note concealed somewhere in your luggage, just in case your cheques are stolen when there is no refund office close at hand.

The biggest problem with carrying cash is that if you are robbed there's no possibility of an immediate refund. So if you decide to risk it, make sure you take out an **insurance** policy that has enough protection to cover any loss; most policies offer very limited cash protection. If you know that you will need to make a claim, go to the police and get a written report of the circumstances from them. This may not be easy if you are in the middle of nowhere and do not speak the language, but few insurance companies are interested in unsubstantiated claims of robbery.

Black markets

If you intend to use black markets you will probably need some cash, preferably American dollar bills which are acceptable to most hustlers. If you cannot get dollars, sterling is usually quite popular, but do not try to exchange less well-known currencies like Belgian francs; there is not usually any market for them.

If you do get involved with black markets, bear in mind the risk of **theft**. If you hand over cash in an illegal transaction and the hustler does not come up with the goods, you cannot run to the police. Many travellers are parted from their money in this way, especially in high risk areas like Nairobi and Dar es Salaam. Never let yourself be hurried into an exchange, and if the money passes backwards and forwards several times keep checking to guard against any sleight of hand. Make sure you know what the notes look like and what denominations they come in, otherwise you may find yourself saddled with invalid notes or even with a completely different currency. Listen out for local tricks: in East Africa many strange incidents involve 'accidentally' dropped envelopes of cash; elsewhere ploys are different. Remember that some of the people who will offer you black market cash will happily ship you to the police as soon as they have their hands on your money, so whenever possible track down a reliable source and stick with it.

Hard currency

You will also need cash if you want to buy goods in socialist 'hard currency' shops like Russian "Berioska" shops where goods on sale cannot be bought elsewhere or for local currency.

Most banks and agents will advise you to take a combination of travellers cheques and currency. This is usually sensible advice, but guarantees them two commissions on the same transaction. If your trip is a weekend trip to France or The Netherlands, you'll probably be fine with cash. In fact, even visitors to the USSR could manage perfectly well with cash since there is very little risk of robbery there. Roubles can only be bought in the USSR but as there's little to spend them on, sterling will do fine.

Cash restrictions

While you can usually take limitless amounts of travellers cheques in and out of countries, the same does not apply to local currency. Many countries, even in Europe, restrict either the import or the export, or both, of their currency.

Import		*Export*	
Bulgaria	Prohibited	Austria	AUS5,000
Cyprus	CYL50	Bulgaria	Prohibited
Czechoslovakia	Prohibited	Cyprus	CYL50
East Germany	Prohibited	Czechoslovakia	Prohibited
Greece	DRA100,000	Denmark	DKK50,000
Hungary	FDR100	East Germany	Prohibited
Iceland	IKR8,000	Greece	DRA20,000
Italy	LIT5,000,000	Hungary	FDR100
Malta	MAL50	Eire	IRL100
Poland	Prohibited	Italy	LIT1,000,000
Romania	Prohibited	Malta	MAL25
USSR	Prohibited	Norway	NOK5,000
Yugoslavia	YUD5,000	Poland	Prohibited
		Portugal	PTE50,000
		Romania	Prohibited
		Spain	PTS100,000
		Sweden	SEK6,000
		Turkey	TUL1,000,000
		USSR	Prohibited
		Yugoslavia	YUD5,000

Do not try and export more currency than allowed, since UK foreign exchanges will only buy the legal amount back and you will end up paying several lots of commission to get rid of the surplus.

Some countries do not allow you to export large currency notes. For example, the SEK6,000 that you can export from Sweden must be in denominations of SEK1,000 or less. The Yugoslavians do not permit the export of anything larger than a 1,000 dinar bill, and the Greeks want to hang on to everything larger than a 500 drachma note. Even the Irish do not want any note larger than IRL20 to leave their shores. Again, do not try and ignore these rules since the exchange outlets will not want to buy the bills from you. Their greatest profits are made on buying currency from returning travellers and selling it to outgoing tourists. It they cannot re-sell a large denomination Greek note, there is little point in their buying it from you, except at a very poor exchange rate.

Currency export regulations
It's always worth checking the currency export regulations before you leave the UK. If you do, you may discover that there are other countries whose large notes you can export but for which you will get a poor reconversion rate. This applies, for example, to Spanish pesetas, Portugese escudos and Icelandic kronor. It pays to check in advance so you can ensure you have only the smallest notes left when you are preparing to come home.

Don't forget that there is no market at all in the UK for certain currencies like the Indian rupee or the Russian rouble, so get rid of all of them before you come home. Also get rid of your small change. Only coins like the French ten franc piece can be re-exchanged in the UK (through some branches of Thomas Cook) and then for only half their value. If you do have coins left over, remember that charities like Oxfam are often pleased to take them from you.

Exchange rates
Exchange rates fluctuate from day to day and depend on various factors—including the states of the relevant national economies. They are not fixed, so if you check the same currency in a bank, a Thomas Cook office and an exchange bureau you will find variations, although they should not be great. Such outlets will also show two exchange rates, one that they use when selling currency to you, **the sell rate**, and one they use when buying currency back from you, **the buy rate**. The sell rate is likely to be lower than the buy rate. For example, when the buy rate for French francs is 11.20, the sell rate will be more like 10.56.

Of course only the rates of exchange for popular tourist destinations will be displayed in these outlets. To find out the value of other currencies, look at the *World Value of the Pound* table in Monday's *Financial Times*. However, the rate shown there only represents an average figure. Do not expect any exchange bureau to offer exactly the amount shown in the paper, but at least it is a rough guide for working out your budget.

CREDIT CARDS
Few budget travellers are likely to own an **American Express** or **Diners Club** card since you have to pay for the privilege of having them. You

also have to settle your debts on a monthly basis which could be awkward if you are constantly on the move.

However, even if you would not normally consider having an **Access** or **Visa** card, these are distinct assets as a means of carrying cash when overseas. Not only can you use them for shopping as you would at home, but you can also use them to draw cash from the bank if funds run low. In general there are more places that welcome Barclaycard or Visa than Access, especially in Africa. But remember if you do draw cash that you will be charged interest from the date of the transaction.

Using credit cards abroad

If you use your card to purchase goods, the exchange rate may seem very favourable, but remember that the charge will not reach your account for some time, and exchange rates could fluctuate for or against you in the meantime.

Guard your credit card as carefully as you do your cash and make sure that you know how to notify the appropriate company quickly if it is stolen. Once again, go to the police and insist on a report of the robbery or you might find yourself liable for the first £25.00 of any purchases made on the stolen card. It is possible to insure your card but that involves extra expense which you may feel is not justified.

Before you leave, work out what you might need your credit card for. If, for example, you are going to carry it as insurance against not being able to afford an air fare home, check that your credit limit is large enough to cover the maximum fare and ask to have it raised if necessary. Remember that if you are going to be away for months, you could miss your payment days and run up interest bills. Either arrange a standing order with your bank or for a friend to settle your bills when they fall due.

In some countries, Access and Visa cards can be used to draw money from **cash dispensers**. Visa can be used in Danish, French, Spanish and American cash dispensers while Midland and NatWest Access cards can be used in Spanish cash dispensers as well. It is dangerous to assume they can be used in all the situations they can at home, though. For example, you cannot always buy petrol with a credit card in Spain. On the other hand if you want to hire a car, especially in the USA, a credit card is invaluable for paying the deposit without having to hand over cash.

If you do use an Access or Visa card abroad there are simple precautions you should take to make sure you are not swindled—once you're home again it will be hard, and costly, to do anything about it if you are.

- Always keep your copy of the transaction voucher safe. Then if the amount on your bill differs from what you actually paid, you will be able to prove it.

- Make sure you either keep the carbons between the vouchers or see that they are destroyed so they cannot be used to impress your number onto another blank.

- Never leave a signed voucher with an incomplete payment space, even with someone you trust.

- Be wary of giving your card number over the phone to restaurants and hotels. They may use it to make out a payment voucher in case you do not show up. Then if you do arrive and sign a normal voucher you could end up paying twice for the same service.

CHEQUES

Cheque books and guarantee cards
Within Europe, more and more people can now use their normal cheque book with its £50.00 guarantee card. You can also use your NatWest cash dispenser machine card to draw out cash in Spain.

Postcheques
In Morocco, there are more post offices than banks and you can cash your travellers cheques in them which is very convenient if you are stuck out in the wilds.

National Girobank account-holders can also buy books of ten Postcheques to be used abroad with a cheque card. There is a set fee of £5.00 for the cheques and 1% commission will be charged on each transaction and debited to your UK account. Usually you can cash up to £100 in local currency at one time, although the amount is smaller in Japan and Turkey.

You can only use Postcheques to draw cash but they can be useful if the banks are closed. You can use Postcheques in most parts of Western Europe and in Egypt, the Bahamas and Hong Kong.

Eurocheques
High Street banks will also sell you Eurocheques to use with a Eurocheque card. They charge between £3.50 and £5.00 for issuing the cards which are valid for two years.

Cheques come in sets of ten or fifteen unless you specifically ask for more. You make them out for sums of local currency up to £100 or use them in banks and shops. In Eastern Europe, Turkey, Israel and Egypt you will be asked to write the cheques in US dollars and can only use them in banks. You can write several cheques for items costing more than £100.

In Albania, Bulgaria, East Germany, Egypt, Gibraltar, Lebanon, Poland, Romania, Czechoslovakia, Turkey and the USSR a counter charge of approximately £1.00 will be levied on your transaction. Elsewhere there should be no extra charge. The 1.6% commission levied on each transaction is debited to your bank account which delays the moment of settlement.

You can use Eurocheque cards issued by **Midland**, **Clydesdale**, **Northern** and **NatWest** Banks to draw money from cash dispensers in Denmark, Germany, Spain and Portugal for the same charges as would be made in the UK. The **Midland** card can also be used in Ireland and the **Allied Irish** in Spain.

If your cheques or card are lost while you are away you will have to wait until you get home to have them replaced.

Ideally, you should take your funds with you in a variety of forms. Carry the bulk in refundable travellers cheques, but also have the equivalent of about £50 of local currency, with perhaps another £20 hidden in your luggage for emergencies. Then, provided you have an Access or Visa card, or both, with you you should be prepared for most eventualities.

SENDING MONEY ABROAD

If you intend to travel for a long time you may want to have money sent out to you so you will not have to carry so much of it at any one time.

Postal orders
Do not be tempted to have money posted directly to you—you'll probably never see it again. However it is worth knowing that British postal orders can be cashed in the following places:

Anguilla	Antigua and Barbuda	Bahamas
Bangladesh	Barbados	Belize
Botswana	British Antarctic	British Virgin Islands
Brunei	Territory	Cayman Islands
Cyprus	Dominica	Falkland Islands
Fiji	Gambia	Ghana
Gibraltar	Grenada	Channel Islands
Guyana	Hong Kong	India
Eire	Jamaica	Lesotho
Malawi	Malaysia	Malta
Mauritius	Montserrat	Namibia
New Zealand	Nigeria	Pakistan

Yemen	Pitcairn Islands	St Helena
St Kitts and Nevis	St Lucia	St Vincent and
Seychelles	Sierra Leone	Grenadines
Singapore	Solomon Islands	South Africa
Sri Lanka	Swaziland	Tonga
Trinidad and Tobago	Turks and Caicos	Western Samoa

Postal orders can be bought for cash at any Post Office, which makes it easy for anyone sending money to you. But do not forget that if your mail is tampered with, a postal order will not be much more secure than straight cash.

Girobank transfers
You can also send money overseas using Girobank. Within Europe there are usually several ways of doing this:

- You can pay money into an overseas Giro account which costs £3.50.
- You can arrange for someone to be paid a cheque at an overseas Girobank. This costs £3.50, but the recipient may also be charged when they collect it.
- You can arrange for someone to be paid in cash at an overseas Girobank but this costs £5.00.
- If you need money sent to you regularly you can open an overseas Giro account. Transfers between UK and foreign Giro accounts are free.

Elsewhere you can only send funds in specific ways, as shown in the chart on page 62.

When money is sent to countries other than those in the chart, payment can be made in US dollars, sterling or any other currency that Girobank thinks appropriate.

Note that if you want to send money through Girobank to India, Pakistan or Bangladesh you will need to know the name of the Post Office where payment is to be made when you apply.

You can pick up a form to send money abroad at any Post Office; but to use this service you must be able to pay in cash. If you want to pay by cheque you must write to International Services, Girobank plc, Bootle, Merseyside, GIR 0AA and allow seven working days for the cheque to clear before the money can be sent. You should keep a note of the **counterfoil reference** number, which can be checked in case the payment is not made overseas, but this is not really a suitable way to send money in an emergency.

EMERGENCY FUNDS

Should the worst happen and you run out of money in the middle of nowhere, you can always have more money sent to you through a

Methods of payment used by Girobank overseas

Country	Cash	Cheque	Giro transfer
Austria	Y	Y	Y
Australia	N	Y	N
Bangladesh	Y	N	N
Belgium	Y	Y	Y
Canada	N	Y	N
Cyprus	N	Y	N
Denmark	Y	Y	Y
Finland	Y	Y	Y
France	Y	Y	Y
Greece	N	Y	N
Hong Kong	N	Y	N
Iceland	Y	N	Y
India	Y	Y	N
Ireland	N	Y	N
Italy	N	Y	Y
Japan	Y	Y	Y
Luxembourg	Y	Y	Y
Malta	N	Y	N
Morocco	Y	N	N
Netherlands	Y	Y	Y
New Zealand	N	Y	N
Norway	Y	Y	Y
Pakistan	Y	N	N
Portugal	N	Y	N
Singapore	N	Y	N
South Africa	N	Y	N
Spain	Y	Y	Y
Sweden	Y	Y	Y
Switzerland	Y	Y	Y
Thailand	Y	N	N
Turkey	Y	Y	N
USA	N	Y	N
West Germany	Y	Y	Y
Yugoslavia	Y	N	N

Y = Possible   N = Not possible

bank, or through a branch of Thomas Cook or American Express. It can be sent by **telegraphic** or **mail transfer**, although the latter takes longer than the former method. You will need to find out which bank the funds will be remitted to, and you may have to wait several days for them to arrive, but arrive they will.

If you know your itinerary it might be wise to call into a local Thomas Cook office beforehand and enquire about the procedure for sending money to the places you will be visiting. Then you can leave advice for whoever will have responsibility for arranging it for you. While you are there, find out what form you can receive the money in; some countries insist you accept it in local currency, which may not suit you at all. If this is the case, limit the amount you have transmitted to that particular place. Bear in mind that payment for mail and telegraphic transfers will have to be in cash or by a bank or building society draft. Make sure that whoever sends the money to you has access to your bank account by signing a bank mandate form. You could also sign a **power of attorney**, a legal document allowing a named person to act for you in legal and business transactions. Standard forms for this are available from stationery shops for about 40p.

In dire emergency you could always try the **British Embassy**, although they are not renowned for their sympathy toward impecunious travellers. You will probably find yourself put on the next flight home with your passport impounded against repayment of the fare. Being female is said to help, but do not depend on it!

BLACK MARKETS

It is worth adding a note about black markets, which flourish in some Third World and most Eastern European countries, where official exchange rates do not reflect the true value of local currency. The 'soft' currencies of such countries are worthless on international exchange markets and the government, and a large proportion of the population, will be desperate to get hold of 'hard' currencies—dollars, sterling, francs, and so on—so that they can buy goods unobtainable with their own money. Attempts to make you change and spend fixed amounts of money are the official response to the need for hard currency. Black markets are the unofficial response. Basically, it is a battle between the government and individuals to see who can get the most out of you.

Black markets come in two forms:

1. Exchange markets.
2. Currency markets.

Exchange markets

Of the two, it is probably safer to dabble in the former. In Eastern Europe, for example, there's great demand for **jeans** and other symbols of western 'youth culture'. People may be prepared to offer you hundreds of zlotys, or whatever, for such items. In Africa, however, although there may be interest in the same items, expect to be offered something made locally in exchange. Sometimes this can work perfectly and may not seem at all illegal. In other cases, expect to be made quite unrealistic offers; our prices are so high that it is impossible for people in poorer countries to imagine them. So in Morocco you might be offered a cheap and tacky ring for an expensive pair of sunglasses.

Currency exchanges

Genuine black market currency exchanges are another matter altogether. Countries like Tanzania regard such arrangements as 'economic sabotage' and have lengthy jail sentences to reflect the severity of the offence. But the Tanzanian black market usually offers exchange rates six times higher than those in the bank. Travellers who play by the rules will find even food outrageously expensive and visits to the game parks and Mount Kilimanjaro prohibitive. However, if you do dabble on the black market, you risk running into an informer. Border checks on the Tazara railway involve body searches for money. If you are caught, expect to pay a hefty bribe at the very least.

Currency declaration forms

Most countries with black markets have currency declaration forms. On arrival at the border, you will fill these out with details of how much money in cash and travellers cheques you are importing. When you go to a bank to cash the cheque, the fact is recorded on the form. In theory, when you leave, Customs officials should be able to match up the **bank receipts** with the money you have left. If there are yawning discrepancies it will look suspiciously as if you have used the black market.

This system, fine in theory, has a number of loopholes in practice. In the first place, few Customs officials ever ask to see your bank receipts and if you say you have lost them there is not a great deal they can do about it. Then, unless they can see where you have spent the money, it's difficult for them to tell how much money you should have changed at the bank. If your currency form shows that you've only changed £20.00 during a two week stay in Tanzania it certainly looks suspicious. But if you say you have stayed with friends and hitched lifts, it is hard to disprove it.

The system works best when, as in Burma, you are not only obliged to have all exchange transactions listed but you must pay for all accommodation and transport through a central tourist office as well. These costs can then be debited against the money you have changed, and when you come to leave the country Customs officers should be able to make a fairly accurate assessment of whether you have cheated. In fact, the Burmese system is so good now that the black market money you get from selling duty-free goods can only really be used to pay for food, souvenirs and jeep trips.

Two tier exchange systems

To discourage black market hustlers, many countries have a two tier exchange system, with a preferential exchange rate for tourists. In some cases governments have even licensed other currency outlets—as has happened in Sudan in an attempt to route at least some hard currency through official channels. In countries where hard currency is in desperately short supply, you may even have to accept currencies other than sterling or dollars (Saudi rials, for example) if you want to resell local currency before leaving. In that case you will have to pay again to re-exchange it at home, so try to avoid changing too much money in the first place. Where there are several exchange rates, you may still have to pay for items like **air fares** at the less favourable rate and have that fact endorsed on your currency exchange certificate.

PUBLIC HOLIDAYS: A WARNING

When you are travelling around, it can be disastrous to run out of funds on a public holiday since all the banks and finance houses will be closed. In Europe this is becoming less of a problem as cash dispensers proliferate, but once you are into the Thirld World, it is quite another matter. If all the banks are closed, you may be forced to exchange money at a hotel or shop at a very unfavourable rate or to resort to the black market even if you do not want to.

The *ABC Guide to International Travel* lists public holidays for each country but be warned that what looks like a one day holiday sometimes turns out to be longer, so it is wise to change more money than you think you need beforehand, to be on the safe side.

HYPER-INFLATION: ANOTHER WARNING

Some countries, particularly in South America, are now suffering from hyper-inflation. In such countries it is advisable only to change your money in small amounts at a time—hopefully, you will get more for it this way.

In countries with intrinsically unstable economies, it is also wise to keep your ear to the ground for drastic measures such as devaluation, revaluation or even complete closure of the banks for several days, as happened in Brazil in 1990.

6

Guarding Against Calamities

For those travelling on a tight budget, it is very tempting to decide to do without insurance—especially after getting a quotation from a high street travel agency. However, remember that if you are travelling to remote areas, and staying and eating in cheap and not necessarily very hygienic surroundings, your chances of falling ill or having your belongings stolen are high—and the longer you are away, the greater the risk.

There are two main methods of taking out insurance:

- Package deals.
- Individual arrangements.

PACKAGE DEALS

Most people automatically opt for the package deal which covers all or most of the following:

- Loss or theft of baggage or money.
- Medical expenses arising from illness or accident.
- Compensation for permanent injury, for example loss of a limb.
- Protection against expenses arising from damage to a third person.
- Compensation for delayed departure.
- Protection against cancellation charges if you are unable to travel.

All insurance policies vary, so *read the details* carefully before committing yourself.

Budget travellers are usually most concerned about costs arising from robbery or ill-health. However, make sure you understand every section of a package insurance policy offer.

Loss or theft of baggage or money

Most policies strictly limit the amount of straight cash that can be refunded, so if you are taking a lot of money, turn it into travellers cheques or arrange to have it sent out to you as you travel. Travellers planning to use black markets should take particular note of the small print of the policy, since they are likely to make the best profits out of cash transactions. Check whether plane tickets, and so on, will be counted as cash and note the number of your tickets in case you need to make a claim.

Some people survive the theft of their luggage better than others. If you are backpacking, remember that everything you own may be in one place, and consider what it would be like to wake up on a train with nothing left but your underwear. The trouble is that even if you are insured, you usually have to pay to replace your belongings and then make a claim against your policy when you get home again. Although the maximum sum covered by the policy may sound a lot, if you estimate the cost of replacing everything you plan to take with you, it may well be more than you think.

Read the 'excess' details carefully. The 'excess' is the amount of each loss you are expected to bear before the insurance company will pay out. What this usually means is that if just your penknife disappears you will not be able to claim because it is worth less than the excess.

Another catch to beware of is the 'one item or set of items' rule. You may find that the maximum you can claim on any one valuable item is £100. A camera can easily be worth more than that and when you add to it the value of additional lenses, and so on, this limitation can leave your insurance cover looking pretty thin. Consider asking a specialist insurance company to insure the specific items for you.

Medical expenses arising from illness or accident

Many budget travellers worry about falling ill and running up enormous medical bills while abroad. Luckily, most package policies provide adequate cover provided you bear in mind the following points:

- Watch out for the 'excess' clause. Minor ailments may result in £20.00 bills which cannot be reclaimed.

- Bear in mind that medical treatment costs more in some parts of the world than others. The USA is notoriously expensive, a fact reflected in the higher premiums for travellers there—prices unfortunately picked up by travellers to less expensive parts of the American continent as well. Ideally, your policy should provide roughly £250,000 of medical cover for Europe, £500,000 for the rest of the world and £1,000,000 for the USA.

- There are parts of the world where medical treatment is free. Citizens of EC countries are entitled to reciprocal benefits in other member countries, which means British citizens can get free or reduced price medical treatment in any other EC country. Eastern bloc countries also offer free medical treatment to visitors. British citizens can also get free medical care in Gibraltar and Hong Kong, and hospital out-patient treatment is free in many countries including Kenya and Thailand.

● Free treatment is provided in public hospitals, so if you are the sort of person who prefers not to trust state-run systems, you may still need that medical cover to allow you to go private.

● Remember that you may have to pay for treatment on the spot and then make a claim when you get home, so make sure you know how money can be sent to you in an emergency. Get a receipt for anything you want to claim for, and a doctor's note justifying the costs of someone staying to help you, and so on.

● Ideally you should look for a policy that allows you to be repatriated by air ambulance if necessary.

Read through the **exclusion clauses** carefully to see if they affect you. The following are usually excluded as grounds for a claim:

● Venereal diseases, including AIDS. More and more insurance companies also exclude the cost of repatriating patients who fear contracting AIDS from medical treatment overseas.

● Pre-existing medical conditions. This can mean either an illness for which you have received treatment in the last year, or one which had begun before you left home or took out the policy. Few insurance policies allow you to travel abroad purely for the purpose of receiving medical treatment. If in doubt, always check with the insurance company directly.

Some policies also include upper age limits and restrict the rights of women reaching the end of their pregnancy. If you want to take part in sports that might increase the likelihood of an accident, your insurance fee is also likely to be higher, so if you plan on mountaineering, paragliding or motorcycling, make sure you check whether such activities are covered first (see also **Ski insurance**, page 75).

Personal accident insurance (compensation for permanent injury)

Few people take out insurance purely for protection against the risk of permanent disablement. However, where two policies offer similar cover at a similar price, this could be an area to help you choose. If you are likely to be taking part in dangerous sports like skiing, it is obviously worth looking into this more carefully.

Typical cover provides for a maximum payment of perhaps £20,000 for the loss of both eyes. Other permanent injuries would attract sums of compensation representing a percentage of the total cover. The following list indicates a common breakdown of compensation for total loss:

Right arm	75%	One foot	50%
One leg	70%	Sight in one eye	30%
Left arm	65%	Right thumb	25%
Right hand	60%	Hearing in one ear	20%
Left hand	50%	Left thumb	20%
Hearing in both ears	50%		

Protection against third party liability
Again, it is unlikely that this would be the sole grounds for taking out a policy, but check how much cover would be provided if you accidentally injure someone or damage their property and they sue for damages.

Compensation for delayed departure
This section is most likely to be relevant if you are going abroad for a short time. It will usually be riddled with let-out clauses covering so-called 'Acts of God', 'government action', and so on. The best policies give you the option of cancelling your holiday without cost if it is delayed for more than 24 hours.

Protection against cancellation charges
This is very important for budget travellers who have bought the cheapest air tickets, as these usually have rules limiting your right to change or cancel your booking, especially close to the date of departure. Without insurance, even a road accident cannot save you from paying the charges if you cannot travel, and these can be very steep—most APEX/PEX tickets carry £25 or £50 cancellation fees.

Package holidays usually carry steep cancellation charges too, so take out insurance at the time of booking to protect yourself. Typical cancellation charges might be:

Length of time between cancellation and scheduled date of departure	*Cancellation fee as percentage of holiday cost*
More than 42 days (6 weeks)	Deposit
29-42 days	30% (or deposit)
15-28 days	45% (or deposit)
1-14 days	60% (or deposit)
Departure date or later	100%

The following general points about insurance are worth bearing in mind:

● Keep receipts if you are likely to want to make a claim.

- Report all losses to the police and get written confirmation that you have done so.
- Take every precaution against theft, like locking your hotel door, wearing a money-belt, placing valuables in the hotel safe, and so on. Insurance companies prefer clients who try to avoid making claims. Do not forget that second and third claims are unlikely to be well-received.
- Ensure that your cover includes both your departure and return days of travel.
- Always read the 'eligibility' and 'exclusion' sections of the policy carefully. The following are examples of typical exclusion paragraphs:

  '1. Suicide, self inflicted injury, alcoholism, use of drugs, pregnancy or childbirth, winter sports, racing, motor rallies, mountaineering involving ropes or guides, sub-aqua diving, pot-holing, motorcycling on machines in excess of 125cc, football, aerial activities other than as a passenger in an aircraft, war and kindred risks.
  Wear and tear, depreciation, confiscation, contact lenses and pedal cycles, business goods, breakage of fragile articles or sports equipment in use, loss of money not carried on the person and losses of money and valuables not reported to the police within 24 hours of discovery.
  Use of vehicles and craft (other than manually propelled), business or trade activity, firearms, control of animals.
  Strikes, riot or civil commotion where warning has been given prior to the application for insurance.
  '2. Money, contact lenses, cycles and other vehicles, mental illness, alcohol, drugs, suicide, racing and hazardous forms of sporting activities (other than winter sports and mountaineering if separate cover taken), the first £10 of each loss. In respect of luggage the maximum payable for any one item is £100. In addition the total payable in respect of valuable articles will be limited to £200.'

- Look around particularly carefully if you are travelling with children. Many tour operators' policies do not offer child insurance discounts, but some private companies do.

- Remember that holiday insurance policies assume that you will be staying away for a limited period of time. If you are making a one-way or indefinite journey, most package policies will not be suitable. Even if the company quotes a price for each extra week, there may still be a maximum length of time—perhaps six months—that you can be away. You should also bear in mind that it is not easy to take out travel insurance once you have left your own country, so this is something that you definitely need to think about in advance.

High street travel agencies sell package policies at reasonable prices for short trips, but their prices are exorbitant for long-stay travellers. Instead, you might do better to take out a policy through **Endsleigh Insurance** whose quotations are usually most competitive. Note that Endsleigh sells one 'travel' and one 'holiday' policy. The 'travel' one is slightly cheaper than the 'holiday' option. Contact Endsleigh Insurance Services Ltd at Endsleigh House, Cheltenham Spa, Gloucester GL50 3NR. STA Travel also sells Endsleigh insurance, but has a slight mark-up on its prices.

Sample package insurance policies for adults (Europe)

	Thomas Cook	Endsleigh	NatWest
1-5 days	£12.30	£6.50	£9.75
6-8 days	£12.30	£10.00	£12.50
9-12 days	£13.40	£12.00	£14.95
12-17 days	£14.50	£12.00	£14.95
18-24 days	£15.90	£14.00	£17.56
25-31 days	£17.30	£17.50	£19.85
Extra week	£3.80	N/A	£5.00

(Note that different companies offer package policies for slightly different durations, so the above comparison is only approximate.)

PLACES WHERE YOU SHOULD NEVER TRAVEL WITHOUT INSURANCE

- USA and Canada.
- Liechtenstein, Switzerland, Turkey, Cyprus, Monaco, Andorra, San Marino and the Faroe Islands.
- Africa, the Indian sub-continent, South America, the Far East, the Middle East and Israel.
- Anywhere near the border of a country which offers free medical treatment. In an emergency you might be taken to a hospital over the border where you do have to pay.
- Any country where only partial refund of medical costs is possible. Your insurance company will then pick up the rest of the bill.

CLAIMING ON YOUR POLICY

With luck, your holiday will go well and you will not have to claim on your insurance. Unfortunately, if you *do* have to, it may turn out to be a trying experience. You can make things easier for yourself by carrying the policy document with you so that you can consult it as soon as you suspect that you need to make a claim, and make sure you have done whatever is required to qualify for cover. If you have been robbed, or have lost something valuable, make sure you have a written report from the police, preferably in English. Even with a medical claim, make sure you can prove your case. When a motorcyclist ran over my foot and broke it on Gibraltar, it was too late at night to get an X-ray and I had no choice but to put up, with my companion, at a hotel neither of us would normally have used. The small print of my policy confirmed that I had cover for someone to stay with me if necessary and the doctor duly wrote a letter the next day confirming the break. But when I tried to claim for the hotel bill I was told there was no proof that I needed someone with me. I wrote back, pointing out that without a companion I would have been on the first flight home with a claim for an air fare rather than a cheap hotel bill. The company paid up by return, so it is worth persevering.

MEDICAL COSTS WITHIN THE EC

UK citizens can receive free or reduced cost medical treatment if they fall ill or have an accident while in another EC country (Belgium, Denmark, France, West Germany, Greece, Ireland, Italy, Luxembourg, The Netherlands, Portugal and Spain, but not the Canary or Channel Islands). To be sure of receiving this you should apply for an **E111** about a month before you intend to go abroad. This can be obtained by filling out form CM1 in the Department of Health leaflet SA40 *Before You Go*, and sending it to your local Department of Health office or to the Department of Health, Overseas Branch, Newcastle-upon-Tyne NE98 1YX.

If you are going to work in another EC country you should write to the Department of Health, Overseas Branch, OVB CONTS (address as above) giving your name and address in the UK, the name and address of your intended employer and your National Insurance Number. Form E111 only covers temporary visits abroad. Similarly, if you are going to study in another EC country you should write to the Department of Health for advice.

In most EC countries, medical treatment is provided through insurance schemes. Obtaining treatment may be more complicated than it is at home, but obviously you have to follow the same rules as local people—and remember that form E111 only covers emergency health care.

Reclaiming medical costs in the EC

In many countries, treatment is free but sometimes you have to pay part of the cost yourself. You may also have to pay for treatment on the spot and then reclaim the costs later. To claim a refund you should apply to the local **sickness insurance fund** of the country you are visiting. You must show all original documents, such as receipts, when making your claim, but it is sensible to make a photocopy of them first. If you wait until you get home to make your claim, you may face a long delay or even lose your right to repayment altogether.

Read the rules for each particular country on the E111 carefully, since if you do not follow the specific instructions, you may forfeit your entitlement to a refund. Wherever possible, take your E111 with you. If it is not essential, take a copy of the DHS leaflet *Before You Go* instead. In Belgium, France, Germany, Italy and The Netherlands, you should also have a copy of the E111.

In most EC countries, the E111 does not cover *all* medical treatment; the cost of dentistry, prescribed medicines and treatment by private doctors or in private hospitals is rarely included. It never covers the cost of repatriating someone who is ill to the UK, or the cost of flying a body home. It may also not cover medical costs arising from an accident while driving. For these reasons, you should still consider taking out a private insurance policy. Drivers should always check their motor insurance to see what it covers. Form E111 is normally valid for two years.

The chart on page 74 summarises arrangements in other EC countries but you should read the information on your E111 for full details.

OTHER FORMS OF INSURANCE

Camping carnets
Holders of camping carnets are automatically provided with limited personal accident and third party liability insurance. Maximum cover under the personal accident insurance is £1,000, while the third party policy covers claims of up to £250,000. The carnet's holder and up to eight members of their family or camping party are protected. Remember that the personal accident insurance covers small medical and dental bills of up to £25.00, with an excess of £1.00.

Credit cards
Should you be lucky enough to hold an **American Express card**, it is worth noting that you automatically receive £75,000 of insurance to cover you against possible accidents at the airport or during your flight. **Access and Visa cardholders** automatically receive £50,000 of similar transit insurance—that is, as long as you have used your card to pay for at least part of your ticket.

Motoring insurance policies
Anyone intending to take a vehicle to the Continent should consider taking out a special insurance policy like the AA's 5 Star Insurance, the

Country	Documents required	What is free	What is not free	Details
Belgium	E111		Hospital treatment, prescribed medicines, other medical and dental care.	About 75% of charges refundable.
Denmark	UK passport	Hospital care or treatment ordered by doctor.	Dentistry, prescribed medicines.	Before you leave, ask Kommunens socialog-sundhedsfor-valtning for refund.
France	E111		Most things.	70-80% refund from French Sickness Insurance Office.
West Germany	E111	Dental and medical care.	Hospital treatment, prescribed medicines.	Details on E111.
Gibraltar	UK passport	Public hospitals, doctors.	Dentistry, prescribed medicines.	
Greece	E111		Most things.	Refunds possible, but insurance sensible.
Ireland	None	Most things.		
Italy	E111	Most things.	Prescribed medicines.	
Luxembourg	E111	Hospital care.	Dentistry, doctors, prescribed medicines.	Partial refund possible.
Netherlands	E111	Medical and hospital care.	Dentistry, prescribed medicines.	
Portugal	UK passport	Hospital care.	Most things.	Mention EC rules.
Spain	E111	Most things.	Dentistry, prescribed medicines.	Follow E111 rules carefully.

RAC's Eurocover or Europ Assistance. These policies offer some or all of the following:

- Break-down assistance on the way to the port.
- A self-drive car if your own breaks down just before you leave.
- Emergency break-down assistance on the Continent, usually through a local affiliated organisation.
- Repatriation of your vehicle if there is no other way to have it repaired in time for your return.
- Limited travel and accommodation costs if you are unable to use your car at all as a result of an accident or break-down.
- A chauffeur if your driver becomes unfit to continue.
- Limited compensation for break-ins.
- Legal assistance following a motoring accident.
- Protection against Customs liability if your car is destroyed abroad and cannot therefore be re-exported.
- Emergency credit to pay for repairs to your car.
- Despatch of spare parts to wherever you are stranded.

Most motoring insurance policies have supplementary personal policies as well. They also have all the same let-out clauses you find on other policies, so make sure you read through the small print carefully, especially if your vehicle is old.

Europ Assistance is at 252 High Street, Croydon CR0 1NF (Tel: (01) 680 1234).

Ski insurance

No-one should ever go skiing without insurance, even though premiums can be three times the normal rates. You will probably be better off buying a specialist ski insurance package rather than a holiday insurance policy with a skiing option. Companies offering suitable policies include:

Perry Gamble and Co. Ltd, Tuition House, 27-37 St Georges Road, London SW19 4EU (Tel: (01) 879 1255).

Douglas Cox Tyrie, 100 Whitechapel Road, London E1 1JB. (Tel: (01) 488 3191).

Fogg Travel Insurance Services, Fullarton House, Crow Hill Drive, Mansfield, Notts NG19 7AE (Tel: (0623) 31331).

NatWest Insurance Services Ltd, PO Box 106, National Westminster Court, Little John Street, Bristol BS99 7NQ (Tel: (0272) 263000).

The best policies cover you against loss or damage to your own or hired skis and against the cost of advance-booked ski-packs if you have to cancel. They also provide compensation if the nearest pistes are closed or avalanches delay your arrival at the resort. Ideally, they should provide a minimum of £50,000 cover against medical costs, £500,000 cover against your liability if you injure another skier, and 24-hour rescue and repatriation cover arranged through Mondial, Medicall or Europ Assistance.

7

Kitting Yourself Out for Your Trip

Some people are happy to travel the world with little more than the clothes they stand up in. For such hardy souls, deciding what to buy before they go is a simple matter. For everyone else time and care are needed, especially if a tight budget makes the price of every purchase important.

What you buy before you go largely depends on:

a) Where you are going.
b) How long you will be away.
c) Where you will be sleeping.

BACKPACKS

For most long-term travellers, a backpack is the mainstay of the trip, a sort of home from home which can double up as seat, pillow or backrest as circumstances demand. Backpacks fall into two main types —those with an **external frame** and those with an **internal frame**.

External frame packs

Nowadays these are usually the cheapest packs on the market, readily available in camping shops for about £30.00. The frames are useful for hanging items like cooking pots where they can be reached easily. Unfortunately, they also catch on doorways, hooks, and so on, and have a nasty habit of coming apart when tossed around by airline baggage handlers. However, for a series of European train journeys they can be ideal.

External frame packs often have useful side pockets into which you can slip knives, books, maps, and so on, for easy access—but bear in mind the equal ease with which pickpockets can then remove these items.

Internal frame packs

These packs have the advantage that no parts jut out to catch on anything. There are also fewer pockets to pick, and they are usually pretty sturdy; mine has doubled as a makeshift seat all round Africa and it survives to tell the story.

Such packs are usually more expensive than those with cheap aluminium frames and must often be bought from specialist shops. However there are a number of excellent stockists to choose from—Karrimor, Berghaus, Vango, Caravan—and a wide selection can be examined at any YHA Adventure Shop. Expect to pay upwards of £50 for a good pack.

Since your backpack will be with you a long time it is worth paying slightly more for a good one. A cheap pack that promptly falls apart and has to be replaced is a very false economy. Always try it for size before buying and make sure the shoulder straps are comfortable and that it has a waistband to help distribute the weight evenly. In the past, women had to make do with packs made for men but Berghaus' new Lady Pulsar model takes their different shape into account. It costs about £45.

Other packs and bags

People who are expert at travelling light sometimes manage with just a small **daypack** which has the advantage that it can be taken inside buses with you and carried onto planes as hand luggage. Even if you need more than that most of the time, it is worth investing in a daypack small enough to fit inside your main bag. Then when you go off on a short side trip you can leave the majority of your luggage at base and just take what you need for the trip. Good daypacks cost upwards of £10.00. Look for one with a lockable zip so no-one can slip it open without you realising. Since **duffel bags** have come back into fashion you could buy one of these instead, but remember that they do not close very securely.

Backpacks are not popular at a lot of border posts, so some travellers prefer to take a **convertible bag** with straps and waistband that fold away to make it look like a normal hand-held bag when appropriate. Interpack, by Caravan, is one such model.

When choosing something for day-to-day purposes bear in mind that although **shoulder bags** are very comfortable to carry, thieves are notoriously good at snatching them, sometimes violently. By all means buy one but carry it tucked under your arm or in front of you where you can keep an eye on it. Sling it over the shoulder which is furthest away from the road and any passing motorcycle thieves.

SLEEPING BAGS

Whether you need to buy a sleeping bag depends on where you are going and where you will be staying. Few campers would set out for Nepal without a good, thick bag. However people hoping to sleep on Greek beaches in the summer could make do with a sheet sleeping bag.

Sheet sleeping bags

If you plan to stay in youth hostels, their rules oblige you to use a sheet sleeping bag instead of, or in addition to, a down one. (An exception is made if you use two sheets and a pillow-case.) Consequently YHA Shops are a good source of solid, well-made bags which cost about £10.00. However, anyone with the slightest skill at needlework should be able to run one up without any trouble. YHA regulations require the bag to measure 210cm by 80cm with a 60cm fold-back from the head section. If you are travelling to somewhere like Egypt where cotton is plentiful and labour cheap, then you could wait till you arrive and have a bag made to your own specifications. It pays to take a drawing with you since the idea of a sheet sleeping bag is not readily understood.

Down and synthetic bags

Anyone intending to travel to colder areas of the world like the Himalayas or the Alps should buy a bag before they go. Once again, this is not an appropriate area for economy; buying a cheap one could mean risking cold, wet nights at best and hypothermia at worst.

Synthetic bags are cheaper than down ones and have the added advantage that they are quicker to dry. If you decide to go for down, buy a bag with a waterproof covering of **Gore-Tex** or **Sympatex**. For maximum warmth you should choose a mummy-shaped bag which you can slide into without undoing and which has a draught-excluding hood.

Even the lightest sleeping bags are bulky. External-framed backpacks usually have a space at the bottom for you to tie your bag to, but with internal-framed packs you may have to squash it inside, so look for ones sold in **compressible stuff bags** which help you squeeze out all the air to take up as little space as possible.

Remember that all sleeping bags provide protection against dirty, bug-infested sheets in cheap accommodation. Travellers in Africa may feel a sleeping bag superfluous as far as warmth is concerned. However, your skin needs to be shielded from beds on offer in most cheap hotels as much as possible. I have also found that carrying a sleeping bag makes it possible to strike a makeshift camp when necessary; for example, at Khartoum airport a sheet bag would not have provided enough cushioning to sleep on a concrete floor—nor would it have offered adequate shelter from inquisitive eyes.

Northern Feather, Karrimor and Vango all offer a wide range of sleeping bags which are on sale at YHA Adventure Shops. Expect to pay upwards of £50.00 for a good bag. Always read the manufacturer's specifications carefully to make sure you are buying the right bag for the conditions you expect to meet.

WALKING BOOTS AND SHOES

Sensible travellers go equipped for all eventualities, so even if you are not planning a long trek, it still pays to pack a pair of sensible walking shoes in case an opportunity presents itself.

If you do not intend to do much walking, you may only need a pair of lightweight, sturdy shoes. **Tennis shoes** with good rubber soles are often ideal, although shoes with ankle supports are best. If possible look for ridged rubber soles since these are good for gripping wet, muddy slopes. If you can get hold of a pair of Israeli canvas army boots, these are ideal for all but the toughest conditions.

However, if you are off on a trek in the Himalayas, this is another area where economy could be a mistake. Buy the lightest but toughest boots you can afford, and make sure that they have thick soles and ankle supports. Practise walking in them first to give the leather a chance to mould to the shape of your foot. Synthetic materials are cheaper than leather and can be better because they don't absorb water or freeze in icy conditions. Berghaus and Hawkins are two manufacturers of good boots on sale at YHA Adventure Shops. Expect to pay upwards of £40 for a good pair of hiking boots.

Remember that you will need good **socks** as well if your feet are to be truly comfortable. Buy the socks first and try the boots on over them to make sure of the best fit. A good, thick pair should cost you about £8.00.

TENTS

If you want to camp while abroad you should certainly buy the tent before you leave.

If you are travelling alone, weight will be important; there are plenty of tents which weigh less than three kilogrammes. If conditions are likely to be wet look for a tent with a flysheet which can be erected first. Then you can set up the tent in the dry underneath. Always buy a tent with built-in groundsheet to keep bugs at bay, and remember to insect-proof all openings in mosquito-ridden areas.

Budget travellers should steer clear of 'novelty' tents; traditional ridge-shaped tents should be adequate for most purposes and those made of nylon or PVC are likely to be longest lasting.

Robert Saunders, Lichfield and Vango are three companies offering a wide range of tents which are on sale through YHA Adventure Shops. Always read their specifications carefully to make sure you choose the right tent for the conditions you will be travelling in. Expect to pay at least £70 for a two-person tent suitable for most camping conditions.

If you cannot afford a new tent, look in the camping magazines for a secondhand one, but if your tent is not brand new always erect it once before setting out to make sure you've got all the pegs and poles. Don't forget that the ground is sometimes very hard and pack a mallet to whack in the pegs.

CAMPING EQUIPMENT

Campers should also buy other vital equipment before leaving home, especially when planning to travel outside Europe. Knives may be readily available everywhere but they are unlikely to be of the quality you get at home, while plastic water bottles are all but unobtainable in Africa. However, tin plates, mugs and cutlery can be picked up almost anywhere at reasonable prices.

However desirable, Swiss army knives are notoriously expensive and this is an obvious area for economy. There are plenty of cheap imitations on the market which should be adequate for all but the purist. Furthermore, ask yourself how many of the various blades you really need; a bottle-opener and knife, certainly, but probably not a device for digging stones out of horses' hooves. Suitable Victorinox knives cost from £7.95 upwards.

A **torch** is also a good investment, but remember that batteries may be hard to obtain elsewhere, so buy spares as well. Buy the smallest, lightest model you can find, or consider investing in the type that sits on a band around your forehead like a miner's lamp, leaving your hands free. Suitable Ever-Ready torches with batteries cost about £4.00.

You may also want to place something soft between you, your sleeping bag and the hard ground, in which case a foam **Karrimat** costing about £14.00 could be ideal. However, foam can feel sweaty in hot climates. Another possibility is to buy an inflatable mattress which will fold up into a tiny space in your pack for about £40.00.

Most campers will also need a lamp, and a basic Camping Gaz model costs about £30.00. A one-ring Camping Gaz stove costs about £18.00, with refill Gaz cartons costing roughly £1.50 each. YHA Shops sell camp cookery pan-sets for £10.25 each, while sturdy plastic water bottles cost about £2.00 each. If you are going to be camping in very rough conditions, you may also want to consider the range of survival equipment produced in the BGB Adventure Series. This includes a matchless fire-making kit, useful for camping in wet conditions.

To find out about the latest developments in travelling equipment, consult the *Gear Up* pages of *The Traveller*, or the *YHA Magazine*. Alternatively you could join **The Backpackers Club** which offers a comprehensive Backpacking Advisory Service to members. Individual membership costs £9.00 a year with a £5.00 joining fee. Write to

Mr. E. R. Gurney, PO Box 381, 7-10 Friar Street, Reading RG3 4RL, Berks (Tel: (04917) 73924).

Stockist information
The following companies specialise in equipment for travellers and it is worth writing to them for their catalogues:

Berghaus
34 Dean Street
Newcastle-upon-Tyne NE1 1PG
Tel: (091) 2323561

Hawkins
Overstone Road
Northampton NN1 3JJ
Tel: (0604) 32293

Northern Feather Leisure (UK) Ltd
1 Newfield Drive
Menston-Ilkley
West Yorkshire LS29 6JQ
Tel: (0943) 74870

Vango
70 East Hamilton Street
Ladyburn
Greenwood PA15 2HB
Tel: (0475) 44122

Karrimor
19 Avenue Parade
Accrington
Lancashire BB5 6PR
Tel: (0254) 385911

Robert Saunders
5 Oaks Lane
Chigwell
Essex IG7 4QP
Tel: (01) 500 2447

Lichfield
John James Hawley Ltd
Lichfield Road
Walsall WS4 2DH
Tel: (0922) 25641

The manufacturers will know your nearest stockist. However, all of them sell their equipment through YHA Adventure Shops in London, Cambridge, Luton, Birmingham, Manchester, Oxford, Cardiff, Bristol and Staines. The YHA also produces its own equipment range at budget prices and a series of useful fact sheets on tents, rucksacks, boots and sleeping bags. These contain sketches, descriptions and prices of many leading models produced by the large companies. So if you want to compare several makes of boot, for example, one letter to the YHA could save you half a dozen to individual manufacturers.

Other major stockists include:

Pindisports
14-18 Holborn
London EC1N 2LJ
Tel: (01) 242 3278

Rohan Designs Ltd
30 Maryland Road
Tangwell
Milton Keynes MK15 8HN
Tel: (0908) 618888
(lightweight trouser specialists)

Travelling Light
Freepost
Morland
Cumbria CA10 1BR
Tel: (09314) 488

Field & Trek (Equipment) Ltd
3 Wates Way
Brentwood CM15 9TB
Tel: (0277) 221259

Cotswold Camping
42-44 Uxbridge Road
London W12 8ND
Tel: (01) 743 2976

CAMERAS AND FILM

If you are off to Hong Kong or Singapore it makes sense to wait and
buy a camera when you get there. Similarly, if you will be transitting
the duty-free lounge at Abu Dhabi airport, prices are very reasonable—
but remember that you will still have to pay duty on the camera when
you return to the UK.

However, if you are going somewhere more remote, you should
certainly buy a camera and as much colour film as you can before you
leave home. Equipment for sale in places like India and Africa is likely
to be expensive, and often ancient. Never risk arriving at a 'sight' like
the Taj Mahal or Victoria Falls without film; prices go through the
roof, partly because there is a captive market but also because film has
to be imported before it can be sold to tourists, bumping up its cost.
Remember that most countries limit the amount of film that you can
import legally; ten or twelve rolls is usually the most you are permitted.

Choosing the right camera

The type of camera you buy may depend on what you can afford, but if
you can rise to something more than an Instamatic it could be an
investment—especially if you sell some of your pictures later (see
Turning Your Travels Into Hard Cash). Good photographers should still
go for an SLR with wide angle and zoom lenses; try secondhand camera
shops or the advertising columns of *Practical Photography* for bargains.
The less experienced should aim for one of the new-generation
automatic cameras. At about £100 these can sound ludicrously
expensive, but the risk of dud shots is greatly diminished, so they
could be viewed as a worthwhile investment. Remember to make sure
your insurance policy covers the full value of photographic equipment.

Some people like to take Polaroid cameras with them so they can
give pictures to people they meet on the way. However in my
experience as soon as you give away one picture you have to give away
ten and this can be extremely expensive. Polaroid pictures are not of the

highest quality either. If you can only afford one camera, stick with an SLR or an automatic.

If you write to Kodak Ltd, PO Box 66, Hemel Hempstead, Herts HP1 1JU, they will supply you with leaflets on tropical photography, choice of film, costs, processing, storage, airport X-ray machines and exposure requirements. They also supply a list of worldwide laboratories able to process Kodak films and of their offices abroad where you can get further advice.

MEDICINES

Now that prescription charges are £3.05 an item, it is sometimes cheaper to wait until you reach your destination before buying pills. This certainly applies in Thailand where lots of medicines like hydrocortisone which can only be obtained on prescription in the UK are readily available over the counter.

NHS doctors are not obliged to prescribe for travellers spending more than six months out of the country. If you would have to pay for a private prescription, it is even more worthwhile considering buying locally. However, bear in mind that drugs are in short supply in some parts of the world and that stocks may be old as well.

Whatever pills you do take with you, transfer them from their heavy glass containers into clearly labelled plastic ones to eliminate the risk of breakage and reduce the weight of your luggage at the same time. Old film cartons are ideal for this, although chemists sometimes sell plastic screwtop bottles for about 50p a time if you are afraid of the lids coming off.

GUIDEBOOKS

Invest in a good guidebook before you leave home. Economy-minded travellers are best served by books in the *Rough Guide*, *Lonely Planet*, *Frommer* and *Let's Go* series, all of which contain advice on where to stay cheaply, how to travel economically, and so on. Books in the Fodor, Michelin, Cadogan and other series are useful for genning up on the history and what to see before you go, but they aim at the middle market and are short on tips for rock-bottom prices.

Lonely Planets

These guides are excellent for information on cheap travel, restaurants, hotels, and so on. They also give a good idea of suitable itineraries for budget travellers. However, the information on sightseeing options is very limited.

If you send in information which can be used in a future edition you become eligible for a free book; write to Lonely Planet Publications,

PO Box 88, South Yarra, Victoria 3141, Australia. The distributor for Lonely Planet in the UK is Roger Lascelles, 47 York Road, Brentford, Middlesex TW8 0QP.

Rough Guides
Although there are fewer *Rough Guides* than *Lonely Planets*, these are also ideal for budget travellers, with similar lists of cheap hotels and restaurants, but also with more information on what to see when you arrive somewhere as well.

If you send in information which can be used in a future edition of a *Rough Guide*, you become eligible for a free book; write to Mark Ellingham or John Fisher, Rough Guides, Harrap Columbus, 21 Ravensdon Street, London SE11 4AQ.

Frommers
The *Dollarwise* series is also full of money-saving tips for travellers. However, these books are written primarily for an American market and reflect slightly different expectations, for example that all hotel rooms will have private bathrooms.

If you want to use Frommer Guides it might be worth joining their **$35-A-Day Travel Club**. Annual membership from the UK is $20 which entitles you to any two of their guidebooks free, together with a free *City Guide*, four copies of *The Wonderful World of Budget Travel* newspaper and a membership card offering 33% discounts on other City Guides and 50% discounts on the other books. Write to $35-A-Day Travel Club, Prentice Hall Press, One Gulf + Western Plaza, New York 10023, USA.

Let's Go Guides
Again these guides are aimed specifically at budget travellers, but like the Frommer guides they have a distinctly American slant. Most volumes cost £9.95 and are updated annually. Publishers are St Martin's Press, 175 Fifth Avenue, New York NY10010, USA.

Traveller's Survival Kits
Although Vacation Work started life publishing books which advised students on how to find work abroad, it now produces a wide range of titles including the excellent *Traveller's Survival Kit* series of guide-books to East and West Europe and to the Far East. Since each volume covers a number of different countries, they are not as detailed as some other guides. However, they are clearly aimed at budget travellers and full of useful tips. Vacation Work is at 9 Park End Street, Oxford OX1 1HJ (Tel: (0865) 241978).

Choosing the right guidebook

Depending on where you are going, you can buy guidebooks to specific countries or to wider areas. Lonely Planet in particular publishes guides to the popular overland routes—Africa, South America, North-East Asia and South-East Asia. These take up less space in your pack, which may be important, and are obviously cheaper than a set of guides to all the individual countries included; but they cover each country in less detail, which can be a drawback. If they also contain information on countries you will not be visiting, you may resent having space in your pack taken up with irrelevancies like information on Nigeria, Niger and Chad when your route crosses Kenya, Tanzania and Zambia. You can, of course, remove the unnecessary pages—but in that case you might have been better off choosing a different book in the first place.

Do not assume that you can find the relevant book on your travels. Most budget guidebooks have UK or US publishers and are hard to come by except in capital cities or airport bookshops elsewhere, especially in the Third World.

A guidebook is only as good as its most up-to-date information, so make sure you are buying the latest edition and check how recent it actually is. If it is several years out of date, find out the inflation rates in the countries concerned and keep them in mind when reading the prices in the book. Guidebooks written for budget travellers depend on travellers to update them, so if you find an error write to the publishers and let them know. You will be doing other travellers a favour, and in most cases will find your efforts rewarded with either the latest copy of the edition you amended or of another book of your choice in the same series, thereby reducing the advance costs of your next trip!

Remember that you can often sell your guidebook to another traveller before you go home. Some bookshops will buy them from you for resale, but a notice on a youth hostel board stating your price is probably the best way of getting rid of it. If you need a book you have not brought with you, try the same noticeboards, or see if you can exchange one of yours.

Where to buy your guidebooks

Most good bookshops have a travel section. However, if you have problems finding a particular text there are also several specialist shops. These include:

• The Travel Bookshop, 13 Blenheim Crescent, London W11 2EE (Tel: (01) 299 5260).
  This stocks brand new and secondhand books as well as first editions and out of print volumes, postcards, magazines and maps. The owner, Sarah Anderson, will also do her best to find books you particularly want.

- Youth Hostel Association Shop, 14 Southampton Street, London WC2E 7HY (Tel: (01) 836 8541), and regional branches.
  This stocks most books for travellers, but with the emphasis on budget and independent travel. It also keeps a wide range of books for walkers and mountaineers, a specialist stock of books on the UK, maps, and so on.

- Chapter Travel, 102 St Johns Wood Terrace, London NW8 6PL (Tel: (01) 586 9451).
  This is a travel agency-cum-bookshop which sells guidebooks and travel literature as well as books on foreign flora, fauna, cuisine, and so on.

- The Travellers Bookshop, 25 Cecil Court, London WC2N 4EZ (Tel: (01) 836 9132).
  The newest travel bookshop to open in London, the Travellers Bookshop sells a full range of modern guidebooks but also specialises in secondhand volumes, including old Baedekers.

If you do not live near a good bookshop you could join the **Travel and Exploration Book Society**. Introductory offers are very good but you are, of course, also obliged to buy another four books before you can terminate your membership. The address is Brunel House, Newton Abbot, Devon TQ12 1XD.

If you will be away for more than two weeks you will probably want to buy a map as well. The best stockists in London are probably:

Edward Stanford Ltd, 12-14 Long Acre, London WC2 9LP
   (Tel: (01) 836 1321).
McCarta, 122 Kings Cross Road, London WC1X 9DS
   (Tel: (01) 278 8278).
See **Appendix 2** for more details of budget guidebooks.

MISCELLANEOUS ITEMS

Toiletries

Items such as toiletries, sun-tan creams and sanitary protection can be expensive and difficult to obtain abroad, so it makes sense to stock up before you leave. 'Own brand' toothpastes, shampoos and soaps are just as effective as their more expensive branded cousins. Make sure you pack anything that could leak, like toothpaste, into a plastic bag before you go. If your trip will be short buy shampoo sachets which are smaller and lighter to pack than the usual bottles and transfer small items like Tampax to plastic bags which are more malleable than boxes.

Many travellers manically stock up on toilet paper whenever they leave England. However in my experience, you really do have to be in the back of beyond not to be able to buy it provided you are prepared to pay the price. Ask yourself whether you could not adjust to the good old hand and water methods popular in so many countries. Not only would this save you money but it would leave space in your pack for more indispensable items.

If you must take loo paper with you, remove the cardboard rolls in the centre so it will squash up more. Use it to double up for tissue as well.

In hot countries buses and trains tend to start out early in the morning, so it is worth investing in an alarm clock, or an alarm watch. Make sure you buy one with a sturdy case that will stand up to rough handling, and avoid the latest models of electronic wizardry; if they go wrong you are unlikely to be able to get them repaired whereas clockwork models can usually be mended more easily overseas than at home.

Laundry
Laundrettes are scarce outside Europe and although hotels in Third World countries often offer a laundry service at knock-down prices, most travellers end up doing more washing than at home. So it is worth investing in a portable washing-line and a few clothes pegs. Chemists sell tubes of concentrated washing powder for travellers, although I have usually found that ordinary soap does just as well—and this is readily available in most places unless you want luxury branded types. If you do want to indulge yourself, a tube of Travelwash detergent costs about £1.00 and will take ten average washes. A little money spent on an adaptable sink plug will also pay for itself over and over again. For some reason even in the most drought-stricken parts of the world, plugs are a luxury hotels like to dispense with, and doing the washing in a stream of running water can be tricky.

Adaptors
If you really cannot leave your electrical appliances at home, then you will need to consider investing in an adaptor plug so they can be used in countries with different voltages (the *ABC Guide to International Travel* lists the voltages in countries worldwide). These are sometimes on sale in travel agencies. The *Go Travel Aids* series on sale in YHA Shops includes travel plugs for about £5.00 and also sells continental plugs with a screwdriver for fitting them to appliances for about £2.00 each. Write to Jack Rogers and Co. Ltd, Building 15, The Paddocks, Frith Lane, Mill Hill, London NW7 1PS (Tel: (01) 346 6885), for a catalogue of items sold in this series.

Guarding your money
Most travellers should also invest in a money-belt or some other kind of concealed purse. Money-belts can be strapped round the waist

underneath your clothing and are particularly hard for thieves to remove without your knowledge, even when you are asleep. Most have pockets large enough to contain your passport as well, although hard-backed British passports are not ideal for concealing in this way. Cotton belts are most suitable for hot countries but soak up sweat, so try to line the insides with plastic to protect air tickets and travellers cheques from damage. A typical belt costs about £5.00.

Some people prefer to hang a purse round their neck and underneath their clothing. This can be easier to get at, particularly for women who like to wear dresses. However, it can also look more conspicuous and thieves manage to cut the neck straps surprisingly often. One way to stop this is to reinforce the neck strap with a guitar string which is hard to cut through. A typical neck wallet costs about £3.00.

Another good way to conceal money is to invest in a length of **tubigrip**, a type of elastic bandage available in different lengths from most chemists. This can be slipped round the arm or leg and doubled over with notes concealed in the fold. Alternatively, you could buy velcro and attach it to your pockets so that it will be difficult for anyone to open them and remove anything without you hearing them. Whichever method of concealing your money you choose, it still makes sense to have one note hidden somewhere separately just in case the worst happens and you find yourself robbed and stranded miles from a bank.

Other miscellaneous bits and pieces to buy before you leave include a simple sewing kit, a padlock, a luggage label and a foldaway holdall. All these items, and many others, are available in the handy *Go Kit Series* stocked by the YHA shops, Salisbury's and other travel equipment stockists for less than £5.00 each.

Protecting yourself from the sun

Tropical travellers should invest in a sun-tan cream with a high protection factor—eight or more for the first few days—since the sun can burn you in a matter of minutes. If you wait until you reach the sun before buying it, you will end up paying much more. Once again, make sure you wrap any lotions in plastic bags—they can make a horrid mess in your pack if they leak. And put in some calamine lotion as well, just in case. A stick of lip-salve costing less than a pound will also save you the discomfort of sun-cracked lips.

It's also worth investing in a good pair of sunglasses before leaving home: the price of these also tends to rocket as the temperature soars, and outside main tourist areas it will be difficult to find polaroid glasses at all. Remember that sunglasses also protect eyes from dirt in dusty areas. Western women travelling in Muslim countries may find they provide some protection against men's stares as well.

Reading matter

Even people who normally manage only one book a year find they get through a lot of reading matter while lazing on beaches, waiting for lifts or enduring long bus rides. So you should start out your journey with at least one good paperback novel, the thicker and more gripping the better. Bear in mind that you will probably get through this book quickly. Your best bet for replacing it will be to swap it for another with a fellow traveller, so now may not be the time to wade your way through something worthy like *Ulysses* that no one else will want to read. Stories set in the country you are currently visiting are often particularly popular, so take Graham Greene to Central America, Lawrence Durrell to Egypt, Elspeth Huxley to Kenya, George Orwell to Burma (now called Myanmar) and so on.

Usually it's easy to find someone to swap with, but if you're desperate a notice in the local youth hostel should fetch results. In towns with a lot of tourists there are often swap-shops where you can exchange books for a small fee; Zimbabwe is especially well-stocked with such shops. If you have to buy books in English in non-English speaking countries expect to pay high prices.

SKIING EQUIPMENT

Hiring equipment

One reason why skiing holidays are so expensive is that you need so much equipment for the briefest foray onto the slopes. First-time skiers are best advised to hire equipment in case they find the sport is not for them. Some tour operators can arrange this for you before you leave and let you pay in sterling. If this is not possible, they should still be able to advise you on the amount you will have to pay in the resort; this is likely to be more in countries like Austria with a high cost of living than in those like Andorra which are generally cheaper. If you *do* have to hire everything in the resort, remember to take extra cash with you to cover the cost.

Alternatively, most British towns have shops that specialise in hiring out sports equipment. They should be able to supply you with moon-boots, salopettes and ski jackets, although you will probably have to buy gloves and goggles and hire the ski boots, skis and poles at the resort. Look in *Yellow Pages* under 'Sports Goods Shops' for the address of your nearest equipment hire shop.

Buying equipment

Those who have survived their first trip and have caught the ski bug might consider buying their own equipment. This guarantees well-fitting boots and salopettes and is likely to work out cheaper over a few seasons. However skis, boots and so on are expensive, so your best bet is to wait until the end of the winter sports season and then scour the sports shops for July sale bargains. Lillywhites, Piccadilly Circus, London SW1Y 4QF (Tel: (01) 930 3181), is one specialist sports shop which regularly sells end-of-season equipment at knock-down prices. Skis, boots and fittings are constantly being developed so if you do buy your own you stand to miss the benefits of the latest changes.

You also need to buy lip salve, thick socks, a hat and even thermal underwear unless you are skiing in the Sierra Nevada in spring. This is another area where you should think carefully before economising. While it makes sense to look for competitively-priced items—for example thermal underwear may be cheaper in large department stores than in sports shops—it would be folly to set out without warm footwear, gloves and something to protect your eyes against the sun's glare. Skiing may be increasingly popular but it remains challenging and potentially dangerous. Do not take unnecessary risks.

It is worth adding a note about lift passes. To get to most ski slopes you will need to use some sort of lift. Tickets for the lifts are sold as passes rather than individually, so make sure you take some passport-sized photos with you to put on the card. These cards are expensive, so guard them carefully; preferably take out an insurance policy that covers you for their loss.

Ski Clubs
Regular skiers might like to join the **Ski Club of Great Britain** to keep up with all the latest developments. This is not especially cheap— annual membership costs £30.00 within London and £22.00 outside London, with a £10.00 joining fee on top. However, it does bring discounts on ski equipment, car-hire and Channel crossings and some ski package holidays. You also receive the Club's magazine *Ski Survey* five times a year from September to February and this is packed with up-to-date information on resorts and equipment to help you make your decisions. The Club also has an information service providing details on over 400 resorts, and a library at its London Clubhouse. The Ski Club of Great Britain is at 48 Eaton Square, London SW1W 9AF (Tel: (01) 235 4711).

8

Keeping Safe and Well on a Budget

It goes without saying that it is cheaper to stay healthy while away than to fall sick and wind up needing expensive medical treatment. Good health is, at least in part, a matter of sensible precautions both before you leave and while you are away.

WHAT TO DO BEFORE YOU GO

1. *Give up smoking.* You are likely to take more exercise while travelling, and it helps to be fit. Cigarettes may be cheaper overseas but think of them as incinerated travelling funds and it may strengthen your resolve.

2. *Get down to your ideal weight.* Not only are you likely to walk more while travelling, but it may be in hotter conditions too. Make it easy on yourself by carrying around only as much weight as you have to.

3. *Build up your walking ability.* This is particularly important if you're planning to trek, in Nepal or Thailand for example. However, all budget travellers to remote areas need to be prepared for the fact that transport isn't always available. In parts of Africa, border crossing points may be miles apart with no transport in between them. It helps if you can walk, preferably carrying your luggage, for reasonable distances.

4. *Ask your doctor for a medical.* You may have to pay for this—usual cost £25.00 plus any extra for tests—but it should give you peace of mind. If you are planning to work on a kibbutz, moshav or American summer camp you will be required to have a medical anyway. Increasingly countries ask visitors to prove that they are not carrying the HIV (AIDS) virus. You can have a blood test done at the same time.

5. *Go to the dentist.* Not only is dentistry overseas expensive, but in some places it is distinctly alarming too; much better to get those fillings seen to before you go. Most students, those under 18, pregnant women, those claiming housing benefit and those on low incomes are entitled to free treatment.

6. *If you wear glasses or contact lenses, go to the optician and get a prescription to be made up if you break or lose a lens.* If you will be travelling in very sunny conditions, consider buying tinted glasses instead of squinting all the time. In dusty conditions contact lenses are not ideal, so visitors to parts of Africa should take a pair of glasses with them as well.

7. *Take out an adequate insurance policy* — see **Guarding Against Calamities** for more details.

8. *Read the Department of Health leaflet SA41: While You're Away... the Traveller's Guide to Health,* which is available in chemists and sets out the latest information on staying healthy while on holiday.

Vaccinations

Six to eight weeks before you plan to leave, find out what vaccinations you need for your trip. Some require weeks to take effect. You can find out what you need from:

- The *ABC Guide to International Travel*—ask in a travel agency.
- *Booklet SA40* which is issued by the Department of Health and is available in doctors' surgeries. This sets out clearly which jabs are compulsory for entry to a country and which are just recommended for your own safety.
- Any of the following Government Health Depts:

International Relations
   Division
DSS
Alexander Fleming House
Elephant and Castle
London SE1 6BY
Tel: (01) 407 5522 Ext 6749

Public Health Laboratory
   Service
Communicable Disease
   Surveillance Centre
61 Colindale Avenue
London NW9 5EQ
Tel: (01) 200 6868

Welsh Office
Cathays Park
Cardiff CF1 3NQ
Tel: (0222) 825111 Ext 3395

Scottish Home & Health Dept
St Andrews House
Edinburgh EH1 3DE
Tel: (031) 5568501 Ext 2438

The Communicable Disease
   (Scottish) Unit
Ruchill Hospital
Bilsland Drive
Glasgow G20 9NB
Tel: (041) 9467120

DSS
Dundonald House
Upper Newtowards Road
Belfast BT4 3SF
Tel: (0232) 63939 Ext 2593

You could also consult your GP but few are very knowledgeable about tropical medicine. Expert advice and inoculation services are available at the following places:

British Airways Immunisation
    Centre
156 Regent Street
London W1R 5TA
Tel: (01) 439 9584
Monday to Friday 0830-1630

British Airways Immunisation
    Centre
Cheapside
London EC2V 60T
Tel: (01) 606 2977
Monday to Friday 0900-1300,
    1400-1630

Liverpool School of Tropical
    Medicine
Pembroke Place
Liverpool LP3 5QA
Tel: (051) 7089393

Thomas Cook Vaccination
    Centre
45 Berkeley Street
London W1A 1EB
Tel: (01) 499 4000 Ext 2156
Monday to Friday 0830-1800,
    Saturday 0900-1200
    (appointments only)

Trailfinders
42-48 Earls Court Road
London W8 6EJ
Tel: (01) 938 3999
Monday to Friday 1000-1300,
    1330-1630

Hospital For Tropical Diseases
4 St Pancras Way
London NW1 0PE
Tel: (01) 387 4411
    (appointments only, except
    yellow fever Monday to
    Friday 1115-1200)

Although most GPs provide vaccination services, they do not stock the vaccines in their surgeries. Instead, they will give you a prescription to take to the chemist, so you need to allow extra time for this. If you only need a booster and they have vaccine available, you may not be charged for the jab. Otherwise, for cholera, typhoid, tetanus, polio, yellow fever and gamma globulin (against hepatitis A) jabs you will only be charged normal prescription fees. However, remember that if vaccination is compulsory to gain admission to a country you will have to have the date that you had it certified on an **International Certificate of Inoculation**. Most doctors charge £3.00 for signing this document. The signature is included in the price charged by the various vaccination centres but these are more expensive in the first place.

Some doctors are reluctant to give hepatitis jabs, and even more so to give you rabies jabs on the NHS. In theory if you are going to work overseas this should be possible. The Department of Health Handbook says 'workers in endemic areas where they may be at special risk... are entitled to rabies vaccination free on the NHS.' However a local surgery may charge up to £50.00 for the course of three injections.

If you live in a town with a university or polytechnic, find out if there is a **Student Health Centre** where you may be able to get cut-price jabs.

The cost of vaccinations

Vaccination	Thomas Cook	British Airways	Hospital For Tropical Diseases	Trailfinders
Cholera	£5.00 (per dose)	£5.00	£5.00	£5.00
Typhoid	£5.00	£5.00	£5.00	£5.00
Yellow fever	£9.00	£10.00	£10.00	£8.00
Polio	£5.00	£5.00	£5.00	£4.00
Rabies	£10.00 (Tuesday 10-11) £25.00 (other times)	£8.00 (appoint- ment only)	£8.00 (Monday) £30.00 (other days)	£27.00
Gamma globulin	£9.00 (2-3 mos) £18.00 (5-6 mos)	£8.00 £16.00	£8.00 £16.00	£9.00 £16.00
Tetanus	£5.00	£4.00	£5.00	£5.00
Meningitis	£10.00	£10.00	£10.00	£9.00

Validity of jabs

	From	To
Cholera	6 days	6 months
Yellow fever	10 days	10 years
Gamma globulin		3-4 months
Polio (booster of childhood jab)		5 years
Typhoid	1 day	1 year
Tetanus	1 day	5 years

Not all injections are equally effective. The yellow fever jab is guaranteed to prevent you catching yellow fever and the typhoid jab is also very effective, but the cholera jab is considerably less effective. Doctors disagree about the benefits of gamma globulin jabs against hepatitis, but it certainly offers less and less protection as time goes by. The rabies jab will not stop you getting rabies, but it will give you a breathing space after being bitten to get to a hospital and start a course of treatment.

Since injections can be expensive, some budget travellers are tempted not to bother, or only to have the strictly compulsory jabs. However this is very short-sighted; in the first place if you have not had a

Areas of yellow fever risk in Central and South America

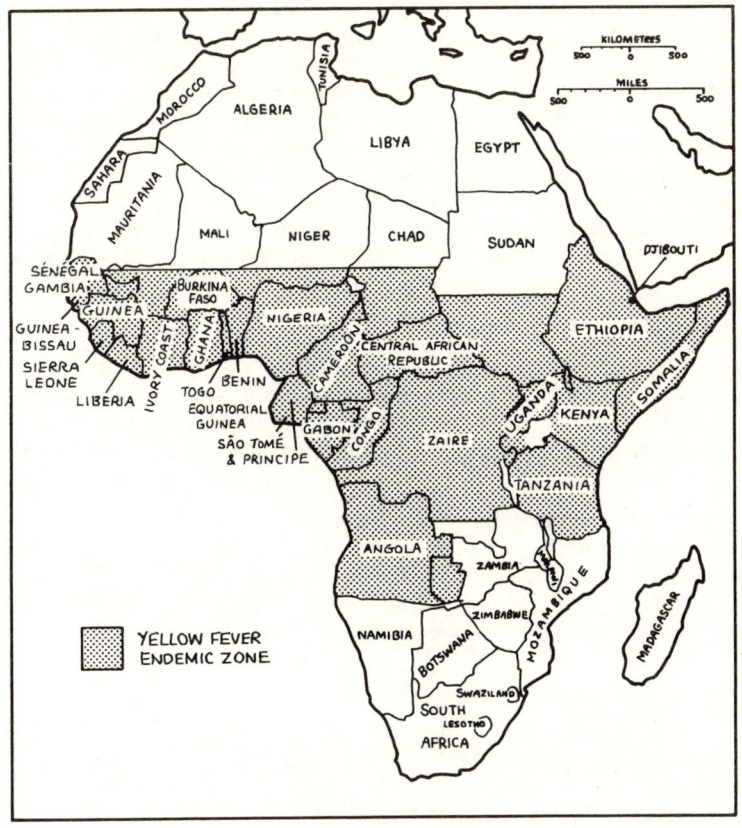

Areas of yellow fever risk in Africa

compulsory jab you may find yourself being inoculated at a border by a non-professional with a none-too-sterilised syringe. This was never a good idea but obviously in parts of the world where AIDS is a serious problem—in particular many African countries—you are now running the risk of contracting a deadly disease for the sake of the cost of a safe injection.

The same applies if you decide to have the jabs at a later stage when outside the UK. In fact, if you are away for a long time you may be forced to have a booster jab away from home. In either case it's worth investing in a medical equipment pack produced by MASTA (The Medical Advisory Service For Travellers Abroad) which contains sterile needles, syringes, alcohol, swabs and dressings. This costs about £10.00 and can be obtained from MASTA, London School of Hygiene and Tropical Medicine, Keppel Street, London WC1E 7HT.

Health briefs

If you do not live within easy reach of any of the specialist overseas medical centres, you might consider writing to MASTA (address above) for one of their **health briefs**. These are specially prepared documents with information and practical advice tailored to the needs of individual travellers. Information can be provided on:

- personal immunisation requirements
- malaria protection
- the risk of encountering specific diseases
- health dos and don'ts
- disease descriptions
- current health news from 230 countries
- suggested lists of things to take with you.

Short Health Briefs cost £4.75, give the minimum information, including a personal immunisation programme and malaria advice, and are recommended for short visits. *Concise Health Briefs* cost £9.50, contain a straightforward guide to health risks and what to do about them, and are ideal for most trips overseas. *Comprehensive Health Briefs* cost £25.00, offer a complete guide and reference for working or living abroad, and are aimed at expatriates or people pursuing a complicated itinerary. Application forms are available from pharmacists at Boots The Chemists. Summary letters are provided with each health brief for you to take to your own doctor.

Some travellers also carry **vitamin pills**. However your diet is unlikely to be so deficient that you need expensive supplements.

Boots sell pre-stocked *First Aid Kits* for about £10.00, while Coghlans sell a *First Aid Kit* with 43 items for £9.25 and a smaller one with 27 items for £4.25. An *Elastoplast Travel Kit* costs £6.50.

Always check that the contents are suitable for your needs. Up a mountain or on a skiing trip you are likely to have more use for support bandages than for eye patches.

First aid kits
All travellers should carry a basic first aid kit containing:

Item	Approximate cost (£)
Waterproof plasters:	
assorted sizes	1.20
continuous roll (do not forget the scissors).	1.00
Triangular bandage	1.30
Eye drops	1.50
Paracetamol or other pain-killers (pack of 24)	0.50
Multi-purpose antibiotic (eg tetracycline)	2.60
Anti-histamine cream	1.35
Inspect repellent gel	0.70
Safety pins	0.60
Antiseptic cream	0.55

Depending on your budget and circumstances you could also include the following:

Clove oil (for tooth-ache)	0.50
Cystitis tablets	1.25
Support bandages	1.70
Antiseptic dusting powder	1.15
Salt tablets—for very hot areas where dehydration is possible	1.55
Sugar and salt measuring spoon to prepare rehydration fluids after diarrhoea, available from MASTA	1.00
Travel sickness tablets	0.75
Water purifying tablets (pack of 48)	1.50
100 anti-malarial tablets (eg Paludrine)	2.50
25ml weak solution of iodine	0.50
Dropper bottle	0.50

Prescribed drugs
Anyone who takes medication regularly should make sure that they have an adequate supply for the journey, preferably clearly labelled and with a doctor's covering note in case of problems at borders. It is sensible to check each country's rules about importing drugs with the embassy or consulate before you leave and you should check with the

Home Office Drugs Branch (Tel: (01) 213 5215) before trying to bring drugs back into the country; your doctor's covering note should ease your path through British Customs on your return.

If you need more than five items prescribed in a four month period because you are stocking up for your travels you can buy a **Certificate of Prepayment of Prescription Charges** from your local National Health Service Family Practitioner Committee (ask at the Post Office for their address). A four month certificate costs £14.50 and a yearly one £40.00. You can obtain the form to apply for the certificate (FP95) from the Post Office. Of course, you may not need to pay prescription charges at all. Leaflet P11, available from your Post Office, doctors' surgeries and chemists, sets out the rules for obtaining free prescriptions.

Contraceptives

Women who use the contraceptive pill should make sure that they have adequate supplies. Most Family Planning Clinics are reluctant to give more than six months' supply at one time, but some will lend a favourable ear if you explain the circumstances. Remember that the pill may not be the best method of contraception if your journey will involve lots of time changes and if there is a risk of sickness or diarrhoea.

If you want to get an IUD fitted instead, do this some time before your trip to give it time to settle down. It would be disastrous to arrive in Sudan just as your new IUD started to cause problems. Bear in mind that condoms are not always very reliable in the Thirld World. If you think you will need them, stock up before you go.

HEALTH RISKS FACING BUDGET TRAVELLERS

In general, the lower your budget the more you are likely to sleep in unhygienic places and eat contaminated food and drink. Drink is a particular problem since many of the world's diseases are spread through the water supply.

Dos and don'ts of safe eating and drinking

To protect yourself, observe the following simple guidelines:

1. Never drink unboiled water.
2. Avoid ice, including ice-cream.
3. Give up salads.
4. Eat only fruit that has been peeled.
5. Look round before you start eating. Do the premises look clean? Has food been cooked and then left to cool? Is it being reheated? Are dishes uncovered so that flies can get at them? Does it look as if old cooking oil is being re-used? If in doubt, err on the side of caution when the food is served.

6. Even if you are normally carnivorous, you may choose to stick to a vegetarian diet when travelling in countries like India since cooked vegetables are less likely to make you ill than badly-cooked meat.

In baking hot conditions the problem of drinking water can seem especially daunting. If you have to drink unboiled water there are several precautions you can take:

- Add water sterilising tablets (Stereotabs, Puritabs, and so on) to it, bearing in mind that most need at least ten minutes to take effect.
- Use an iodine solution which should kill even the bugs causing giardia and amoebic dysentery. Ask your chemist to prepare a solution of 3% tincture of iodine. Then add five drops to a litre of water (ten if the water is very cloudy) and allow at least twenty minutes for it to take effect.
- Buy a filter and use it to remove impurities from the water. Ideally you should still boil it afterwards.

It's easy to become paranoid about your health. I have met Egyptians who would not touch koshari for fear of hepatitis, and yet provided the restaurant was clean this seemed no riskier than any other food. The best advice is probably to use your common sense and avoid becoming careless just because you have been travelling for a long time.

Malaria
Malaria is becoming a serious problem for travellers as more and more mosquitos develop resistance to prophylactic drugs. In most countries you can still use **chloroquine**—also sold as Nivaquine or Avloclor—but this is one subject that you should certainly get expert advice about as soon as you have a definite itinerary. If you plan to visit coastal Tanzania or Zanzibar, for example, you should bear in mind that a particularly virulent strain of malaria flourishes there. Similarly, on the paradise beaches of South Thailand, chloroquine-resistant mosquitos are common. In fact it is worth visiting Bangkok hospital for the latest advice on the most effective drugs to take.

If you know you will be visiting a malarial area, invest in:

- *Mosquito coils* which burn during the night and give off a scent that keeps mosquitos at bay. Take care if sleeping in a wooden building. Cost: about £1.50 for a packet of ten from YHA stores.
- *A mosquito net.* Some fold up small and are worthwhile if you do not like the smell of coils. Cost: single net, £25.00; double net, £27.50 (from MASTA).
- *Needle and thread.* If you plan to rely on local nets remember that they tear easily and that insects always find the gaps.

Map of the world showing

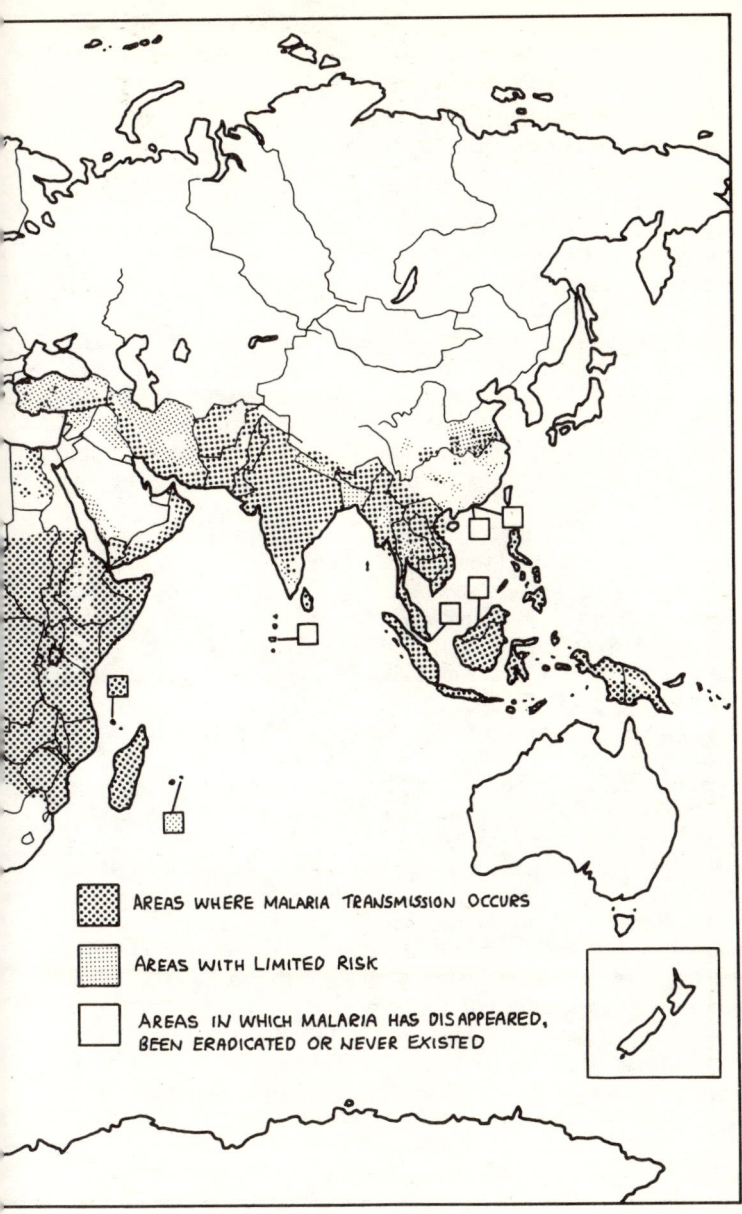

AREAS WHERE MALARIA TRANSMISSION OCCURS

AREAS WITH LIMITED RISK

AREAS IN WHICH MALARIA HAS DISAPPEARED,
BEEN ERADICATED OR NEVER EXISTED

areas of malarial risk

● *Insect repellent.* You can buy repellent to put on your skin in any chemist but MASTA also sells neat DEET repellent for use on clothing in 125ml plastic bottles. Cost: £4.75.

The Hospital for Tropical Diseases advises that you should start taking **malaria prophylaxis** a fortnight before leaving for the malarial area and continue taking it for up to six weeks after returning home.

Visitors to Sub-Saharan Africa, the Indian subcontinent and Central America are advised to take two tablets of Paludrine each day and one tablet of chloroquine once a week. Those going to South-East Asia should take one tablet of Maloprim and one tablet of chloroquine once a week. Visitors to North Africa and West Asia should take two tablets of proguanil each day or one tablet of chloroquine weekly. You should never continue to take chloroquine regularly for more than five years.

The symptoms of malaria include shivering, fever and flu-like feelings. If you do contract it you may have to get treatment locally, in which case your insurance company should reimburse the costs if you keep the receipts. Some types of malaria are killers so do not be tempted to do nothing.

Specialist advice on malaria prevention is available from The Malaria Reference Library (Tel: (01) 636 7921).

Paludrine is available from chemists without a prescription but you need to see a doctor for a chloroquine prescription. Since you need to take both regularly it helps to establish a set time in the day or week to do so, preferably after a meal since, taken on an empty stomach, they can make you feel sick.

AIDS

AIDS is another problem which should concern travellers, especially in parts of the USA—California and New York in particular—and East and West Africa. However, cases of AIDS are being recorded all over the world so do not be complacent just because you are not in the worst affected areas.

AIDS is spread through the exchange of blood or sexual fluids, so one way to make sure you do not catch it is to steer clear of unprotected sex with anyone, and particularly with prostitutes of either sex (you save money that way too).

Avoiding exchanges of blood may not be so simple since you cannot predict when you might have an accident requiring a blood transfusion or an injection. Protect yourself as far as possible in non-Western countries by carrying your own supply of sterile syringes.

Hepatitis

Another disease to avoid is hepatitis which comes in two forms: **infectious hepatitis** (Type A) is carried by contaminated food and drink while **serum hepatitis** (Type B) is caught through sexual contact with an infected person or from infected needles. A gamma globulin jab before you leave may help protect you against Type A, but the onus is on you to take care over where you eat and drink. To protect yourself against Type B you should take the same precautions as you would to avoid AIDS.

Symptoms of hepatitis include fever, nausea and complete lethargy. Unfortunately if you do contract it, the only treatment is rest and improved diet: in other words, it probably means the end of your trip.

Bilharzia (Schistosomiasis)

This is a debilitating disease, prevalent in Africa and carried by fresh-water snails. To avoid it, you should never swim in African rivers (including the Nile) or lakes; even when you see local people doing so, do not be tempted to copy them. Nor should you walk barefoot or in open sandals if it is likely to bring your feet into contact with river-water. If you have any cuts in your skin the disease will take a grip even more easily so take extra care. Although sea-water is perfectly safe, even some mineral pools seem to be contaminated.

If you see blood in your urine or faeces and you do not have diarrhoea, you might have contracted bilharzia. Treatment is expensive and difficult to obtain in the countries where the disease is prevalent. If you suspect you may have caught it, see a tropical medicine specialist at home as quickly as possible and explain your suspicions; the damage done by bilharzia is cumulative.

Giardia

Giardia is another common tropical illness. Symptoms include a feeling of fullness, indigestion, wind and frothy, yellowish diarrhoea with no blood or mucus. Sometimes it clears up of its own accord. Failing that it can be treated quite easily with a course of Flagyl.

Rabies

Animal-lovers are particularly at risk from rabies which is contracted from the saliva of an infected mammal, often a dog but just as easily a monkey or cat. A course of three prophylactic injections offers some protection, but not enough for complacency. Since rabies is incurable and leads to prolonged and agonising death it is advisable to steer well clear of all animals away from home and particularly in Third World countries. The worst risk is when a cut in your skin comes in contact with infected saliva, so if you have a wound take even greater care.   If you are bitten, wash the wound thoroughly with disinfectant and see a doctor immediately. Try and find the animal's owner so that you will know if it develops symptoms of rabies or dies. If the animal is rabid you will need to have a series of booster injections. Should you develop any unusual symptoms after returning home and you know that you have been bitten, *always* tell your doctor since they would not normally think of diagnosing rabies.

Mountain sickness

Several places like Machu Picchu, Lhasa and the Nepali Himalayas, which are popular with long-haul budget travellers, also lie above 11,500 feet, the point at which it is estimated 50% of people show symptoms of mountain sickness. Such symptoms include headaches, excessive weariness, sickness, dizziness and a pounding heart-beat. Normally if you rest and do not go any higher until the symptoms subside you should make a natural recovery. Headaches can be treated with paracetamol and other conventional pain-killers.

However, there are two more dangerous forms of mountain sickness which require immediate descent if the sufferer is not to die. **High-altitude pulmonary oedema** shows itself in breathlessness even when resting and in frothy or blood-stained sputum. People suffering from **cerebral oedema** seem confused and may lurch as if drunk. If anyone in your party shows these symptoms make sure they are removed from the mountains as quickly as possible.

Dysentery

Like hepatitis, dysentery comes in two forms. The least worrying is **bacillic dysentery** which is characterised by extreme diarrhoea, fever and stomach cramps. However, this can be treated quite easily with antibiotics and should clear up in a couple of days.

Amoebic dysentery is more alarming and harder to shake off. If the diarrhoea persists and you see blood and mucus in your faeces then you may have contracted amoebic dysentery and will need to be treated, perhaps with Flagyl.

If you have suffered from any stomach disorder while in the tropics it is worth going to your doctor for a stool test when you return to make sure that it has been cleared up completely.

Snakes, scorpions and other bugs

Whilst sleeping rough on a Greek beach, I remember the horrifying experience of waking up with a scorpion on top of me. Fortunately it turned out to be harmless but that did not save me from a very nasty shock. Travellers off the beaten track are bound to come into contact with all manner of creepy-crawlies, some of them well worth avoiding. Here are some precautions you can take to protect yourself:

● *Inspect rooms carefully before renting them.* Look for blood-stains on the bedding or walls which could indicate the presence of bed bugs.

Watch out for cracks in the windows, particularly in malarial areas where mosquitos can get in. If there are too many ants around, consider putting the bed legs in shallow bowls of water to stop them climbing up. Many cheap bathrooms are infested with cockroaches; they look alarming but do not usually cause much harm unless they come into contact with your food.

● *Put insect repellent on exposed parts of your body* and remember to renew it after a swim. In the evenings, in malarial areas, you should wear long-sleeved shirts and trousers for added protection.

● *Wear sandals at all times* to avoid the sorts of insects that burrow into your feet, such as jiggers, hookworms, and so on.

● *Look inside your shoes* before putting them on in case an insect or snake has made a home in them.

● *Read up about your particular destination* so you will know if there are poisonous spiders, or snakes, and what they look like.

● *If you are bitten by a snake, try not to panic*; surprisingly few are actually killers. Wash the wound out thoroughly but do not ask anyone to suck the venom out. Try and kill the snake so it can be identified. Contact a doctor or hospital as quickly as possible for expert advice. Avoid snake bites in the first place by wearing boots and long trousers in areas of thick vegetation where they could be hiding.

EMERGENCY TREATMENT IN NON-EC COUNTRIES

(For information about EC countries, see **Guarding Against Calamities**, page 72). Whilst it is always wise to take out insurance against emergency health costs while travelling, it is sometimes possible to get treatment abroad free. The chart below summarises the possibilities:

Anguilla   Minor emergency treatment is free on proof of UK residence, for example an NHS card or UK driving licence. However, you have to pay for all hospital treatment, medicines, dentistry, ambulance transportation and treatment at out-patient clinics.

Australia   Hospital treatment is free on proof of UK residence and of legal entry to Australia. You must enrol at a Medicare Office, although this can be done retrospectively. Some doctors' charges may be partially refunded if you apply to Medicare before you leave. But you pay for use of ambulances and for medicines.

Austria	On production of a UK passport, you will be treated free as a hospital in-patient on a public ward, but out-patient services and all other medical services must be paid for.
British Virgin Islands	People over 70 and school-age children are treated free on proof of UK residence.
Bulgaria	All treatment is free on production of a UK passport and NHS medical card, but you pay for medicines.
Channel Islands	Treatment is generally free, but medicines must be paid for. If you are staying for less than three months, you should be able to produce proof of your UK residence.
Czechoslovakia	Medical treatment is free on production of a UK passport, but you pay for medicines.
Falkland Islands	All costs are free on proof of UK residence.
Finland	Consultations at health centres are free if you show a UK passport, but actual treatment, including medicines and ambulance costs, must be paid for. If you claim at the Finnish Sickness Insurance Institution before you leave, you may be able to get a partial refund.
East Germany	Medical costs are free on production of a UK passport, unless you are involved in an accident while driving.
Hong Kong	In-patient hospital treatment is free, but you must pay for meals and the supply of appliances. Out-patient treatment is not free. Emergency dental treatment is free at certain clinics.
Hungary	Treatment is free on production of a UK passport, but you must pay for medicines, dentistry and ophthalmic treatment.
Iceland	Only hospital in-patient treatment is free, although children between 6 and 15 receive emergency dentistry free. You need your UK passport.
Malta	Only emergency treatment in a Government hospital is free to UK passport-holders.
Montserrat	People over 65 and children under 16 will be treated free on proof of UK residence. Children also receive free dentistry.

New Zealand	In-patient hospital treatment and prescribed medicines are free to UK passport-holders. Children under 16 also receive free dentistry.
Norway	UK passport-holders pay for everything except hospital in-patient treatment, use of ambulances and dental extractions. However, if you take your receipts to the social insurance office in the district where you were treated before you leave, you may be able to get a partial refund.
Poland	If you show your NHS medical card, you only have to pay for doctors' visits and 30% of the cost of prescribed medicines.
Romania	If you show a UK passport and NHS medical card you only need to pay for medicines.
St Helena	You can be treated free as an out-patient at hospitals during normal clinic hours if you have proof of UK residence.
Sweden	You can be treated as a hospital in-patient free, including medicine costs, if you have a UK passport. Dentistry for children is also free.
Turks & Caicos Islands	People over 65 or under 16 are treated free on proof of UK residence. Others may have to pay for in-patient treatment.
USSR	If you have a UK passport, you will only have to pay for prescribed medicines.
Yugoslavia	If you have a UK passport, you will only have to pay for prescribed medicines.

In some parts of the world drugs are in short supply, so always make sure you take enough for your own needs. In such circumstances items like malaria tablets even make acceptable presents. You may also be able to exchange them for local craftwork of low value.

SAFETY HINTS FOR BUDGET TRAVELLERS

However careful you normally are at home, the risk of being robbed or mugged while abroad increases simply because everyone knows that travellers have money, cameras and other valuables with them. In poorer parts of the world even passports are tempting to thieves.

Not only are you vulnerable because you are a guaranteed source of goodies, but also because you are unfamiliar with your surroundings and with the nuances of daily life in a strange country. You may also be in a generally relaxed, free and easy mood engendered by holiday-making—and suddenly it is easy to see why problems occur. However, by following simple guidelines you can do a lot to protect yourself and your belongings:

1. Never walk along unlit streets or in parks or on deserted beaches at night. If you must do so, go with a group of people.
2. If there are hedges or anything which could conceal an assailant, walk as far from them as possible—ideally on the other side of the road.
3. Try not to keep pulling out a map in shady-looking areas. Every time you do so, you are telling someone that you are a stranger.
4. Always wear a money-belt or concealed wallet, even at night and especially when sleeping on public transport.
5. Walk briskly and look confident even if you do not feel it. Most muggers pick on easy targets.
6. If you suspect that someone is following you, cross over to find out if the other person does the same. If they do, it is probably best to run.
7. Keep keys or a pen in your hand if you feel unsafe. Both turn your fist into a more dangerous weapon than skin and bone alone.
8. Always lock your bedroom door and all windows. Carry a padlock with you in case there are no locks. Tie your backpack to the bed if in doubt.
8. If you are staying in a hotel where the staff seem trustworthy, put your valuables—such as camera, passport, tickets and money—into the safe and get a receipt for them. Some insurance companies will only honour loss claims if you have done this wherever possible.
10. Beware of trusting people too readily, particularly if you are a woman travelling alone. This can be difficult, because outside Western Europe strangers are often eager to befriend you. If you do go to visit anyone, make sure someone knows where you have gone and when you will be back, and let your host know that you have done so as subtly as possible. If possible, try not to reveal that you are completely alone.
11. Read up about your destination. That way, you will know which countries have notorious mugging problems like Colombia, and you can recognise black spots to avoid like River Road in Nairobi and Moshi and Arusha bus stations in Tanzania.
12. If you find out about your destination you can understand likely causes of aggravation; for example avoid political arguments in Israel and Morocco, and be aware of what constitutes unseemly behaviour in Muslim countries. With luck, you will avoid making unnecessary enemies.

13. Do not be greedy. Many people come unstuck simply because their desire to make a killing on the black market leads them to take foolish risks. Although you will not want to be seen changing money outside a police station you do not have to let yourself be led down dark alleys. Watch what goes on carefully; you could well be dealing with some very dodgy characters.
14. If someone grabs your bag, let go of it, otherwise you may suffer injury as well as financial loss. Likewise if someone threatens you with a knife or a gun; give them your money or passport.They can be replaced, unlike your skin!
15. If you must use prostitutes, remember that you are putting your money as well as your health at risk. Leave your valuables in the hotel and only take as much money with you as you are willing to spend.

Self-defence courses

Budget hotels are often in the seediest parts of towns, so as part of your preparations for a trip, consider taking a simple self-defence course. Women especially may feel more confident alone on alien streets if they know what to do to escape from an assailant. You can find out about courses from:

- the local police
- the local library
- a Women's Centre
- a Local Education Authority evening classes programme.

9

How to Choose the Best Value Package Deal

At the budget end of the market it is often cheapest to make your own travel arrangements. However, many people still prefer to book a package deal, sometimes because, with only two weeks to take a holiday, it is the best way to make sure of reaching your destination and seeing what you want in the time available. For travellers with children, the elderly or the disabled it may also be the best way to avoid unexpected problems.

So, faced with the multitude of brochures on offer in the average agency, how can you make sure you choose the best deal available?

Reading the brochures – additional costs

The front covers of most holiday brochures are emblazoned with rock-bottom price tags. This certainly does not mean all the holidays inside the brochure are as cheap as this—in fact it is often hard to track down this **lead-in price** at all. When you do find it, it will probably be attached to a week's self-catering in Benidorm in February flying from Gatwick, which may not suit you at all. So the first rule is, do not be misled by 'come-on' offers.

Inside the brochure will be a number of **price grids**. You can calculate the cost of any given holiday by finding the name of the accommodation along the top of the grid and then reading off the price against your planned holiday date along the lefthand side of the grid. Sounds simple? Well, it is—except that you must normally add several compulsory or semi-compulsory extra costs to this basic charge.

So to work out the real cost of your holiday you should always add together all the following items:

1. **Basic cost** as given in the price grid.
2. Any **flight supplements**—for example, for flying out of regional airports or for leaving Gatwick at a reasonable hour. These are usually listed either beside the price grid or at the back or front of the brochure with the other flight details.
3. **Insurance**. Prices usually appear underneath the price grid or at the back or front of the brochure. Most companies insist that you take out some insurance even if you do not take their own.

4. **Room supplements**. If you want a sea-view you usually have to pay for it. Prices are generally quoted per person per night beneath the hotel details. Single rooms usually cost more as well.
5. **Board supplements**. If you want meals other than those included in the basic cost you will have to pay a supplement, again usually quoted per person per night beneath the hotel details. BB is bed and breakfast, HB (half board) is breakfast and evening meal, FB (full board) is breakfast, lunch and evening meal.
6. **Supplement for a smaller than maximum number of people sharing an apartment**—for example, two people sharing an apartment which could accommodate four. These supplements are usually listed under the apartment details or on the actual price grid.

Only when you have added all these costs together do you have a realistic idea of the price of the holiday that interests you, and these extras can make quite a lot of difference.

The following example shows how the price of a seven night stay in Palma Nova can rise as you add the incidental costs to the basic price:

Basic grid price	£117.00
Insurance	£13.90
Total	£130.90

Optional extras

Single room	£14.70
Full board	£18.20
Saturday flight from Gatwick	£7.00
Friday day-time flight from Gatwick	£14.00

To find the real price for you, you might need to add one or more of the optional extras to the £130.90. If you wanted to fly from a provincial airport, the flight supplement would probably be even higher; and the company may reserve the right to increase the holiday cost by up to £15.00 if the price of aviation fuel rises.

Additional costs on a skiing holiday

With a skiing holiday you also need to take into account the cost of hiring the equipment, buying a lift pass and attending ski school if you are a beginner. These items cannot always be paid for in advance, but the best operators provide an indication of the costs you should expect in their brochures. So the price of a typical ski holiday in Mayrhofen could be calculated in this way:

Basic grid price for 14 nights	£193.00
Insurance	£23.50
Shower/wc	£18.20
Boot hire	£13.00
Ski hire	£30.50

Ski school	£35.50
Lift pass	£83.50
Total	£397.20

The price of this holiday could be reduced by £40.00 for coach travellers, but those flying from regional aiports would pay about £10.00 more for the privilege. In these examples the hotels selected represent low budget accommodation at low season prices.

Of course a good travel agent will make these calculations for you. However when you are combing through the brochures at home, knowing how to add up the price could save you setting your heart on something outside your price range.

Hidden reductions

On the bright side, brochure prices do sometimes have hidden reductions as well. The basic price may be lowered for:

- **Children**, usually between the ages of 2 and 11 and sharing a room with their parents. However child discounts do not apply to all holidays and sell out early in the season. Always check the conditions at the front of the brochure very carefully. A few companies also offer reductions if the child is sharing a room with just one parent.

- **Three people sharing a room**. Some hotel rooms can accommodate an extra bed, in which case there may be a discount to make up for the crowding.

- **Special offers**. Always check the brochure carefully for special discounts. These may include a third week for the price of a fortnight, no single supplement on certain dates, larger child reductions for certain dates, and particularly low prices for holidays of unusual length, such as nine days at the start or end of the season, when airline flight patterns change. Such special offers are usually described in the front of the brochure and then highlighted on individual pages.

Surcharges

In recent years most tour operators have reserved the right to increase their prices if aviation fuel rises in price or currency exchange rates fluctuate badly against them. In most cases a **no surcharge guarantee** limits the extra amount that you could be charged to either 10% of the holiday cost or to a flat £10.00 or so. In 1988, fuel surcharge increases caused so much resentment that in 1989 large companies like Thomson and Intasun offered cast-iron guarantees that their prices would not be increased. It is possible that smaller operators will follow suit; always read the conditions at the front or back of the brochure carefully before signing the contract, since each company has its own policy on surcharges and these can change from season to season.

Also remember that all tour operators exclude 'government action' from their guarantees. Should you be unlucky enough to book a holiday to a country which then starts a civil war, you may have to bear some of the loss yourself.

When you have found the holiday you want and calculated its price, look in the *St James Press Holiday Guide* to see what other companies feature the same hotel. Then you should do the same calculations again for each of them to check that you are getting the cheapest deal.

THE CHEAPEST PACKAGE HOLIDAYS

Self-catering

One way to reduce the cost of your holiday is to opt for a self-catering deal either in a villa or an apartment. The more of you who are prepared to share, the better the bargain.

However not all self-catering packages automatically offer the best deals. Quite often large tour operators negotiate such good all-in hotel arrangements that paying for your apartment and then paying for food on top of the cost will make the price the same or even more than if you had used a cheap hotel. This is particularly likely to be the case in places with a high local cost of living. Bear in mind also that if your apartment is in an isolated area there may be only one shop, and its prices are likely to be high. You can, of course, help yourself by bringing some staple goods with you, especially if you are driving to the resort.

The real benefits of self-catering are that you are not restricted to hotel dining times, and that children may be less restricted than they would be in a hotel with other guests to worry about.

If you do opt for self-catering, check carefully to find out what household goods are provided—such as linen, crockery, and so on—and whether there are any arrangements for the accommodation to be cleaned during your stay.

Square deals

If you know where you'd like to go but are not fussy about where you stay, you could consider buying a **square deal** holiday. These are organised by the large companies who offer reduced prices to people prepared to wait until they arrive at their resort to find out where they are staying. Usually the company guarantees the grade of accommodation and it may even be a hotel featured in their brochure. Sometimes you can even choose between a rock-bottom one star deal or a slightly more expensive two or three star version offering classier accommodation. Ask a travel agent for details.

Late bookings

More and more people are putting off their holiday decisions until the last moment in the hope of getting a bargain. If you do not mind where you go, and can travel out of season, this is a good way to save money. However if you have set your heart on Rhodes in July, not booking until June is risking disappointment. Travel agencies keep details of late availability but are not always prepared to spend the time needed to find what you really want. The London newspaper *The Evening Standard* is an excellent source of information for those who like to make their own late bookings.

To encourage people to book earlier, some operators offer **no surcharge guarantees** if you pay by a specific date, perhaps the end of February. Some only ask for a low deposit, perhaps even £5.00 a head, in an attempt to secure bookings. If you know where you want to go and will have to travel in the peak season, either of these options might be better than waiting until the last moment.

Special offers

More and more tour operators are throwing all sorts of 'extras' in with their packages. You may, for example, see offers of free insurance, free transport to and from the airport or free airport car parking. In most cases these are genuine offers and worth snapping up, but always check these prices carefully against those of other companies featuring the same resort to make sure they have not covered the cost of the 'free' items by raising their basic prices.

Even if you have avoided the big tour operators in the past, remember that their products are constantly changing and there can be some exceptionally good deals around. For example, in summer 1989 Intasun offered cheap holidays to Barbados, Bangkok and Acapulco at prices individuals would have been struggling to match. There is nothing to stop you buying a package, to take advantage of a large company's bulk buying power with the airlines and hotels, and then doing your own thing once you get there.

Several of the operators are also starting to offer smaller, less overwhelming hotels—often featured in a separate brochure—and 'unpackaged' packages, perhaps involving a flight with hotel and ferry vouchers thrown in but with some of the dates and details left for you to sort out once you arrive at your destination.

The best ways to find out about the latest developments are to read the travel pages of quality newspapers, or to befriend a good and well-informed travel agent.

Specialist and long-haul tour operators

Many people intending to join a long-haul overland expedition do not realise that they can pick up the brochures of specialist companies in many travel agencies. ABTA agents only stock the brochures of ABTA operators, but student travel shops often have an even wider range on offer.

Some of the main specialist companies are:

Encounter Overland, 267 Old Brompton Road, London SW5 9JA (Tel: (01) 370 6845).

Transglobal, 64 Kenway Road, London SW5 0RD (Tel: (01) 370 5136).

Hann Overland, 201-203 Vauxhall Bridge Road, London SW1V 1ER (Tel: (01) 834 7367).

Guerba Expeditions Ltd, Freepost Dept L, 101 Eden Vale Road, Westbury, Wilts BA13 3YB (Tel: (0800) 373334). Africa specialists.

Dragoman, 10 Riverside, Framlingham, Suffolk IP3 9AG (Tel: (0728) 724184).

Exodus Expeditions, 100 Wandsworth High Street, London SW18 4LE (Tel: (01) 870 4814).

Explore Worldwide (OB), 7 High Street, Aldershot, Hants GUH 1BH (Tel: (0252) 319448).

Tracks, 12 Abingdon Road, London W8 6AF (Tel: (01) 937 3028).

Journey Latin America, 16 Devonshire Road, London W4 2HD (Tel: (01) 747 3108).

Once again, the prices quoted in these operators' grids do not usually include insurance. Often there is also a 'kitty' for meals and other extras which everyone has to pay on departure. Details of the kitty usually appear at the start or end of the brochure and the sum involved can be surprisingly large.

Remember that signing up for a long-haul expedition usually commits you to paying for a large number of **visas and injections**. Again, make sure you have taken these into account when adding up the cost.

If you look through travel advertising pages, you will find that there are plenty of other companies offering overland expeditions. Their prices may look attractively cheap compared with some of the bigger companies. However, on expeditions like this there are many things which can go wrong, and the price you pay often reflects the company's experience; the larger companies are more likely to have a network of contacts for resolving unexpected difficulties along the way. Once again, this is an area where economising can be counter-productive; if you end up having to buy all your visas again because you are so behind schedule, and then miss places out altogether because time has run out, you may feel you would have been better off paying more in the first place.

Cruises
On the whole, cruises are too expensive to interest most budget travellers. However, if you are determined to push the boat out on a floating holiday, ways to economise include:

- opting for a cheaper inside, lower-deck cabin
- sharing with other people to benefit from third or fourth person sharing discounts
- choosing a shorter three or four day cruise, perhaps out of Miami or round the Mediterranean or the Canary Islands
- applying for standby space on a P and O cruise. In return for the uncertainty of a berth you will be offered a reduced fare.

FINANCIAL PROTECTION OF PACKAGE HOLIDAYS

When you book a package holiday, you want to be sure not only that you have found the best deal but that your money will be safe if the company offering the holiday collapses. The best way to do this is to book through an **ABTA (Association of British Travel Agents)** travel agency. ABTA agents can only sell the holidays of ABTA tour operators who pay money into various bonding schemes to make sure that holidaymakers can be compensated if they cease trading.

Student and independent travel agents like STA Travel and Campus belong to **ISTC (The Independent Student Travel Confederation)** instead of ABTA. A cornerstone of ISTC's policy has been the financial protection of its customers. It boasts that no one has suffered as a result of the financial collapse of one of its members in the 38 years of its existence.

If you book with an agent that does not belong to ABTA or ISTC, you need to be particularly careful since your money is not necessarily safeguarded in the same way. *Never* send money to an address you have seen in an advertisement when you do not know anything about the company making the offer apart from what it says in the advertisement.

10
Paying for Your Travels Without Paying Through the Nose

There are several ways of paying for most travel services.

CASH

The most straightforward way is to pay in cash, but this may mean drawing out your savings and losing interest on deposit accounts. Instead, you could put off payment briefly by using a credit card. If you are paying for a package holiday less than eight weeks before it is due to depart, travel agents usually insist you pay by cash, building society cheque or credit card rather than with a bank cheque. This is because cancellation charges start to rise steeply at this point and they will want to be sure they are holding enough money to cover themselves.

CHEQUE

Most purveyors of travel services will accept cheques for sums of up to £50 provided that they are backed by a guarantee card. If the sum is more than £50 you may have to allow ten or more days for your cheque to pass through the banking system. Bank or building society drafts can be made out for larger sums, and do not need time to clear since they will only have been issued after a check that you had adequate funds in your account.

Since most cheques take three days to be debited from your account you have, in effect, three days' credit which can be useful if, for example, you want to pay for a holiday just before pay-day, and do not have enough cash in your account to do so.

CARD PAYMENT

Access or Visa

Most travel services can be purchased with credit cards like Access or Visa, and both these cards are at present available free to anyone whose application is accepted by the card company. If you pay your account promptly each month they allow you to make your purchases with approximately six weeks' free credit. After that, interest is charged on the outstanding balance. However this is not an economical way to purchase foreign currency or travellers cheques, since you will be charged interest on these immediately (see **Thomas Cook Credit Card** below).

If you book a holiday costing more than £100, try and pay for it with a credit card. If the company then collapses you will be able to claim against the credit card company as well as against the tour operator. In order for you to do this, the payment voucher must have been made out to the operator rather than to the agent who sold you the holiday. ABTA agents have special credit card vouchers to fulfil this requirement.

Travel and entertainment cards

Few budget travellers will have American Express or Diners Club cards since you have to pay an annual fee to own these. They are also travel and entertainment cards rather than true credit cards, which means that outstanding accounts must be settled in full every month. Anyway, they are only useful to pay for a limited range of package holidays whose operators accept them. American Express travel agencies obviously welcome their card for all services.

You can use American Express, Diners Club and major credit cards to pay for scheduled air tickets, although discount agencies may levy a service charge to cover the card company's commission. High street agencies do not charge an extra fee.

Budget account cards

Another way to pay for your holiday is to open a **Creditcharge Budget Account** which permits you to pay a fixed sum of £8.00 or more into an account each month. Once you have opened the account you can make purchases costing up to 24 times your monthly payment. As long as you are in credit—that is, you are paying money in but do not have any outstanding debts—interest will be added to your balance. However, once you have purchased something, interest will be added to the cost to be cleared. Before committing yourself to such an account, find out the APR (Annual Percentage Rate) charged. For example, on a creditcharge account in August 1988 the APR was 32.9% compared with 23.1% charged by Access or Visa. In other words, if you paid by either of those cards the total repayable sum was less.

Globetrotter Accounts

Mercantile Credit offers a Globetrotter Account which operates in a similar way. Every month you pay between £15 and £170 into your account. You can then borrow up to 30 times that amount to pay for a holiday. Once again, interest is paid on your account when it is in credit and you pay interest once you have taken out your loan. However the interest paid to you is usually 2% below current base rates, while the

APR you pay will be more like 23.1%, depending on current rates. Contact Mercantile Credit for more details at Elizabethan House, Great Queen Street, London WC2B 5DP. Their leaflet gives local telephone numbers for most large towns in the UK.

SPECIAL CARDS FOR TRAVELLERS

Thomas Cook Credit Card

If you intend to pay for your holiday, foreign exchange or other travel arrangements through a branch of Thomas Cook, you could apply for a Thomas Cook Credit Card. This works in much the same way as an Access or Visa card and you can pay as much or as little of your bill each month, subject to a minimum payment of £10.00 or 10%, whichever is the greater. You can apply for the card when you book your holiday, provided you have a formal means of identification and another credit or charge card with you. So applying for a Thomas Cook Credit Card could save you from losing a last-minute holiday that you must pay for instantly. As with Access and Visa you will have up to six weeks' free credit if you pay off your account each month. With a Thomas Cook card you can also buy foreign exchange on interest-free credit for that length of time. If you do not settle your bill each month, check the APR to see how it compares with using Access or Visa.

Universal Air Travel Plan (UATP)

UATP cards can be used to pay on credit for air and air-related services (excess baggage, MCOs, and so on). They are available to regular travellers on application to The Credit Controller, BA, E10 9T BC (S83), PO Box 10, Heathrow, TW6 2JA (Tel: (01) 562 0382).

Airplus cards

Airplus cards can be used to purchase air and air-related services on credit but can also be used to pay for hotel and car hire bookings, rail tickets and restaurant bills. They also permit their holders emergency cheque cashing facilities, cash advances and a 25% discount on vaccinations at British Airways immunisation centres. Apply to The Credit Controller, BA (address above) (Tel: (01) 562 0078).

UATP and Airplus cards work like American Express cards. You are charged an annual subscription fee and must settle your bills in full on a monthly basis.

SAVING YOUR MONEY

If you know that you are going to have to pay for fares and accommodation, the most economical way of doing so is to open a building society savings account or a bank deposit account and pay regular sums into it each month. You will be paid interest on your balance at regular intervals and while rates are high you stand to gain quite a bit for your foresight. The best accounts are those which pay your interest monthly, so that each month you receive compound interest on your deposits and on the interest they have already earnt. Since bank and building society rates vary, shop around for the best deal before committing yourself. Also remember that the higher your initial deposit, the higher the rate of interest you are likely to be able to earn.

11
How to Reach Your Destination Without Busting Your Budget

One of the largest items on most travellers' bills is the cost of reaching their destination. However, there are ways of keeping this to a minimum.

HITCH-HIKING

Of course it is sometimes possible to reach your destination by thumbing a lift for free.

Getting a lift

Hitching in the UK is usually simple, especially if you stick to the motorways and main roads. However, there are also ways you can increase your chances of getting a lift:

- *Prepare a card with your destination clearly printed* on it so that drivers can make up their mind whether to stop well in advance. The only drawback to this strategy is that someone going part of the way might decide not to stop. Some people like to add a representation of their national flag to the card, but before doing so check just how popular your home country is on the route you plan to travel.

- *Stand somewhere where cars can pull in safely* without menacing other road-users, for example near a lay-by. Never stand on a bend, on the brow of a hill or anywhere else where it would be dangerous to stop.

- *Try to look clean and presentable.* It goes without saying that lone women should never hitch in short skirts, low-neck blouses or anything else that could encourage the wrong kind of offer.

- *Keep your luggage to a minimum* so you can squeeze into already crowded cars.

- *Do not try to hitch while still in a town or its suburbs.* It will be quicker to take a bus or train to a village on the outskirts where drivers are more likely to stop for you.

Points to remember about hitching

Not every motorist's insurance covers unexpected passengers; this is especially true if you hitch a ride with a lorry driver whose company does not approve of unauthorised lifts. So make sure you are adequately insured yourself.

There are hidden snags to hitching as well. In the first place, if you wait a long time for lifts it may take longer than you expected to reach your destination. In that case you may end up with larger bills than you anticipated for food and accommodation. Such problems can be minimised if you contact one of the organisations that arrange lifts in advance. However, if you do this you will have to contribute something towards the cost of petrol, so it is a 'swings and roundabouts' situation. If you *do* decide to go for a pre-arranged lift you could also check university and college noticeboards for people going your way. Alternatively you could place your own advertisement there, usually for free.

Women in particular may also experience problems with road 'romeos'. To minimise the risk try to travel in pairs. Lone women should never accept lifts in cars with several male occupants. If the worst comes to the worst insist on getting out again; it usually works.

WALKING

The very energetic can always try walking to their destination. This is, of course, free. However, it takes a long time and means you spend more money on en route accommodation and meals. You do get to see more of the countryside though. The major snag for UK travellers, obviously, is that at some point you have to at least cross the Channel if you want to reach anywhere other than Wales and Scotland.

CYCLING

Cycling is only slightly more expensive and far faster than walking. Once you have met the initial cost of buying and equipping the bike, the only cost will be to your leg muscles.

The law prevents cyclists using motorways for obvious safety reasons, so progress is likely to be slow and steady. A good road map is essential.

Taking your bike on public transport

British Rail charges a £3.00 advance reservation fee for carrying bikes on 125 Inter-City and Sprinter trains—there is no charge on other types of passenger trains—and space is often limited. If you want to take your bike on an Inter-City Europe boat train you must register it at Victoria or Liverpool Street station and pay a nominal fee, although on local services to the ferry ports there is often no charge. Detailed information on British Rail's services for cyclists appear in the leaflet *The British Rail Guide to Better Biking.*

Most airlines will carry bikes free of charge provided the total weight of the bike and your luggage does not exceed the free baggage allowance. If it does, you will be charged excess baggage fees which can be astronomical. If you decide to take your bike by plane, always tell the airline at the time of booking and find out well in advance what arrangements must be made. Often you have to partially dismantle it before it will be accepted, especially when flying to the USA. If this is the case you should find out whether the airline can supply a suitable box for packing the bike, and whether it will be padded to protect delicate parts like brakes and gears. If possible, check with the airline office at the airport itself; they are the people who will have to handle it.

You usually have to pay to take a bike on the cross-Channel ferries.

Choosing your bike

If your bike is going to cover hundreds of miles, it needs to be in excellent working order and equipped with gears. Choose it carefully. You will also need spare parts as well—on a long journey, the Cyclists' Touring Club advises that you should take all or most of the following with you:

- screwdriver
- 3-way socket-spanner
- adjustable spanner
- small pliers
- Allen keys
- puncture kit
- pump
- cone spanner
- chain rivet tool
- cotterless crank remover/ spanner
- freewheel remover
- pedal dustcap spanner
- spoke nipple key
- small nail punch
- flat multi-hole spanner
- inner tube
- brake cable
- bulbs
- batteries
- rear gear cable
- brake straddle cable
- brake blocks
- chain links
- spokes
- ball bearings
- grease
- oil
- PVC insulating tape
- small nuts and bolts

Most towns have reputable cycle dealers; to find your nearest, look in *Yellow Pages* under 'Cycle Shops'. One particularly good stockist is Madison Cycles plc, 4 Horseshoe Close, London NW2 7JJ (Tel: (01) 452 5401).

Do not forget that you will also need to choose your clothing carefully. Make sure you have waterproofs if you are likely to encounter rain on the way, that you have comfortable, sturdy shoes and that you have lightweight clothing if you are going to be cycling through a heat-wave.

Cycle clothing stockists include:

Bertram Dudley and Son Ltd, Wickham Buildings, Brooke Street, Cleckheaton, West Yorkshire BD19 3RZ (Tel: (0274) 873015)

Cycling 2000, 218 Dallow Street, Burton-on-Trent, Staffordshire (Tel: (0283) 44669)

Pedersen Cycles, 21 Parsonage Street, Dursley, Gloucestershire (Tel: (0453) 46755)

The Cyclists' Touring Club Shop, 69 Meadrow, Godalming, Surrey GU7 3HS.

The Cyclists' Touring Club

If you intend to do a lot of cycling, it might be worth joining **The Cyclists' Touring Club**. Their Touring Department has fact sheets on cycling in the following countries:

Algeria and Tunisia, the Arabian Peninsula, Australia, Austria, Belgium, Bulgaria, Canada, the Canary Islands, the Channel Islands, China, Corfu, Corsica, Crete, Cyprus, Czechoslovakia, Denmark, East Germany, Egypt and Sudan, the Faroe Islands, Finland, France, Gambia, Greece, The Netherlands, Hong Kong, Hungary, Iceland, India, Indonesia, Iran, Ireland, Israel, Italy, Japan, Jordan, Luxembourg, Malawi, Malta, Mexico, Morocco, New Zealand, Norway, Pakistan, the Philippines, Poland, Portugal, Romania, the Sahara, Sardinia, the Seychelles, South Africa, South America, Spain, Sri Lanka, Sweden, Switzerland, Syria, Thailand, the United States, West Africa, West Germany, Yugoslavia, Zambia and Zimbabwe.

The staff are helpful with planning and information if you send an SAE with your enquiry. In addition the club has a list of cycling correspondents overseas who have offered to help members with information in return for an International Reply Paid Coupon.

The Technical Department can advise on buying a new bike and accessories and can supply members with information sheets on such matters as touring cycle specifications, hybrid gearing, cycling with children, cycle care, suggested gears, cycle luggage, cycling for the disabled and saddle sores. Members receive a Handbook listing all the Club's facilities and free bimonthly copies of the Club magazine *Cycletouring*, which contains feature articles on cycling in the UK and overseas, details of the latest bike developments and readers' letters with tips on all sorts of topics of interest to cyclists. The Classified Ads columns are also ideal if you want to buy a secondhand bike or parts.

There is even a section where members can advertise for a cycling companion at no cost.

Membership of the club costs £15.00 a year for anyone over 20 and £7.50 for anyone under 20, and entitles you to an AIT International Cycletouring Club card which can be used to obtain introductions at affiliated clubs abroad. You will also receive discounts at YHA Adventure Shops (except on books and maps), at repair shops recommended in the Handbook and on Sally Line ferries. Contact The Cyclists' Touring Club, Cotterell House, 69 Meadrow, Godalming, Surrey GU7 3HS (Tel: (04868) 7217).

LONG DISTANCE COACHES

Another reasonably cheap possibility is to book a seat on a long-distance coach from the UK. Taking a coach has several advantages: intense competition means that most are now equipped with essentials like air conditioning and toilets, and with luxuries like videos and hostesses, and, provided you book with a reputable company, you are likely to leave and reach your destination at predictable times.

But there are drawbacks too:

- Long-distance coach travel can be very uncomfortable. There are regular stops but timed for the drivers' convenience rather than yours. Feet tend to swell, and loose clothing is essential.

- There is the food problem. If you have chosen a coach for economy, you will not want to see the money you have saved melting away in expensive motorway service stations. To take advantage of these, you will also need small change in the currencies of the countries you are travelling through. This can sometimes be obtained through branches of Thomas Cook, but by the time you have paid their commission and accepted the unfavourable exchange rates, you could find yourself paying a great deal for your sandwiches.

- The alternative is to take enough food to last the journey. If so, choose your food carefully. Take cheese spreads instead of meltable margarine or butter, biscuits rather than rolls that will go stale, and apples and bananas which are less messy to eat than oranges.

- Most important of all, take plenty to drink in cans or plastic bottles. You can run up a surprisingly large bill for liquid refreshment in three days.

- Do not assume that travelling by coach will save you from border hassles. If anything, they can be worse because there are so many people to process.

What to take with you on the bus

- Washing things, pills, combs, razors and anything else you need overnight. Once your luggage is stowed in the hold you will not be able to get at it again until you reach your final destination. This applies to your passport too—don't make the mistake of packing it in your bag so that it's inaccessible when you reach the border.
- Layers of clothing. It can get cold at night, even if it was sweltering during the day.
- Travel sickness pills.
- Plenty of reading matter. Magazines are usually more restful than books on long journeys.
- Personal stereo and cassettes, especially if you don't like watching somebody else's choice of video.

The following coach companies operate long distance routes out of the UK:

Name of Company	Head Office	Routes
Eurolines	Victoria Coach Station, 164-172 Buckingham Palace Road, London SW1W 97P	Belgium, France, West Germany, Holland, Spain, Greece, Italy, Hungary, Poland, Morocco, Turkey, Portugal, Yugoslavia, Scandinavia.
Miracle Bus	408 The Strand, London WC2R 0NE Tel: (01) 379 6055	Amsterdam, Paris, Athens, Dublin, Berlin, Madrid, Stockholm, Helsinki, Barcelona, Brussels, Scotland, Istanbul.

Eurolines also offers a four or five journey **bus pass**, valid for two months and costing from £98.00, and **Capital Tripper** tickets costing £52 or £58 for the circular routings London/Paris/Amsterdam/London, or London/Paris/Brussels/London.

RAIL

Travelling by rail is more comfortable than travelling by bus but can be expensive, particularly if you are over 26.

Inter-Rail Cards

If you are under 26 and intend to be away for at least a month, you can buy an **Inter-Rail Card**. This costs £145 and entitles you to free rail transport within Europe and Morocco, to half price travel in the UK and to reduced fares on Sealink, Hoverspeed and some other ferry services. Holders of **British Rail Young Persons Railcards** are eligible for a further £10.00 discount.

If you want to stay away longer you can buy a second or third card. If you plan to use the boats in the Mediterranean, Scandinavia or Ireland, an extra £30.00 entitles you to an **Inter-Rail + Boat Card**.

Cards can be bought from:

- main line British Rail stations
- British Rail-appointed travel agencies—although they may need notice to stock the cards.

To buy an Inter-Rail Card you need your passport to prove that you will be under 26 on the first day of the card's validity. You should also be able to prove that you have been resident in the UK for the six months preceding your purchase of the card.

Once you have bought the card, you must write the routing of each journey on it. Guards will stamp the card to validate it for every journey. If you return the card to British Rail, correctly stamped, within one month of its expiry date, there is even a £4.00 rebate for helping them compile their statistics.

If you only want to use a train on a specific route but you are still under 26, you can buy **Eurotrain** rail tickets offering up to 50% discounts on journeys within Europe. Eurotrain tickets are on sale at 52 Grosvenor Gardens, London SW1W 0AG (Tel: (01) 730 6525), and through branches of Campus Travel.

Sample Eurotrain fares

	£(return)		£(return)
London to Paris	45.90	London to Madrid	102.00
London to Brussels	38.00	London to Rome	133.80
London to Amsterdam	35.00	London to Oslo	165.50

Eurotrain also offers reduced price tickets for use on set routes. These **Explorer tickets** are valid for two months and start at about £50.00 for a London/Rotterdam/The Hague/Amsterdam/Brussels/London routing.

Other ways to economise on rail fares

If you're over 26, rail fares from the UK to the Continent look exorbitant. But before you rush for a bus there are ways to economise.

- There are **special fares** for journeys of five days or less to Belgium, Denmark, France, Luxembourg, The Netherlands, Switzerland and West Germany.

- 'Sejour' tickets offer discounts to people travelling 1,000 kilometres or more on French Railways—for example, en route to Spain.

- **'Night Sejour'** tickets are even cheaper for journeys combining overnight travel from the UK to Paris, and at least 1,000 kilometres on French trains.

- **'Starlight'** fares offer discounts to parts of South Germany, Austria and Switzerland on direct overnight trains.

- Women over 60 and men over 65 who hold British Rail Senior Citizen Cards (£15.00) can buy **Rail Europ Senior Cards** (£5.00) offering discounts in Austria, Belgium, Denmark, Finland, France, West Germany, Greece, Hungary, Italy, Yugoslavia, Luxembourg, The Netherlands, Norway, Sweden and Switzerland.

Families can get reductions by buying a **Rail Europ Family Card** for £5.00. This offers discounts on trains and on some shipping lines in 15 different countries to groups of three to eight people living at the same address. The term 'family' is interpreted broadly, so there is no need for all party members to have the same surname.

If you intend to use British Rail services to get to a port or airport remember that there are a variety of different fares available on most routes. The cheapest are **Saver Return** tickets which come in two forms: **Blue Savers** and **White Savers**. Blue Savers are cheaper and can be used on Sundays to Thursdays inclusive. They can also be used on Saturdays except in July and August. White Savers can be used on Fridays as well but cost slightly more. All Saver tickets are valid for up to one month, but you cannot use them to travel on rush hour services to and from London. Savers from provincial cities to London are often cheaper than those in the opposite direction.

Indispensable handbooks for rail travellers are:

- British Rail's twice yearly *International Passenger Timetable* which includes a European rail map. Cost: £1.50 from British Rail or selected newsagents.
- Thomas Cook's monthly *European Timetable*. Cost: £4.95 from any branch of Thomas Cook.
- Thomas Cook's *Rail Map of Europe*. Cost £2.75 from any branch of Thomas Cook.

FLYING

There are several reasons why you may have to fly to your destination:

- It may be a long way away and you do not want to spend your limited holiday time in transit.
- It may only be accessible by air, like Burma (now known as Myanmar).
- Cheap air fares may actually cost less than travelling by other means; for example, London to Cairo is more expensive by bus and boat than by air.

Air couriers

Some lucky souls manage to fly to their destination at little or no cost by finding work as an **air courier**. As the business world gets more frenetic, there are more and more documents and articles that need to be transported from A to B and cleared through Customs urgently. Obviously, firms that have a lot of these sorts of deliveries employ full-time air couriers. However, there are also opportunities for enterprising and reliable freelancers.

To find work as an air courier it helps to be between the ages of 18 and 22 so you are eligible for any youth discounts. You may have to dress more respectably than you would normally when travelling, and you will have to be travelling light since the firm employing you is actually after your free baggage allowance.

Some firms let you have a completely free ticket in return for seeing their packages through Customs; others charge you a small part of the fare. Either way, you are getting a bargain.

One firm that uses freelance couriers is **Securicor Air Couriers** who recruit them through Tickets Anywhere, 2 Lower King Street, Royston, Hertfordshire SG8 5AL (Tel: (0763) 45722). Another is **Jupiter Travel** (Tel: (01) 751 3323), who advertise in *TNT*.

Finding bargain flights

If you have to pay for a flight there are several options available:

- You can try a **high street travel agency**. Many tour operators now have *seat-only* programmes to popular European holiday destinations like Majorca, the Algarve and Corfu. Some of these can be very attractive, especially if you book at the last moment—however, this is not a good idea in peak season if you have a specific destination in mind. Watch out for extras like airport taxes, insurance and surcharges which bump up the initial cost. In theory, these seats are only meant to be sold as part of a package deal. In the past vouchers for basic accommodation, often in dormitories far from the resort, were issued with the tickets but clients were not actually expected to use them. However, several European governments are now cracking down on these regulations and in future it may not be wise to show up, particularly in Greece, unless you can prove that you have proper accommodation booked in advance.

- In addition to the large tour operators like Thomson and Intasun, there are several companies that specialise in 'seat-only' deals. These include Scantours, 8 Spring Gardens, London SW1A 2BG (Tel: (01) 839 2927), which specialises in flights to Scandinavia, and Slade Travel Ltd, Slade House, 15 Vivian Avenue, London NW4 3UT (Tel: (01) 202 0111) which has a more general programme. Unlike tour operators, these companies offer seats on scheduled flights out of Heathrow as well as on charters.

- Large travel agencies like Hogg Robinson, Pickfords and Thomas Cook also offer **discounted air fares** to popular long-haul destinations like Singapore at prices well below those published in the airline tariffs.

- Ask about **Round The World (RTW)** air fares. These are special fares which allow you to use the services of one or more carriers—for example, TWA and Air New Zealand—wherever they fly in the world for a fixed price. All sorts of rules apply to RTW fares; usually they must be booked in advance, and you can only fly in one direction without backtracking. To find a suitable service you will need the help of a good travel agent. You could also consult *Round the World Air Guide* by Katie Wood and George McDonald, (Fontana, £9.95), bearing in mind that rules and prices change all the time. Hogg Robinson also publishes the useful *Around The World Fares Planner* (free).

Sample RTW fares

Airline	Fare	Rules
Singapore Airlines and TWA	£1,028	14 days advance booking. Valid one year. Minimum three stops.
Delta Airlines and Thai Airways	£1,028	As above. Valid six months.
Alia, Korean Airlines and American Airlines	£1,028	As above. Valid one year.

- Many agencies specialising in long-haul travel also offer ad hoc round the world tickets routed through specific points and usually with Australia or New Zealand as the ultimate destination. These fares are advertised in magazines like *TNT* and offered by agencies like Trailfinders and STA Travel. Other agencies to ask are Reho, 15 Oxford Street, London WC1A 1BH (Tel: (01) 242 5555) and Pan Pacific, 16A Soho Square, London W1V 5FB (Tel: (01) 734 3094).

- Ask about cheaper IATA tickets. **Standby** tickets normally offer the best prices; you get a cheap fare in return for no certainty of a seat on a specific flight. These fares are most popular on North American routes. 'APEX' and 'SuperAPEX' tickets are also cheaper than normal economy fares, but have lots of limitations on their use. Usually you must book and pay for them in advance—often three weeks—and you will have to pay to change your reservations. There are also hefty cancellation charges, so insurance is essential. APEXes and SuperAPEXes are usually available on long-haul routes. Within Europe there are also **PEX** and **SuperPEX** fares with similar restrictions on booking and alterations. They are usually only available on a limited number of flights each day, and often involve a Saturday night stay at your destination. If none of these possibilities suits you, normal excursion fares are also cheaper than economy return fares. The rules attached to excursion fares depend on your destination; however, they usually involve minimum and maximum stays. All these fares are offered by IATA airlines and can be bought in high street travel agencies.

● You can also contact a **bucket shop**, a smaller, usually unlicensed agency, which exists primarily to sell cheap air tickets. These shops are able to undercut high street travel agency prices because their non-membership of IATA allows them to operate out of cheaper premises, for example from an upstairs back room with lower rent than a shop-front office. By saving money on overheads they are able to trim fares to the bone, especially to popular destinations like Bangkok.

How to find a bucket shop
● Look in the back pages of newspapers like *The Guardian*, *The Telegraph*, *The Times* and *The Independent*.
● Pick up a London listings magazine, *Time Out* and *City Limits* both carry bucket shop advertising. So does *TNT*, which is distributed free through bins outside Central London Underground and railway stations. There are listings magazines in other towns too, but London is one of the world's discount air fare capitals.
● Ring the **Air Travel Advisory Bureau** (Tel: (01) 636 5000) for the phone numbers of reputable agencies.

Precautions when buying a bucket shop ticket
Bucket shops operate on the fringe of the law since technically they are selling illegal tickets. However, it is not an offence to buy their tickets, and the airlines are keen to fill their seats at any price. So the risk is relatively small provided you follow these guidelines:

● Visit the shop in person rather than telephoning or writing. Then you can check that it is operating in a business-like manner.

● Ask for the numbers of all flights you book and check them with an agency or airline, or by consulting the *ABC World Airways Guide* in the library before parting with any money. If in the slightest doubt, ring the airline and get them to check that your name appears on their central reservations list.

- Check which airline you will be flying on. Many cheap flights are on Eastern bloc carriers such as Aeroflot, Tarom, Lot, and Balkan Bulgarian which are desperate for hard currency. They may involve long stopovers in Moscow, Bucharest, Warsaw, and so on. Alternatively, they may be on hard-up Third World carriers such as Sudan Airways, Bangladesh Biman, with a poor reputation for in-flight service and safety. Recommended carriers include:

  – Thai Airways International
  – Philippine Airways
  – Singapore Airways
  – Most Middle Eastern airlines offer a reasonable service, although there may be long stopovers in places like Kuwait. Alcohol may not be available.

- Remember that if you pay more than £100 with an Access or Visa card, you can claim from the credit card company if the agency or airline goes bust. However, even the best bucket shops may make a charge for accepting a credit card, since their profit margins are too thin to absorb the card companies' commission charges.

- Check that the price you pay cannot be increased after you have paid the full fare agreed.

- Check that your ticket has 'OK' written in the status box. This means the reservation is confirmed, whereas 'RQ' simply means it has been requested and confirmation is awaited. Standby tickets have 'SA' for 'space available' in the status box.

- If your journey involves long stopovers, check whether you will need a visa for your stopover point, and whether you can leave the airport.

One particularly well-known and well-established bucket shop is Riaz Dooley's Travel Bazaar, 221 Westbourne Park Road, London W11 1EA (Tel: (01) 221 1729).

Losing your ticket

Airline tickets are valuable documents and losing them can be a problem. Always make a note of your ticket number so that if it is stolen you can ask the airline to cancel it and issue you with another. You will be asked to sign an indemnity form, promising to return the ticket should it eventually come to light. The more complicated and cheap your ticket is, however, the harder it may be to get it replaced. Some insurance policies include the loss of air tickets, but read the small print carefully to find out how much cover is offered.

SHIPS AND FERRIES

The days when sea travel was cheap and simple may be over, but you can certainly start your journey by boat. The following services currently operate out of the UK:

Route	Company	Crossing time
Harwich-Gothenburg	Scandinavian Seaways	24-27 hours
Harwich-Hamburg	Scandinavian Seaways	21 hours
Newcastle-Gothenburg	Scandinavian Seaways	26 hours
Plymouth-Santander	Brittany Ferries	24 hours
Aberdeen-Lerwick	P & O Ferries	14-31 hours
Harwich-Hook of Holland	Sealink	6¾-7½ hours
Hull-Rotterdam	North Sea Ferries	14 hours
Sheerness-Vlissingen	Olau Line	7-8½ hours
Harwich-Kristiansand	Fred Olsen Lines	23½ hours
Harwich-Oslo	Fred Olsen Lines	36½ hours
Newcastle-Bergen	Norway Line	22-25 hours
Newcastle-Stavanger	Norway Line	19½ hours
Cairn Ryan-Larne	P & O Ferries	2¼ hours
Liverpool-Belfast	Belfast Car Ferries	9 hours
Stranraer-Larne	Sealink	2¼ hours
Fishguard-Rosslare	B & I/Sealink	3½ hours
Holyhead-Dun Laoghaire	Sealink	3½ hours
Holyhead-Dublin	B & I	3½-4 hours
Liverpool-Dublin	B & I	8¾ hours
Swansea-Cork	Swansea Cork Car Ferries	10 hours
Dover-Ostend	P & O Ferries	3½-4½ hours
Dover-Zeebrugge	P & O Ferries	4 hours
Felixstowe-Zeebrugge	P & O Ferries	5-8 hours
Hull-Zeebrugge	North Sea Ferries	15 hours
Portsmouth-St Helier	British CI Ferries	8-11½ hours
Portsmouth-St Peter Port	British CI Ferries	6½-11¾ hours
Torquay-Alderney	Torbay Seaways	5½ hours
Torquay-St Helier	Torbay Seaways	9¼ hours
Torquay-St Peter Port	Torbay Seaways	6-13 hours
Weymouth-St Helier	British CI Ferries	10½ hours
Weymouth-St Peter Port	British CI Ferries	8 hours
Harwich-Esbjerg	Scandinavian Seaways	20-21 hours
Harwich-Hirtsals	Fred Olsen Lines	27 hours
Newcastle-Esbjerg	Scandinavian Seaways	21-23 hours

Dover-Boulogne	Hoverspeed	40 minutes
Dover-Boulogne	P & O Ferries	1 ¾ hours
Dover-Calais	Hoverspeed	35 minutes
Dover-Calais	Sealink	1 ½ hours
Dover-Calais	P & O Ferries	1 ¼ hours
Folkestone-Boulogne	Sealink	1 ¾ hours
Newhaven-Dieppe	Sealink	4-5 hours
Plymouth-Roscoff	Brittany Ferries	6-7 hours
Poole-Cherbourg	Truckline Ferries	4 ½ hours
Portsmouth-Caen	Brittany Ferries	5 ¾ hours
Portsmouth-Cherbourg	P & O Ferries	4 ½-6 ½ hours
Portsmouth-Cherbourg	Sealink	4 ¾-7 hours
Portsmouth-Le Havre	P & O Ferries	5 ½ hours
Portsmouth-St Malo	Brittany Ferries	8 ½-10 hours
Ramsgate-Dunkirk	Sally Line	2 ½ hours
Weymouth-Cherbourg	Sealink	4-6 hours
Heysham-Douglas	Isle of Man Steam Packet	3 ¾-5 ½ hours
Liverpool-Douglas	Isle of Man Steam Packet	3 hours
Stranraer-Douglas	Isle of Man Steam Packet	6 hours

The short sea crossings are usually fairly cheap, especially in the low season, because of intense competition. However, the longer crossings to Spain and Scandinavia where you have to have a cabin can be costly; air fares are often cheaper. On the other hand facilities on board these ships are excellent. North Sea Ferries actually include the cost of breakfast and dinner in their ticket prices, which makes them more reasonable than they initially appear.

You can book ferries:

- Through a travel agency.
- Through the ferry company directly.

Addresses of UK ferry operators

Sealink UK Ltd, 163-203 Eversholt Street, London NW1 1BG (Tel: (01) 387 1234).

P & O, Enterprise House, Channel View Road, Dover CT17 9TJ (Tel: (0304) 203388).

Hoverspeed, Maybrook House, Queens Gardens, Dover CT17 9UQ (Tel: (0304) 216205).

Sally Line, The Argyle Centre, York Street, Ramsgate CT11 9DS (Tel: (0304) 595522).

IOM Steam Packet, PO Box 5, Imperial Buildings, Douglas (Tel: (0624) 72468).

Brittany Ferries, Millbay Docks, Plymouth PL1 3EW (Tel: (0752) 221321).

North Sea Ferries, King George Dock, Hedon Road, Hull HU9 5QA (Tel: (0482) 795141).

Fred Olsen Lines, Fred Olsen Travel, Victoria Plaza, 111 Buckingham Palace Road, London SW1W 0SP (Tel: (01) 828 7000).

Truckline Ferries, New Harbour Road, Poole, Dorset BH15 4AJ (Tel: (0202) 672153).

Torbay Seaways, Beacon Quay, Torquay, Devon TQ1 2BG (Tel: (0803) 214397).

British Channel Island Ferries, Norman House, Albert Johnson Quay, Portsmouth PO2 7AE (Tel: (0705) 864431).

Scandinavian Seaways, Scandinavia House, Parkeston Quay, Harwich CO12 4QG (Tel: (0255) 552000).

Norway Line, Tyne Commission Quay, North Shields NE29 6EA (Tel: (091) 258555).

Olau-Line (UK) Ltd, Sheerness, Kent ME12 1SN (Tel: (0795) 663355).

Swansea Cork Car Ferries, 55 Grand Parade, Cork, Ireland (Tel: (021) 271 1166).

B & I Line, 54 Grosvenor Street, London W1X 9FH (Tel: (01) 734 4681).

Belfast Car Ferries, Langton Docks, Bootle, Merseyside BT1 3ED (Tel: (01) 922 6234).

Ferry fares are usually based on:

1. The **time and date** of the sailing.
2. The **length of the vehicle**.
3. The **age of the passengers**—children under 4 are usually carried free; between 4 and 14, they pay a reduced fare.

Finding bargain sea crossings
The cheapest fares on the short crossings will usually be for early morning or late night crossings. Obviously fares are higher in July and August, and over Christmas and the New Year when car passengers should reserve their places. Always check the cost of sailings a day, or just a few hours, earlier or later than your ideal travelling time. Sometimes you will be able to save quite a bit by travelling at a slightly different time.

There are usually special **excursion fares** for people intending to stay less than five days on the continent. These offer discounts of up to 50% so are well worth considering.

Night sailings on the longer routes are not always cheaper since many people use them as floating hotels to get a good night's sleep before starting a lengthy journey.

On most ferry routes, foot passengers can book a **through rail or coach ticket** from their point of origin to their final destination, for example, from London to Copenhagen.

Worldwide shipping routes are listed in the *ABC Shipping Guide*, available in travel agencies or your local library. This is also the book to use if you hope to find a berth on one of the few cargo ships still sailing from the UK.

It remains to be seen what the combined effects of the opening of the Channel Tunnel and the abolition of duty-free allowances within Europe in 1992 do to ferry fares.

DRIVING

Since the oil price rises of the seventies, driving is no longer a bargain way to travel. However, taking a car abroad means that you can go exactly where you want to, with as much baggage as you like, and if you have a campervan you may even be able to eliminate accommodation costs.

If you are planning to take a vehicle to the Continent, there are a number of items you need to take with you:

1. A **GB identification sticker**, provided free by ferry companies, motoring insurance brokers, and so on.

2. **Green card insurance** to extend your UK cover to the Continent. This can be done by your home insurance company. In Austria, Belgium Czechoslovakia, Denmark, Finland, France, East and West Germany, Hungary, Ireland, Italy, Luxembourg, The Netherlands, Norway, Sweden and Switzerland, normal UK insurance provides you with minimal third party cover. However, you will still not be protected against damage, theft or personal accident. In other European countries, your UK policy provides no cover at all. The motoring organisations therefore recommend that you take out green card insurance wherever you are going. Make sure that any caravans or trailers are included on the policy and that it is valid on ferries and motorail if you will be using them. Always arrange cover for a couple of days longer than you expect to be away in case of delays.

3. **Your car log-book**. If this is not available get a *Certificate of Registration (Form V379)* from the local vehicle licensing office, allowing ten days for it to arrive. If you are not the vehicle's owner, get a covering letter from the person in whose name it is registered. If you are hiring a vehicle, get one of the motoring organisations to arrange a **Vehicle on Hire Certificate** for you.

4. An **International Driving Permit (IDP)**, if required. The IDP is needed in the USSR, Bulgaria (unless you have a Bulgarian translation of your UK licence) and Hungary. It is also needed in Finland for hired cars or if you are staying longer than a normal holiday, while visitors spending longer than three months in Poland also need one. Visitors to Spain also require an IDP unless they have a translation of their UK licence obtained from the Spanish Consulate (which costs more than an IDP), or a pink EC licence. An IDP is also required for Algeria and recommended for East Germany, Morocco and the USA. Permits are valid for one year and should bear the holder's photograph. They cost £2.50 from RAC European Services, MLPD Reservations, PO Box 92, Croydon CR9 6HN or from the AA, Fanum House, Dogkennel Lane, Halesowen, West Midlands B63 3BT.

5. Your **UK driving licence** (with a translation for Italy unless you have a pink EC licence, and an authenticated translation in Bulgaria).

6. **Bail bond** (Spain and Portugal only) to prevent you being imprisoned until your trial after a serious car accident.

7. **Customs documents** (carnet de passages en douane). If you want to take any kind of boat abroad on tow with you, you will need a Customs carnet to allow you to import it temporarily without paying duty. People taking campervans to Morocco also need a carnet as do visitors to Turkey who are importing motor vehicles for more than three months. These carnets are available from the AA for £9.00.

You might consider taking out **break-down insurance** in case of an accident. **Europ Assistance**, the **RAC's Eurocover Motoring Assistance** and the **AA's Five Star insurance** provide for spare parts to be flown to you in an emergency, which can make all the difference between your trip being ruined and saved. These insurances are only available to people motoring in Europe and around the Mediterranean. RAC and AA insurance is available to non-members of these associations, but you must pay a temporary registration fee on top of the normal premium.

Vehicle checks to make before a long journey
1. Check the air and water filters.
2. Flush the engine with flushing oil and put in fresh lightweight oil.
3. Remove the water thermostat or replace it with a summer one.
4. Replace the plugs and points.
5. Replace the fan belt. Keep the old one as a spare.
6. Flush the radiator and change the top and bottom hoses.
7. Check the brake linings. Replace the brake fluid and cylinder rubbers.

8. Tune the engine.
9. Check the tyres, including the spare. Make sure they all have a minimum of at least 1.6 millimetres tread.
10. Check that you have the correct wheel brace for the wheels.

Spare parts

It also makes sense to take a **spares kit** with you. Purpose-designed kits can be hired on a 'per day' basis from garages, the AA (The Automobile Association Hire Service, Snargate Street, Dover, Kent CT17 9XA (Tel: (0304) 203655) or the RAC (Selectacar Touring Ltd, 10 Plaistow Lane, Sundridge Park, Bromley, Kent BR1A 3PA (Tel: (01) 460 8972/3)). A refundable deposit of about £35.00 will be charged for each spares kit. If you need to use any of the parts, you pay for them on your return home. A typical spares kit should contain:

Set of plugs, points, condenser, rotor arm, HT lead, stop lamp bulbs, side lamp bulbs, indicator bulbs, fuses, fan belt, top/bottom hose, tow rope, adhesive tape, distributor cap, ignition coil, headlamp bulb or sealed beam unit, fuel pump points.

You should also make sure you take a jack and your own tool-kit with spanners, and any other tools you think may be necessary.

Depending on the countries you will be driving through you may also need:

- One or two red danger warning triangles.
- Headlamp deflectors.
- First aid kit—compulsory in Austria, Bulgaria, Czechoslovakia, Greece, USSR and Yugoslavia and recommended in Algeria, East Germany, Iceland and Tunisia.
- Fire extinguisher—compulsory in Greece, Bulgaria and the USSR and recommended in East Germany and Iceland.
- Spare lamp bulbs—compulsory in France, East Germany, Hungary, Spain and Yugoslavia.
- Rear seat belts.
- Emergency windscreen.
- Snow chains.
- Ski racks.

Once again most of these items can be hired on a 'per day' basis through the motoring organisations.

Where to buy a campervan

London has a market specialising in the sale of campervans. On weekdays it is at Bermondsey Square, near London Bridge, while at weekends it is at Provost Street — Old Street is the nearest tube station.

Alternatively, you could look in *Exchange and Mart* or *Thames Valley Trader*, or try a **car auction**. But make sure you know what you are doing when you buy, or take someone along with you who does.

The most popular vans are Volkswagens because they are cheap to drive and spares are available all over Europe. You should expect to pay upwards of £1,000 for one of these. Bedford Commers and Ford Transits are also popular but use more petrol than VWs.

Whilst the initial outlay for a van may seem high, you will probably be able to recoup some of the cost by reselling it on your return. However, if the cost really is beyond your means but you still fancy the idea you can also hire campervans from companies like Apex Leisure Hire, 90 High Street, Hampton Hill, Middlesex TW12 1NY (Tel: (01) 977 2117). Magazines like *TNT* also carry adverts for firms hiring out vans.

Motoring regulations

Although in general motoring regulations are fairly similar throughout Europe, there are local differences and it is always worth consulting the AA or RAC to check on regulations about minimum driving ages, children travelling in the front seats of cars, drinking and driving, and so on before setting out. They have offices in most large towns in the UK so a local phone call should be possible.

Transporting your car overseas

Taking a car with you obviously increases the ferry fare so it makes extra sense to travel at off-peak times and dates.

Travellers to France, West Germany, Austria, Italy, Portugal, Spain, Switzerland and Yugoslavia could consider using **Motorail** to reach their destination. Motorail is a railway system adapted to carry passengers and their cars, and although it is not particularly cheap, driving to the South of France costs a lot in petrol and motorway fees; taking the train does at least mean you arrive rested. There are Motorail routes to the following European towns:

Brive-la-Gaillarde, Bordeaux, Biarritz, Narbonne, Avignon, Evian, St Raphael, Gap, Grenoble, Lyon, Marseille, Moutiers, Mulhouse, Nice, St Gervais, Toulon, Tarbes, Salzburg, Villach, Munich, Bologna, Milan, Rimini, Lisbon, Madrid, Brig, and Ljubljana.

Not all these services are available from the Channel ports but they can all be booked from the UK through the RAC European Service. Some services only operate in peak season.

How much will it cost?

When calculating the cost of motoring to your destination, include the following:

- **Ferry fares** for car, passengers and accompanying pets.
- **Insurance.**
- Hire of **spare parts**.
- Purchase of items like **warning triangles**, and so on.
- **Petrol** in the UK and abroad. RAC offices can provide an indication of comparative costs. Remember that credit cards are usually only accepted for petrol in main towns and on motorways. In Algeria, Gibraltar, Iceland, Malta, Norway, Spain and Tunisia, credit cards are never accepted for petrol purchases, while in West Germany, Italy, Greece, Portugal, Turkey, Yugoslavia, The Netherlands and Switzerland they are rarely accepted. **Lead-free petrol** is often cheaper than leaded petrol on the Continent, but make sure your car is adapted to use it before filling up.
- **Motorway tolls**. RAC/AA offices can provide an indication of costs, but to drive a car from Calais to Nice could set you back about £33.00; with a caravan the charge rises to nearly £50.00. Tolls apply in France, Italy, Spain, Portugal, Greece, Yugoslavia and parts of Austria. Make sure you have a supply of local currency to pay them.
- En route **meal costs**.
- En route **accommodation costs**.
- **Motorway tax** for Switzerland (SFR30—roughly £11.50).
- **Tunnel tolls**, for example when traversing the Alps. The AA can supply free discount vouchers for the Grand St Bernard Tunnel on application.

Cutting petrol costs

You can cut the cost of motoring in Italy by obtaining **petrol coupons** from the AA before leaving home. Visitors to Eastern Europe can also obtain discounted petrol with coupons. These are essential for obtaining supplies in the USSR, Bulgaria, Poland and Romania, but can also be used in Czechoslovakia, East Germany and Yugoslavia. Coupons for Yugoslavia and the USSR are only on sale at border posts; in the other countries they are also on sale within the country itself. Usually you must pay for them with hard currency like sterling.

While it may be tempting to stock up on petrol in countries where it is cheaper, remember that this is not always legal; you should not, for example, carry full petrol cans on ferries. Poland forbids the export of petrol in cans while Bulgaria, Finland, Sweden, the USSR and Yugoslavia charge import duty on petrol brought in in cans. In Greece, Hungary, Italy, Spain and Turkey it is against the law to carry petrol in cans inside a car.

CARAVANNING

You can take a caravan to Ireland, France, The Netherlands, West Germany or anywhere else on the Continent that you can drive to.

Obviously, this increases both your ferry fares and petrol costs, so although you save on hotel bills it is unlikely to be a rock-bottom option even if you already own the caravan.

If you're taking a caravan with you, make all the usual checks on the mechanical worthiness of your car and then check the suspension, bearings and hitch assembly for the caravan. Also take heed of the following tips:

- **Book space on the ferry** crossing earlier than usual since you will need extra space.
- **Stock up on tinned foods** to keep costs down; although Customs officials frown on food imports, their border checks are usually pretty cursory.
- **Inform your insurance company** that you will be taking a caravan with you so it can be entered onto your green card policy.
- **Take out a breakdown insurance** that caters for caravans. It may be best to use the Caravan Club's own policy to benefit from their specialist expertise.
- **Stock up on road maps**. If you are crossing mountains, find out the height of the passes and whether there are alternative ways of crossing that would be easier.
- Make sure you **pack a 16 foot cable** for connecting your caravan to mains supply electricity on sites. Decide on a fuel for cooking and lighting, bearing in mind that Calor gas is in short supply on the Continent whereas Camping Gaz is readily available.

When calculating the cost of caravanning, add in site fees and the charge for connecting your vehicle to the gas supply. With the extra weight for your car to pull, it makes even more sense to make use of any petrol discounts available.

MOTORCYLING

Travelling by motorbike is faster than cycling but more costly. However, a motorbike costs less to buy than a car and might be a good alternative for those who want the advantage of being able to get exactly where they want without the expense of a car. Once again, taking a motorbike increases your cross-Channel costs but petrol costs much less.

Bear in mind that long-distance motorcycling can be dangerous and is only really an appropriate choice of transport for experienced riders.

12
Travelling Around Without Busting Your Budget

If the cost of getting from home to your destination can make a big hole in your budget, the cost of travelling from place to place can be just as high; but once again, there are ways to reduce the expense.

HITCHING

Once you get out of the UK you can continue to hitch your way from place to place. This has the obvious advantage of reducing your transport costs, but may mean you take longer to reach your destination and end up paying more for meals and accommodation. You may also lose the freedom to choose where you eat and so on—for example, if your chauffeur stops at an expensive café along the way, you can hardly refuse to eat there. Often you will be offered meals and drinks as well, but do not depend on this. Accepting may not always be the best response to a free ride anyway.

Autostop agencies

One way to bring more certainty to your arrangements is to organise lifts through international **autostop agencies**, although this means you will have to pay some of the costs of your transport. For example, **Mitfahrzentrale** (Lammerstrasse 4, 8 Munich 2 (Tel: 594561)) is an autostop agency for Germany with offices in Hamburg, Frankfurt and Berlin. For a fee of no more than £7.00 they will put you in touch with drivers going your way on an 'expenses' basis. In France, contact the **Allostop-Provoya** organisation (84 Passage Brady, 75010 Paris (Tel: 42460066)) which runs a similar scheme. In Belgium you need a **Taxistop** office. Hitch-hiking is positively encouraged in Poland where drivers get points for carrying extra passengers. Enquire at a **Polorbis** office for more information. It is possible to find such organisations outside Europe; in Perth, Australia, for example, a company called **Travelmates** (496 Newcastle Street, West Perth) does its best to match hitchers with rides.

The best and worst places to hitch

You should also bear in mind that in some parts of the world where there is relatively little traffic, almost any vehicle will stop for passengers—but the driver will expect you to pay, just as you would for a bus or taxi. This is particularly likely in Africa, even in parts of North Africa like Morocco and Tunisia with a flourishing tourist industry. If you think you will be charged make sure you agree the price in advance; it is no good trying to argue about it later.

It is definitely easier to hitch in some parts of the world than others. There are many sad stories of hitchers trapped for hours at Andalucian road-sides, whereas you are unlikely to wait for long in West Germany. According to *Vacation Work* editor Simon Calder, Yugoslavia and Scandinavia in winter are other hitching black spots to be avoided; nor is Portugal the best bet for hitchers. Where traffic is thin on the ground you may wait ages just because nothing comes along—although when it does you are almost certain to be squeezed in even if the vehicle already looks crammed to capacity.

Hitching is rarely popular with the authorities. If the police appear, try and find something better to do with your thumb until they've gone away again.

Potential problems for the hitcher
For lone women travellers there is *always* some risk attached to hitching; this obviously becomes higher in Muslim countries, and areas with a pronounced 'macho' culture. In such places it is usually best to stick with the buses where drivers, conductors and other pasengers can guarantee some protection.

Also remember that, once outside Europe, the same **insurance regulations** are unlikely to apply. This is particularly important when you consider that more people are injured or killed on African roads than die of any of the well-publicised diseases. In some countries drunken driving is also a serious problem which goes virtually unheeded.

WALKING

Once again you could choose to walk everywhere, which would mean slow progress. However it would also bring you into closest contact with the people around you.

Footwear
If you plan to walk, make sure you have the best possible footwear. This need not necessarily mean hefty boots—it depends on the terrain. It could mean canvas shoes or trainers. However, if you want the shoes to last, you will have to invest as much as possible in them. This is an area where false economy could be painful. Whatever shoes you decide on, make sure you try them out for a while to get your feet accustomed to them. Take some spare laces with you if appropriate; they wear out more quickly in tropical conditions.

In hot areas sandals may seem more suitable than shoes. Indian-style thong sandals are ideally comfortable, but do not expect them to last forever. Nor should you assume that similar sandals will be readily available elsewhere. In Africa, for example, most people wear sandals but in many places the only ones on sale are made out of remoulded tyres.

Ideally walkers should have two sets of footwear: one sturdy pair of boots for hard walking and sandals or canvas shoes for towns and easier terrain. Remember that your choice of socks to go into the boots is also important. Once again, this is not an area for economy; outside Europe, sturdy socks will be hard to come by.

Additional walking equipment

Walkers also need to take specific equipment with them. Again, this depends on where they intend to walk, but items to consider include:

- **Maps**. The best ones are not always available in the country concerned, especially if there are any border disputes such as those in Kashmir, and Southern Morocco, for example. If you are going to use your maps a lot, especially in wet or windy areas, cover them with plastic to protect them against wear and tear.
- **Compass**. If you intend to wander off the beaten track this could come in handy. Compasses cost about £10.00 each.
- **Water bottle**. Wherever you plan to walk, you will always need more to drink than you think. So take the largest plastic container you can comfortably carry. Again, do not assume that you will be able to buy one on the trip. In many Third World countries such containers are like gold dust.

Even if your trip is not planned around hiking, there are bound to be circumstances when you want to walk; after all, part of the fun of being abroad can include short treks, whether in the Samaria Gorge on Crete, the Himalayas or the hills of Northern Thailand. In parts of the world where transport is sporadic, it pays to assume that you will have to walk occasionally. For example in Africa many border posts are quite far apart with no transport in between them, and foot-slogging is an enforced activity.

Bearing this in mind, try and carry as little as possible. If you are weighed down by your luggage, walking can be a nightmare. So the golden rule should be—*if in doubt, leave it behind.*

CYCLING

This is a more reasonable option than many people imagine. Clearly, it is not easy to take a bike across a desert or over a glacier; however, you only need to read the exploits of Dervla Murphy to realise that almost anything is possible provided your bike is sturdy and you are fit and ready to persevere. After all, bikes can always be loaded onto trains, buses and the backs of trucks if the going really gets too tough.

Cycling is faster than walking, and costs, after the initial outlay for the bike, are minimal. Obviously some parts of the world are more conducive to cycling than others. Denmark and The Netherlands, for example, have plenty of cycle-tracks which make life easier. You can even hire bikes in Beijing now, and what better way could there be to explore China?

In most European countries you can take your bike on the trains, but the regulations depend on where you are. On many local French trains you can take your bike free as accompanied luggage. On major routes you may be expected to register it as unaccompanied luggage and pay for the privilege. Contact The Cyclists' Touring Club for information on other countries (see page 127).

FERRIES

Ferries are often a sensible alternative to long overland journeys, and sometimes they may be the only possibility available. In most countries ferries have several classes—at least some of which will be cheap. However, in Third World countries, expect 'deck class' to be crowded and often dirty. Some ferries are also dangerously overloaded, which can be disastrous if there is an accident—and there tend to be more of these than there are in Europe.

The ABC Shipping Guide

To find out all the ferry routes available, consult the *ABC Shipping Guide* which has a quick summary of European Car Ferries, followed by pages of information on worldwide services, including times and dates of sailings and approximate fares. However, the dates and times should be treated with caution; in many parts of the world, the regularity of the service depends on how many tickets have been sold. Of course ferry services may also be cancelled at short notice if the weather is particularly bad.

Finding bargain sailings

Where there are a number of shipping offices all selling ferry tickets, ask around before you buy a ticket. You may be able to persuade someone to offer you a discount, especially if you have a student card. A typical example of somewhere where it pays to ask around is Piraeus, the Athenian port, which is crammed with competing companies. Do not buy tickets for any routes, apart from your trip out of the UK, before you leave; you may end up paying more for them than you would on arrival at the port.

Wherever there is water, there is usually a ferry as well as more expensive cruise and excursion boats. In Venice, for example, it is cheaper to visit the lagoon islands of Murano, Burano and Torcello by ferry than by excursion boat. And at Aswan, no matter what the *felucca* boatmen try to tell you, there is a perfectly good and cheap ferry out to Kitchener's Island. Local tourist offices will not always tell you about these things, however—they want to make money out of you.

TRAINS

Most budget travellers use trains at some point on their travels; but whether there are many trains to use, and whether they represent good value for money or not, depends on your destination.

In India, for example, the rail network is extensive and trains frequent. However, it would be a mistake to assume that going by train guarantees either a quick or a comfortable journey. Third class carriages are jammed with people and baggage, and the trains sometimes move so slowly that you have time to inspect every field you pass. In contrast Japanese bullet trains are luxurious but pricey.

The best guide to worldwide train services is the *Thomas Cook Overseas Rail Timetable* which is published twice a year and costs £5.95.

If you intend to use a lot of trains, find out about any **rover tickets** first. Most rovers allow you unlimited travel on a specific rail network for a fixed period of time for a set fee, and are available for many European countries and some non-European ones as well. The *Thomas Cook Railpass Guide* is published annually, costs £1.50 and contains an excellent summary of the possibilities.

European Rail Rovers

- **Swiss Regional Holiday Season Tickets** are available in the summer months and entitle the holder to 2, 5 or 7 days of unlimited travel in specific regions, like the Bernese Oberland. The tickets are issued for a longer period and on the other days the user can purchase tickets at half price.

- **Swiss Holiday Cards** entitle the holder to unlimited travel on a large number of rail, boat and post coach services and to an unlimited number of reduced price tickets for private funiculars, and so on. They also allow free transport on buses and trains in 24 towns. Cards are available for 4, 8 or 15 days, or one month, and can be bought in the UK or at rail border crossings and at Geneva and Zurich airports. A second class adult ticket for one month currently costs £127.

- **Swiss Half Fare Travel Cards** offer half price fares on trains, boats and post coaches for one month or a year. The one month card costs

£27.00 and you must buy it before arriving in Switzerland. Holders of this card who then buy a Swiss Holiday Card get a further 20% discount on their fares.

- **Netherlands Railways Season Tickets** are available for 3 to 7 days and entitle the holder to unlimited travel on Dutch railways. There is also a one-day rover for £16.25. Purchasers of these cards can extend them to cover urban trains and metros for a small extra fee—about £6.00 for 7 days, for example.

- **Nordic Tourist Tickets** give unlimited travel for 21 days on Danish, Finnish, Norwegian and Swedish Railways as well as on some ferry routes. A second class ticket currently costs £128.

- **DB Tourist Cards and DB Junior Tourist Cards** entitle their holders to unlimited travel on the West German railways, and to exemption from TEE and Intercity supplements. They are valid for 4, 9 or 16 days. A 16-day second class adult card currently costs £113.

- **West German Regional Rail Rovers** are available to people who will be making a return rail journey of 250 kilometres or more in each direction, at least partly on the German rail network. They are valid for 10 days and cover 73 separate areas of 1,000 kilometres, each for a cost of DMK46 (£15.00).

- **Tramper-Monats Tickets** are available to anyone under 23 and to full-time students under 27 and offer one month's unlimited travel on West German trains and rail-operated bus services for DMK228 (£72.00).

- **Greek Tourist Cards** entitle their holders to unlimited second class travel on Greek Railways and bus services operated by the Railways. They are available for 10, 20 and 30 days. A 30-day card currently costs £52.00.

- **French 'Vacances' Passes** give unlimited travel on French Railways for 9 or 16 days in a month or for 4 days in 15. A 16-day pass currently costs £130. You can also get 50% discounts on Hoverspeed services between the UK and France with one of these passes.

- **Belgian Railway Season Tickets** entitle their holders to 16 days' free travel on Belgian railways. The second class cost is currently £53.50.

- **Belgian Tourrail Tourist Season Tickets** are valid for 5 or 8 days' unlimited travel within a 16-day period. An 8-day second class ticket currently costs £37.50.

- **Belgian Fixed Rate Reduced Fare Cards** are valid for one month and entitle you to 50% reductions on any Belgian rail journeys. Their current cost is £8.80 for a second class card.

- **Benelux Tourrail Tickets** offer 5 days' unlimited travel in a period of 17 days on the Belgian, Dutch and Luxembourg railways for £46.70.

- **Austria Tickets** are available to people aged 6 to 25 and give unlimited second class travel on Austrian Federal Railways. They are valid for 9 or 16 days. A 16-day ticket currently costs £71.50.

- **Austrian General Season Tickets** entitle you to unlimited travel on Austrian Federal Railways, and to reduced fares on some shipping services. They are valid for 9 or 16 days or for one month. A second class ticket for one month currently costs £163.50.

- **Portugal's Bilhete Turistico** offers 7, 14 or 21 days' unlimited travel on Portugese railways. A 21-day pass costs ESC21,600 (£83.00).

- **Spain's Tarjeta Turistica** offers 8, 15 or 22 days' unlimited travel on Spanish railways with no supplementary charges. A 22-day pass costs PTA19,000 (£96.00).

- **Italian Tourist Cards** offer 8, 15, 21 or 30 days' unlimited travel on Italian State Railways. A 30-day pass costs £97.00.

- **Polrailpasses** offer 8, 15, 21 days' or one month's unlimited travel on Polish railways. The one month pass costs £48.00.

- **Hungarian Rail Runaround Tickets** offer 10, 20 or 30 days' unlimited travel on Hungarian Railways for the equivalent of SFR81 (£29.00) for 10 days.

- **Freedom of Scotland Tickets** entitle you to 7 or 14 days' unlimited standard class travel on ScotRail. The 14-day ticket currently costs £66.00. There are also rover cards for the Northern Highlands, Western Highlands and Central Highlands and a Highlands and Islands Travelpass. Railcard-holders can get discounted prices.

- **Freedom of Wales Tickets** cost £24.00 for 7 days and entitle you to use all Welsh trains. Welsh travellers should also enquire about the North Wales Rover, the Pass Cambria and the Great Little Trains Wanderer Ticket.

- **Irish Overlander Tickets** offer 15 days' unlimited standard class travel on Northern Ireland's trains, Bus Eireann and Ulsterbus Ltd for £98.00.

- **Northern Ireland Rail Runabout Tickets** offer 7 days' unlimited train travel between April and October for £19.00.

- **Rail Ramblers** offer 8 or 15 days' train travel in Ireland. A 15-day rambler costs IRL73.00 (£61.00).

- **Irish Rail and Road Ramblers** offer 8 or 15 days' train travel plus the use of Bus Eireann services. A 15 day pass costs IRL90.00 (£76.00).

- **Isle of Man Rovers** offer 2, 3 or 7 days' train travel on the Isle of Man. The charge for 7 days is £10.50.

- **British Rail** offers the following rail rovers for 7 days' standard class travel between April and October:

Cornish Rover	£15.00
Devon Rover	£15.00
Wessex Rover	£15.00
Hants and Dover Coast Rover	£15.00
Sussex Coastway Rover	£15.00
Kent Rover	£15.00
Heart of England Rover	£18.00
Freedom of Midlands Rover	£21.00
Freedom of North West Rover	£24.00
Freedom of South West Rover	£30.00
Freedom of North East Rover	£30.00
Freedom of East Anglia Rover	£30.00

These rovers are available from **British Rail stations** in the appropriate areas or at seven days' notice from other main British Rail offices.

Non-European Rail Rovers
- Australia offers:
  - a) A **Budget Austrailpass** for one or three months' second class travel, including sleeping accommodation on some trains. A three month pass costs AUD730 (£348).
  - b) A **Nurail Pass** for 14 days' first class travel in New South Wales for AUD130 (£62.00).
  - c) A **Sunshine Rail Pass** offers 14, 21 days', or one month's travel on Queensland railways. A one month pass costs AUD260 (£124).
  - d) A **Victoria Pass** offers 14 days' first class travel on Victoria railways for AUD99 (£47.00).

- **Canrail passes** offer 8, 15, 22 or 30 days' coach class train travel and use of VIA-operated intercity buses. A 30-day national pass in high season costs CAD560 (£276) and CAD430 (£212) in low season. There are also east, west and corridor area passes.

- **Indrail Passes** for Indian railways are available for periods of 7 to 90 days in air-conditioned, first and second class. You must pay for them in dollars or sterling. Charges for the passes include reservation and sleeper fees; in a few cases they even include the cost of meals on the train. A 90-day second class Indrail Pass currently costs USD150.00 (£87.00). Passes can be obtained from S D Enterprises, 21 York House, Empire Way, Wembley, Middlesex HA9 0PA (Tel:

(01) 903 3411), who can also make reservations for you. A few other UK travel agencies like Cox & Kings and Thomas Cook can also make your reservations, or you can wait until you arrive in India to buy your pass and make the reservations. Indrail recommends booking a month in advance, but three or four days is usually adequate.

- **Japan Railpasses** offer 7, 14 or 21 days' travel on state railways. The ordinary 21-day pass costs £261. These passes are available from JAL offices.

- **Malaysian Railpasses** offer 10 or 30 days' train travel (including use of trains to and from Singapore). The 30-day pass costs MAD175 (£38.00) and is only on sale in Malaysia.

- **New Zealand Travelpasses** offer 8, 15 or 22 days' use of trains, buses and inter-island ferries. The 22-day pass costs £238 in high season (£176 in low season).

- **South African Visitor's Exclusives (SAVEs)** offer 40% discounts on off-peak train travel for a period of up to three months. They may not be used on the Blue Train. Students get a 50% discount. SAVE tickets are available from SAR Travel, 48 Leicester Square, London WC2H 7HX (Tel: (01) 839 2764).

- **USA Railpasses** offer unlimited coach class train on Amtrak national and regional (Northeastern, Eastern, Western, Far Western and Florida) networks for 14, 21 or 30 days. A 30-day pass for the entire system costs USD525 (£305).

Where to buy Rover tickets

Branches of Thomas Cook can sell the following rovers at seven days' notice:

Austria Ticket*	Nordturist Card
Belgian Tourrail	Spanish Holiday Card
Belgian Sixteen Day Ticket*	Swedish Holiday Card
Finnrail Pass*	DB Tourist Card
France 'Vacances' Pass	Inter-Rail Card
Greek Tourist Card	Rail Europ Senior Card
Italian Tourist Card	Rail Europ Family Card

(*voucher to be exchanged on arrival in appropriate country)

The following are available from Compass Travel, 46 Albemarle Street, London W1X 4EP (Tel: (01) 408 4567):

Austrailpass	Canrailpass
New Zealand Travelpass	USA Railpass

Surcharges on train tickets

If you will be using trains a lot, but will not have the advantage of a rover ticket, remember that different train tickets can cost different amounts, especially in Europe. To save money, avoid travelling on **TEE** and **rapide** trains which carry surcharges because they are quicker and more comfortable. Sometimes people buying tickets outside the country are exempt from paying surcharges.

Local ticket offices may try and persuade you to travel on the faster trains, but ultimately it is a choice between speed and economy. The following list indicates which trains are best avoided by budget travellers, but the *Thomas Cook European Timetable* is the best source of up-to-date information which can be found at the start of each national section:

Country	Type of service with surcharge	Notes
France	Eurocity, Intercite, most TGVs, some rapides.	
The Netherlands	EC and D trains.	
Italy	Intercity, Rapido.	
Spain	Rapide, Talgo, Inter-City, TER, Electrotren.	
Finland	Some Express and Rapide services.	
UK	Pullmans.	
West Germany	Eurocity and Intercity (5DMK), express (3DMK).	No charge for tickets bought abroad, or for people travelling more than 50 kilometres. Extra DMK1 if you pay on the train.
Austria	Eurocity, International Express, express (AUS30).	No charge for tickets bought abroad.
East Germany	Expresses and semi-fast trains.	
Yugoslavia	Internal expresses.	No charge for tickets bought abroad.
Czechoslovakia	Internal expresses.	No charge for tickets bought abroad.
Romania	On rapides and expresses, reservation plus fee compulsory.	No charge for tickets bought abroad.
Poland	Fast and express trains.	No charge for tickets bought abroad.
USSR		Charge for bedding.
Scandinavia		Reservation fee often compulsory.

Other pointers for train travellers

- Trains cross **borders** and the problems can be just as bad as if you approach on foot. On the Tazara railway between Tanzania and Zambia you can expect a good deal of hassle.

- **Thefts** on trains are common, so you should always sleep with your money and passport strapped to your body. In some countries there are also conmen who give travellers drugged food and then rob them while they're sleeping. This has become such a problem in Thailand that guards on popular tourist routes come round with a notice warning travellers only to eat food bought from railway officials.

- **Sleeping** in crowded trains can be a problem, and ticket inspectors have a nasty habit of coming around at night-time. Paying for sleeping accommodation pushes up the price and may not always be possible. In some countries, such as Egypt, it is quite acceptable to sleep in the luggage racks or, in Burma (Myanmar), under the seats. Avoid sleeping on the roof though—you may roll off if the train jolts.

- In countries where people regularly travel on **train roofs** you may be able to avoid paying for a ticket at all; but this can be at the risk of exposure to blazing sun, so make sure you have a hat on before you embark on such an adventure.

- Many trains—including the original Orient Express—don't have a dining car or buffet. However, finding **snacks** en route is rarely a problem since everywhere the train stops people will rush to the window selling all sorts of food and drink; take all the usual health precautions when experimenting. In countries where the drinking water is unsafe, stick to hot tea or bring your own drink along.

- If you intend to use trains, but do not have a rover, remember that **buying tickets** may not be the simple matter it is at home. Queues at Delhi Central will make those at Victoria look non-existent, and it's never easy to make yourself understood if you do not speak the language and there are hundreds of people crowding round all trying to get served before you. Sometimes, however, simply being a foreigner entitles you to queue separately, or to buy tickets elsewhere. Women should find out if there is a separate queue for them before joining the never-ending main one. In somewhere like India it may be worth tipping someone to stand in line for you.

- **Train ticket prices** may depend on where you buy them. For example some travellers have managed to buy tickets for the Trans-Siberian Railway very cheaply in exchange for hard currency at the IBUSZ office in Budapest. Always read up the latest literature before committing yourself to a hefty fare.

Sleeping on trains

You can always save money by travelling overnight on trains, thereby eliminating some accommodation costs. European **couchettes**, which are fold-down, shelf-like beds, cost a standard £7.80 (six berth) or £10.00 (four berth) and can be booked through British Rail or rail-appointed travel agents.

Sleeping cars can be far more costly and are not usually for budget travellers. However some offer exceptional value for money and are worth a splurge. For example the Nairobi to Mombasa train still offers Orient Express-style luxury even to second class ticket-holders. You wake up in the morning rattling through the Tsavo Game Park, a pleasure well worth paying slightly more than the bus fare to experience.

BUSES

Most budget travellers also resort to local buses at some point in their travels; but although buses are cheaper than trains in the UK, this is not always the case elsewhere; when both options exist, always compare prices. Nor is it always true that trains are more comfortable; in Sudan buses are a much better bet.

Tourist offices rarely have much information about buses, and there are no comprehensive guides to the services available. Basically you have to play it by ear and ask around when you arrive. Fellow travellers are often the best source of up-to-date information.

Where several bus companies operate on the same route, make sure you check all the prices to find the best deal.

Bus Rovers

Once again, if you intend to use buses a lot in one area or country, find out if there are any Rover tickets available. The following are some examples:

- **Greyhound Ameripass** allows up to 30 days' use of America's Greyhound bus network for USD225 (£131) (+ USD50 (£9.00) to include Canada). These tickets must be purchased before you arrive in the States. Greyhound Lines is at 14-16 Cockspur Street, London SW1Y 5BL (Tel: (01) 839 5591).
- **Trailways USA Pass** offers a minimum of 5 days' travel on the Trailways network throughout the States for USD10 (£6.00) a day, provided the pass was bought abroad. It is available at selected UK travel agents.
- **Greyhound Bus Pass** allows up to 60 days' travel on the Australian Greyhound network, with a break of up to 7 days allowed during its validity. The 60-day pass costs AUD735 (£350) and must be bought before you reach Australia.

- **Down-Under Coach Pass** allows 9 days' travel on Greyhounds in Australia and Mount Cook Lines in New Zealand for AUD210 (£100).
- **Ansett Pioneer Aussiepass** allows up to 60 days' travel on Ansett Lines for AUD690 (£329) when bought abroad. It also offers free and discounted sightseeing tours.
- **Deluxe Coachlines Koalapass** offers up to 90 days' travel on Deluxe Coachlines round Australia for AUD990 (£471).
- **Kiwi Coach Passes** offer 7 and 10 days' travel at a discounted price when bought overseas.
- **Egged Round About Bus Tickets** offer unlimited travel on Israeli buses for 7, 14, 21 or 30 days at a time. The 30-day pass currently costs USD80 (£47). The passes also offer 10-15% discounts in Egged restaurants.
- **Singapore Explorer Tickets** offer 1 or 3 days' unlimited travel in Singapore and come complete with a map to help you find your way around. They are on sale at the YMCA and a 3-day pass costs SID12 (£4.00).
- **Iceland Omnibus Passports** offer unlimited bus travel for 1, 2, 3 or 4 weeks. A 4-week pass costs USD310 (£180).
- **Iceland Full-Circle Bus Passport** allows you to make one complete circuit of the island by bus with no set time limit on the journey. It costs USD145 (£84.00).

The cons of travelling by bus

The main problem with buses, apart from overcrowding and the risk of breakdown, is that in some parts of the world they are driven with a reckless disregard for the terrain. Kashmiris are fond of terrifying travellers with lurid stories of buses that fell into ravines, but they do have a point; if you are a nervous passenger, think twice before embarking on a transmontane bus ride in one of the world's poorer countries.

Another snag with buses is that they have limited space for baggage inside. Normally you have to put your bag into a boot or onto the roof, which means that you will not see it again until journey's end. Make sure you have everything you need for the journey with you, and make absolutely certain that you have any valuables inside the bus with you; there are plenty of stories about items removed from bags on roofs. If possible, empty all backpack side pockets since it's easy to slip items out of those without it being obvious. Make absolutely sure you see your bag put onto the bus and accept that you will probably have to pay for the privilege of doing so. In Morocco the bus companies actually issue tickets for bags. Elsewhere the 'fee' will be negotiable, but make sure you agree the price in advance.

PLANES

While it may not sound the most economical way to get around, you may sometimes have to fly from place to place because of the distance involved, because of the terrain, or because of political disturbances somewhere along the route. In some countries like Peru, however, air fares are actually very good value for money and well worth considering. In Burma (Myanmar) travellers often opt for flying simply because with only seven days to look round the country, there is not much time for getting around by unreliable forms of overland transport. In the USA competition as a result of deregulation has caused fares to fall, and some are remarkably good value for money. Within Europe deregulation is only just creeping in. When it does, expect to see some air fares fall here too.

Pointers for travelling by air

- It may be cheaper to buy the ticket before you leave the UK, even if it is for a longer journey than you intend to make, since there are plenty of cheap tickets available out of the UK and very few out of places like Khartoum. So, for example, a ticket from London to Nairobi can actually work out cheaper than one from Khartoum to Nairobi. So long as it is routed via Sudan, you can simply take out the unwanted London to Khartoum coupon and throw it away.

- In countries with a flourishing black market, you will usually be expected to pay for air tickets with hard currency and then have the fact that you have done so endorsed on your currency exchange certificate. Once again, this means that buying a ticket on the spot can work out more expensive than you had expected.

- Find out where the world's bucket shop capitals are. Amsterdam, Nairobi and Bangkok are examples. If you do have to buy a ticket, these will be good places to try.

- Bear in mind that airlines like Aeroflot offer cheap fares from places other than the UK. Flying out of Nairobi, they may not seem the most obvious carrier; in fact they are often the cheapest.

- Beware of very cheap travel agencies. If you think bucket shops have a shady image in England, similar shops open and close with surprising frequency in other cheap fare centres like Nairobi and Bangkok. Check with other travellers, and go somewhere with a *recent* recommendation. Even good guidebooks go out-of-date quickly.

- Look out for **discounted return portions** of tickets being sold by travellers who can't use them. These will often be offered on hostel noticeboards. In the past, few check-in desk staff compared ticket names with passports, so it was sometimes possible for someone other than the legal owner to use them, even though this was not strictly legal. However, with increased security at airports, the likelihood of getting away with this now is greatly reduced, and it may not be wise to try. If you *do* decide to risk it, arrange to hand over payment for the ticket *after* checking in and before going through passport control. The real ticket owner can then check in and you will only need to go through passport control, where officials usually only look at your boarding pass.

- While it is harder to find out definite prices for cheap air tickets out of countries other than the UK, organisations like Trailfinders and STA Travel can offer up-to-date advice on many routes. Their prices may not be rock-bottom, but they will still represent reasonable value for money.

- If you are a frequent flier, try to befriend an expert air fares agent. Since exchange rates fluctuate so frequently, you can sometimes take advantage of cheaper fares from other towns than the one you are actually in, if you are prepared to remove flight coupons you do not really need to use from the ticket. For example, when it was cheaper to fly from Dublin than London to the Far East, some agents issued ex-London passengers with tickets from Dublin and simply removed the unwanted Dublin to London coupon. IATA frowns on 'cross-border' ticketing but it is not necessarily illegal and can be a way of bringing down steep air fares.

- Always check the status box of your ticket. If it is endorsed 'OK', then you hold a confirmed booking. 'RQ' means a booking has been requested but not confirmed. Ideally, you should not show up at the airport unless the 'RQ' has been amended to 'OK'. However, return flights from Rangoon to Bangkok usually read 'RQ', as do many Indian Airline and Royal Nepal Airline tickets, and there is nothing you can do about it. If the status box says 'SA' you will only be carried if there is space available—in other words, you have a standby ticket. 'NS' indicates that no seat will be available and should only appear on an infant's ticket. If the agent says your name is on a 'wait list' 'WL', don't panic—it does not mean you are overweight. What it does mean, however, is that the flight is full and your booking will not be confirmed unless somebody cancels. Again, try not to arrive at the airport without first checking that you have been cleared from the wait list onto the confirmed seat list.

- Remember that many airlines require you to reconfirm that you will be using the return portion of your ticket no later than 72 hours before you intend to do so. Failure to do this can result in the reservation being cancelled. If possible reconfirm directly with the airline, since most travel agencies charge for doing this for you.

Airpasses

If you are going to do a lot of flying while away, investigate the possibility of an **airpass**. Airpasses are similar to railpasses, although they usually restrict you to a limited number of flights within a set period of time. The price of passes is unlikely to compare with that of bus or train tickets. However if you are heading for the USA or Australia, where you may wish to cross huge areas with few specific sights to stop for then you may feel that the extra cost is justified in terms of the time saved. Furthermore, when you work out the true cost of long overland journeys, you have to add in the price of meals and accommodation en route to make a fair comparison.

The following air passes are available:

- **Go Australia Airpass**. A pass allowing five stopovers costs AUD600 (£286) while one allowing eight stopovers costs AUD950 (£452). These prices represent roughly a 40% discount off economy fares. They are available to overseas residents visiting Australia on APEX or other promotional air fares, and you can purchase them overseas or within 30 days of arrival in Australia. They are valid on Ansett and Australian Airlines, with a minimum validity of 7 nights and a maximum validity of 45 nights.

- **East-West Transcontinental Airpass**. This pass is available to East-West Airlines passengers travelling from Cairns to Brisbane, Gold Coast, Sydney, Ayers Rock and Perth or vice versa. It costs AUD469 (£223), is valid for 60 days and is only available to non-residents.

- **East-West Coastal Airpass**. This is available to East-West Airlines passengers flying from Cairns to Brisbane, Gold Coast, Sydney, Albury, Hobart, Devonport and Melbourne or vice versa. It costs AUD469 (£223) to non-residents and is valid for 60 days.

- **East-West East-Side Airpass** This is available to East-West Airlines passengers for a maximum 14 days for unlimited travel as far north as Maroochydore, as far south as Hobart and as far west as Ayers Rock. It costs AUD469 (£223).

- **Kendell Country Airpass** This costs AUD380 (£181) and offers international travellers 14 days' unlimited travel on Kendell Airlines network.

- **Visit New Zealand Pass**. This costs NZD280 (£100) for four sector flights on Air New Zealand and NZD380 (£136) for six sectors. It is valid for 60 days and can only be bought overseas.

- **Mount Cook Line Kiwi Air Pass**. There is also a one-month Mount Cook Airlines pass which must also be bought overseas and can be used once on each airline sector.

- **Brazil Airpass**. A 21-day pass costs USD330 (£192) and a 14-day pass USD250 (£145). Both passes allow unlimited travel on Brazilian domestic airlines and both must be purchased before you arrive in Brazil.

- **Discover India Airpass**. This offers unlimited economy class travel on domestic Indian airlines for 21 days for USD400 (£233). No backtracking is allowed.

- **South India Excursion** tickets permit 30% discounts on economy class air fares for up to 21 days. Holders must be flying from the Maldives or Sri Lanka and entering India via Madras, Tiruchirappalli or Trivandrum. It is valid for flights between Madras, Tiruchirappalli, Madurai, Trivandrum, Cochin, Coimbatore and Bangalore.

- **India Wonderfares** permit unlimited economy class travel for 7 days for USD200 (£116) in any one of North, South, East or West India flight networks. Travellers wishing to include Port Blair (Andaman and Nicobar Islands) in their itineraries must pay USD300 (£174).

- **Visit Norway Passes** are valid for one month and offer either two or four discounted flight coupons to be used on Braathaus SAFE domestic flights. They are only available to non-residents of Norway and can be bought from UK travel agents (you may have to accept an MCO to be exchanged on arrival in Norway). The four-coupon pass costs £113.

- **American Airpasses.** There are so many North American airlines, all with different fares, that it would be impossible to list all the passes available. However the following carriers all offer them and your travel agent can supply details:

American	Piedmont
Continental	Presidential
Delta	Republic
Hawaiian	TWA
Northwest	United
Ozark	US Air
Pacific Southwest	Western
Pan American	

In general these 'VUSA' (see page 161) passes must be bought before arrival in the USA. Normally you have to buy a set number of flight coupons for use within a set period of time, and your itinerary must be set out on the same ticket as your transatlantic journey.

When deciding which pass to buy, you obviously need to check that they fly to the cities you want to visit, since the smaller carriers will only have limited networks. Then there are several ways to make sure you get the best bargain:

1. Start your airpass on the eastern seaboard to save paying the higher transatlantic fare to the west coast.
2. Check whether the airline will want one or two of your coupons for transitting an airport simply to make a connection.
3. Buy a standby pass for rock-bottom prices.

Some VUSA passes even allow you to fly to Mexico, Canada or the Caribbean, but you are unlikely to find this sort of deal without the help of a good travel agent with an even better computer.

Other discount flights

Even if you will not do enough flying to justify the cost of an airpass, you do not necessarily have to pay the full fare for routes you choose to fly. In several countries overseas visitors are entitled to **discounted domestic air fares**. Frequently these must be paid for in the country of origin and the routing must appear on the same air ticket as the international flights. However, you may still be able to change your bookings at a later stage.

The following regular discounts are available:

Australia
- **Air Queensland Overseas Visitors Fares**. 15% discounts are available on all Air Queensland routes.
- **East-West Visit Australia Fares**. 30% discounts on economy fares are available on all East-West Airlines routes except to Norfolk Island and Canberra.
- **Air New South Wales Network 30 Fares**. 30% discounts are available on all Air New South Wales routes except to Norfolk Island.

USA
'Visit USA' (VUSA) tickets are available on most routes and offer approximately 20% discount off normal economy fares. You must book and pay for them before you arrive in America.

Canada
Most Canadian airlines also offer 'VUSA' fares. Again, you must book and pay for them before you reach the country.

CAR HIRE

While travellers to Europe may decide to take a vehicle, those travelling further afield are very unlikely to have their own transport with them. Hiring a car is certainly not the cheapest way to get around; however, sometimes it may be the best option in spite of the cost, especially if you want to reach places that might otherwise be inaccessible.

Points to consider when hiring a car

- The well-known firms like Avis and Hertz may not offer the cheapest rates; however, their cars will be maintained to a reasonable standard, and you may have some come-back if anything goes wrong. Hire from a smaller firm and you may pay less but risk having a car with mechanical defects.
- If you will be driving a long distance, look for a company offering an **unlimited mileage** tariff. If you accept a **time and mileage** deal and then drive a long way, the price will rapidly mount up.
- If you only want to drive the car from A to B, look for a company which does not levy a surcharge on one-way trips; this is often only the case with a larger company.
- Check the car for defects and make sure the company has a record of them before driving it away; then you cannot be charged for them when you return.
- Make sure the petrol tank is full when you drive off, if you are expected to return it full.
- Try and carry a credit card to pay the deposit; otherwise you will need a lot of cash with you.
- Think carefully before economising on **collision damage waiver (CDW)** fees. These are a form of insurance to cover the first part of the cost of damage following an accident. Unless you have a major accident, damage to the car is likely to be slight—but the bill may still be considerable, and not covered by normal insurance. For a few pounds extra, CDW puts your mind at rest.

Shipping a vehicle

If you take a vehicle with you or buy one while abroad, you may have to consider the possibility of shipping it from one country to another. This is never likely to be cheap, but could cost less than selling one vehicle, shipping its contents on and then buying another.

It is difficult to predict the cost of shipping, since the only reliable prices are those quoted by agents at the ports. Often the charge will be based on the weight, length or area of the vehicle. Take these dimensions from your handbook, without mentioning towbars and other extras unless specifically asked. If the car has to be packed in a container rather than driven on and off the ship, the cost will rise substantially because you may have to pay for packing and unpacking and also for any unused space in the container. It makes sense to take out maritime insurance since a fire at sea could cost you dearly.

It is probably unwise to book and pay for your passage before reaching the port since overland itineraries often come unstuck somewhere along the route.

Remember that if you want to import a vehicle into another country permanently, it may have to be adapted to suit local regulations. In countries like Australia and the USA such adaptations can be very expensive indeed. You should also remember that it may be illegal to sell your vehicle, so unless you allow enough time for driving it home again, you could end up having to pay a hefty bill for shipping anyway.

For up-to-date information on shipping routes worldwide, consult the *ABC Shipping Guide*. It can be particularly tricky to ship vehicles between Africa and Australia or between South America and Australasia.

Motorcyclists may also have to ship their bikes unaccompanied on a few routes. Sometimes they will be asked to pack them in crates, which can cost more than the actual charge for passage. One way round the problem is to make your own crate, checking on specifications first. Another is to find a motorcycle dealer who can sell you one secondhand.

Safari vehicles
Travellers to Africa who hope to visit the game parks should consider hiring a vehicle. Not only are organised safaris expensive, but some of the remoter parks are rarely included in tours. Since these are least congested with other vehicles, having your own transport to visit them is a distinct advantage. Hiring a Land Rover in Nairobi is fairly straightforward and you can cut the cost by looking for companions. It is not strictly legal to place advertisements on noticeboards seeking safari partners, but asking around should bring results.

'Driveaway' cars in America
Visitors to North America who are over 21 and hold a current driving licence can take advantage of the marvellous 'driveaway' system where car owners who need to move their vehicle from A to B sometimes employ an agent to find a driver for them.

Once you have arrived in the States and decided you would like to drive across it, find a copy of *Yellow Pages* and look up 'Automobile Transporters and Driveaway Companies'. Someone may need a driver for your route immediately but, if not, most companies will take a note of your name and contact you when a car becomes available.

The driveaway system offers you the use of a car for little more than the price of petrol, although you will be expected to leave a refundable deposit. To keep costs down, look for as small a car as possible, although in the States this could mean waiting a very long time! Alternatively, try finding other people who want to make the same journey to share the cost with you. Provided their names are registered when you take the car away, there will be no objection to this. Once again, check the car for obvious defects before you take over responsibility for it.

You will usually be given a date for delivering the car to its owner, but are not normally expected to drive like the clappers to get there.

SELF-DRIVE EXPEDITIONS

Of course some people do set off to drive great distances, for example across Africa. This is unlikely to be a cheap way to travel because petrol is expensive almost everywhere. It can also be in very short supply, leading to monopoly prices. However, you can always buy a vehicle to see you through the trip and then sell it again on your return, thus recouping some of the costs.

Choosing a vehicle

When choosing a vehicle you will need to consider:

- The kind of terrain you will be crossing. Two-wheel drive vehicles are adequate for all but the trickiest expedition ground.
- The availability (and cost) of fuel en route. If it is likely to be scarce you will need a vehicle capable of carrying large quantities at a time.
- How important the living space is going to be. A Range Rover will be good for desert driving but is not ideal for living in. A Volkswagen Kombi or Ford Transit will be more comfortable.
- The height of the vehicle. Ferries charge more for tall ones.
- Whether a diesel or petrol engine will be best. Diesel is often cheaper outside Europe, although the engines cost more in the first place and are harder to repair if anything goes wrong.

Obviously, you should think twice before setting off on a long overland trip unless you are an excellent and experienced driver. Even in Europe there are some nightmarish places to drive in—Naples is a good example—and once outside Europe the hazards are too numerous to mention. In Turkey, expect to be forced off the road by oncoming lorries hogging the centre of the carriageway. In parts of Africa, expect to have to follow sand tracks across desert rather than tarmac roads. In Africa, Iran and Afghanistan be warned that injuring someone in an accident could result in a lynching party; and almost everywhere you will have to contend with sheep, goats, chickens, children, rickshaws and other unprecedented obstacles.

Before setting off to drive outside Europe, consult a reliable guidebook for details of what to take with you and for information on potential problems. Contact your vehicle's manufacturer for advice about the conditions you expect to encounter. If you write to Volkswagen, c/o VAG (UK) Ltd, Yeoman's Drive, Blakeland, Milton Keynes, Buckinghamshire MK14 5AN (Tel: (0908) 679121), they will supply you with information about driving in tropical conditions.

One final point—remember that it is usually illegal to sell a vehicle in a country other than your own, although there are ways round this, like selling to a diplomat, for example. If you *do* want to sell, consult the AA or a Customs Office before you leave the UK for up-to-date advice.

13
Staying Away for
Next to Nothing

Budget travellers can choose from a wide range of possibilities when it comes to somewhere to stay. They can camp on recognised sites or on beaches, stay in hostels or dormitories, take refuge in Sikh temples or Italian monasteries, or live in hope of being befriended by someone they have met on a train or while hitching who will invite them to stay in their own home.

CAMPING

The cheapest form of accommodation is obviously camping rough either on beaches, in parks or on private land. This does have drawbacks, including a lack of privacy, shortage of sanitary facilities and danger of theft. However there are places like Sharm El Sheikh and Nuweiba beaches in Sinai which have semi-permanent travellers' camps and where these difficulties have been overcome with a little help from local café owners.

Free camping

Free camping, with the farmer's permission, is permitted in Iceland, and you can camp anywhere that you can put up a tent in Italy. But in most places camping anywhere apart from on authorised sites is technically illegal and best thought of as an emergency measure. If you do want to try it *The Hitch-Hiker's Guide to Europe* contains lots of tried and tested tips about parks, stations, riverbanks and so on sent in by readers.

Campsites

There are plenty of campsites throughout Europe, America, Australia and New Zealand. However, outside these areas they may be few and far between and it is best to find out well in advance rather than risk being stranded in the middle of nowhere. Tourist offices can usually tell you where the sites are and some, like the Danish one, provide excellent touring and camping maps. Otherwise, consult an up-to-date guidebook or the Camping and Caravanning Club of Great Britain.

It is always worth asking about discounts. For example, in Denmark you can buy a cheque for DKK75 (£6.50) which covers as many as six people for one night. Many sites offer cheaper rates in low season; in Hungary you can save up to 20% of the usual cost by camping off-peak.

Camping carnets often entitle you to discounts too, for example in Greece. These are identity documents which, if fitted with a photograph, can be used as a substitute for a passport on sites which like to keep campers' identification papers. Carnets also offer personal accident and third party liability insurance to holders. They are compulsory for camping in Denmark and Portugal and on most Swedish sites, and may be asked for in Austria, France, West Germany, Greece, Italy, The Netherlands, Norway, Spain, Switzerland and Yugoslavia. However the carnet is not recognised in Algeria, Cyprus, Czechoslovakia, East Germany, Ireland, Romania, Turkey or the USSR. Carnets are available to members of the Camping and Caravanning Club for £1.40 (see address below), at RAC offices for £1.25 (personal callers) or from the AA for £1.95.

In a few places, particularly islands with limited spare ground space, camping is not really feasible. Malta, Gibraltar and Antigua are three countries where there's little point in taking a tent.

Camping equipment
One of the main drawbacks with camping is that it necessitates carrying a lot of equipment. At the very least you will need:

- Tent with ground-sheet.
- Sleeping bag.
- Torch or gas lamp.
- Mallet to hammer pegs into dry ground.

More serious campers will also want to take cooking equipment with them, and some people will not feel comfortable without an air-bed or Karrimat.

Camping clubs
Regular campers should consider a subscription to the **Camping and Caravanning Club**. Members receive a handbook listing thousands of sites all over the UK and Ireland, some of them only open to members. There is also a special map showing UK site locations. The **Carefree Foreign Touring Service** is also available to help with booking ferries and camp-sites overseas, arranging insurance (often with Europ Assistance) and collecting camping carnets. Annual membership costs £23.00 from the Membership Department, The Camping and Caravanning Club, 6 Greencoat Place, London SW1P 1PL (Tel: (01) 828 4321, ext 123).

The monthly magazine *Camping and Caravanning* is delivered free to all members and contains useful articles on sites at home and abroad,

surveys of the latest equipment, advertisements for equipment stockists,
and so on. The *Classified Advertisements* section is also an ideal place to
look for secondhand equipment. To advertise in it yourself costs a
minimum of £7.00 and you should send cheques to The Classified
Advertisement Manager, *Camping and Caravanning*, Jackson House, 12
Merton Park Parade, Wimbledon SW19 3NT. General enquiries to the
Club should be referred to its headquarters at 11 Lower Grosvenor
Place, London SW1W 0EY (Tel: (01) 828 1012).

Remember that campsites are usually quite far away from town
centres. In countries where rented rooms are very cheap, camping may
cost almost as much by the time you have added the cost of transport to
the site charges.

HOSPITALITY

If you travel beyond Europe, you may find yourself 'adopted' by local
people and invited to stay in their homes. This is a lovely idea but does
present certain problems. For women, of course, there is the dilemma
of whether it is wise to stay with people when you have only just met
them, particularly since the low public profile of women in many
countries means that most invitations come from men. If you do decide
to take up an offer, always make sure that there are women staying in
the house as well and that someone knows where you are going.
Remember that in Muslim countries in particular, your own image may
suffer if you are seen to behave in a way that local women would not.

For men, of course, the dilemmas will be different. However, you
should never forget the risk of robbery; protect yourself by listening
into the grapevine to discover if you are in an area well known for
drugged food, theft of travellers cheques, and so on. However
hospitality towards lone men, particularly in Muslim countries, can
be amazing and it would be a shame to miss out on it whenever
possible.

Living conditions

If you are adopted on a bus or in the street, remember that many
people live in conditions far removed from those you are accustomed to
at home. Houses may be infested with bugs and have limited furniture
and sanitation. If you do not think you can grin and bear it, make your
excuses and check into a hotel instead. Since people who can afford cars
are usually wealthier, they will normally—but not always—have homes
that reflect their higher standard of living.

Presents

If you are invited to stay with anyone, remember that hospitality works
two ways. However hard up you feel, you should still offer some token

of your thanks. Money may not always be appropriate, but depending on your hosts' circumstances presents for their children, food or household items will be welcome. Even postcards of home, badges, balloons, perfumed soap, malaria tablets, foreign stamps, coins or biros may make acceptable gifts if you have nothing else.

It pays to adopt a non-materialistic approach when staying with people, in case your host takes a particular interest in your books, camera, sun-glasses, personal stereo, or jewellery. There are parts of the world where etiquette demands that the host parts with anything greatly admired by a guest. Be careful what you say and decide what you can bear to part with yourself before the situation arises. If you take photos and promise to send copies, make sure you do so once you are home.

Never outstay your welcome, particularly in parts of the world where food and drink is in short supply and someone may be going without to support you. This also applies when you turn up on the doorstep of a friend of a friend. They may be very pleased to put you up for a day or so; any longer might be asking a bit much.

In spite of all the caveats, the chance to stay with local people is usually a wonderful opportunity, offering the best chance to find out what life is really like in other parts of the world. I've stayed in a luxury high-rise apartment in Bombay, in a doctor's surgery in Malawi and in a village hut on Tuti Island in Sudan. All three experiences were eye-opening and all three will linger in my memory long after I have forgotten the names of cheap hotels.

HOSTELS

Hostels usually make good, cheap alternatives to staying in hotels or pensions. Facilities are generally fairly basic, and accommodation is often in dormitories which can make for a noisy stay, especially in places like Egypt where whole families actually live in the hostels.

The main criticisms travellers have of hostels are that they often have evening curfews, are sometimes closed during the day and usually segregate the sexes unless special family rooms are available.

International Youth Hostel Federation
The **International Youth Hostel Federation** has more than 5,000 hostels worldwide. The British **Youth Hostel Associations**—for England and Wales, Scotland and Northern Ireland—are affiliated to this body and their members can use all these hostels at discount rates. Many hostels give preference to people under 26 but will accept people of any age if there is space available. Hostels are occasionally on the outskirts of town, but are usually more central than campsites and cost very little more.

There are as many different types of hostel as there are cities equipped with them. Some are simple dormitories with only basic cooking facilities as at Port Sudan, while others may be in architecturally splendid buildings and equipped with modern bedding as in Toledo, Spain. In the UK and Ireland you are still expected to pay for your keep with work as well as money, but elsewhere this tradition has been dropped. In the UK traces of a 'hardy' ethic which elevates walking and cycling above car driving also linger on. Again, elsewhere this is rarely mentioned.

Membership of the **YHA** (for England and Wales) costs:

Young (5-15)	£1.60
Junior (16-20)	£3.70
Senior (over 21)	£7.00
Family	£14.00 for both parents with children under 16 enrolled free.
	£7.00 for single parents.

Members receive a handbook listing all English and Welsh hostels. *The International Youth Hostel Handbook* (Vol. 1: Europe and Mediterranean, Vol. 2: Africa, America, Asia, Australasia. Cost £3.50 per volume) lists the affiliated hostels worldwide. There are hostels in the following countries:

Argentina	Hong Kong	Mexico	Sudan
Australia	Hungary	Morocco	Sweden
Austria	Iceland	The	Switzerland
Belgium	India	Netherlands	Thailand
Bulgaria	Ireland	New Caledonia	Taiwan
Canada	Israel	New Zealand	Tunisia
Chile	Italy	Norway	Turkey
Colombia	Japan	Pakistan	Uruguay
Cyprus	Kenya	Philippines	West Germany
Czechoslovakia	Korea	Poland	USA
Denmark	Lesotho	Peru	Yugoslavia
East Germany	Luxembourg	Portugal	Zimbabwe
Egypt	Libya	Saudi Arabia	
France	Malaysia	Spain	
Greece	Malta	Sri Lanka	

Technically, you must already be an Association member to stay at any of these hostels, so if you mean to do a lot of hostelling, it makes sense to join in advance, particularly since possession of a youth hostel card is sometimes enough to get you student discounts, for example on Egyptian trains. However in practice you can usually take out temporary membership.

Most hostels have either on-site canteens or facilities for self-/ catering. Some even have shops selling basic foods and equipment. Many also have excellent noticeboards which help travellers keep in touch with each other.

YMCA/YWCA

The **Young Men's Christian Association (YMCA)** is a movement operating in 90 countries. It also has a network of hostels which are often classier than YHA hostels, but may be more expensive. YMCAs in different countries act independently and so standards can vary considerably. You do not have to be a Christian to stay in these hostels but you may find stricter behavioural rules than in non-denominational hostels. Like YHAs, many YMCA hostels have either cooking facilities or canteens. Unlike YHAs they tend to be in towns rather than in the country. They also let rooms on a regular basis where YHAs usually only let people stay for three or four days at a time.

The **Young Women's Christian Association (YWCA)** is a partner association with similar aims and also operates a network of hostels. In some countries men are allowed to stay in YWCA hostels but in other places only married men travelling with their wives are admitted.

You do not need to be a member of the YMCA/YWCA movement to stay in their hostels although non-members may have to pay a local membership fee.

Accommodation for transient guests is limited, so you will probably have to book in advance, sending an International Reply Paid Coupon. During the summer the YMCA offers cheap accommodation to Interrailers at **YMCA Inter-Points** throughout Eruope. You can also buy a **YMCA Inter-Point Card** which qualifies you for further discounts by sending a £2.00 cheque to YMCA Training For Life, Unit 2A, Roundthorn House, Floats Road, Wythenshawe, Manchester M23 9PQ.

The *YMCA Directory* which lists all the YMCAs round the world costs £3.75 from the National Council of YMCAs, 640 Forest Road, London E17 3DZ (Tel: (01) 520 5599). The *World YWCA Directory* is available from YWCA, Clarendon House, 52 Cornmarket Street, Oxford OX1 3EJ (Tel: (0865) 726110). It costs £2.00 plus 25p postage and packing. The YWCA also sells *Pack For Europe* which lists addresses of YWCAs, YMCAs and other hostels and inexpensive hotels throughout Western Europe for £1.50 plus 20p postage and packing.

The YWCA also send lists of hostels in the USA, Canada, France, West Germany, Italy, Ireland, Switzerland, Scandinavia and Greece to anyone sending an SAE with their request. A separate list gives the addresses of hostels in the following countries:

Argentina, Australia, Bangladesh, Barbados, Belize, Botswana, Brazil, Burma (Myanmar), Colombia, Egypt, Fiji, Ghana, Guyana, Hong

Kong, Jamaica, Japan, Jordan, Kenya, Lebanon, Liberia, Madagascar, Malaysia, Mexico, New Zealand, Nigeria, Pakistan, Papua New Guinea, Philippines, Sierra Leone, Singapore, Solomon Islands, South Africa, Sri Lanka, Surinam, Taiwan, Tanzania, Thailand, Turkey, Uganda, Zambia and Zimbabwe.

For a complete list of hostels in India, write to the YWCA International Guest House, Parliament Street, Delhi, India.

Other hostels
During the long vacations **university hostels** are sometimes available to tourists and offer bargain rooms. This is certainly one way of finding cheap accommodation both in Budapest and Prague in the summer. The tourist offices should be able to provide you with further information.

ACCOMMODATION IN RELIGIOUS BUILDINGS

It may be less conventional to take overnight refuge with a religious community, but this option is bound to offer an interesting experience.

Sikh temples
The Sikhs have a long tradition of hospitality to travellers and until the recent troubles flared in the Punjab, staying in the **Amritsar Gurdwara** was an experience not to be missed. Thousands of people would be sleeping on the hostel floor, but at least one room was always kept free for foreigners. Hospitality even extended to free dahl and chapatis and lockers to ensure your baggage was safe. Sadly the Golden Temple is now closed to foreigners.

There are, however, plenty of other **gurdwaras** all over India for you to try. Even outside India this is a possibility; the Sikh temple in Lusaka is always full of foreigners and there is a fine temple on the Nairobi to Mombasa road at Makindu which is also very popular.

In theory you can stay in these temples for nothing, but in practice a contribution towards your keep is expected. In Lusaka you will be presented with a guest book listing previous visitors' contributions, which helps give you some idea of how much you should give. You should also take care to abide by the rules which include not smoking or eating meat on the premises, covering your head and going barefoot within the temple itself. However, such privations are more than compensated for by the chance to attend exotic temple services, and you are bound to be counted in when the sweetmeats are being shared out. If you eat in the **langar** or gurdwara kitchen a small donation or help with preparation of the food is likely to be appreciated.

In Algeria men can spend the night in a **hammam**—a public bath— which will have a rest-house attached.

Churches

In some countries the church provides private accommodation. For example in Malawi, which still bears the stamp of its Scottish missionaries, there are several excellent church guest-houses which offer cheap, comfortable places to stay, with resident housekeepers to do your cooking and ironing. There are such hostels in Blantyre and Livingstonia which also offer the rare luxury of hot water baths too.

Even in Europe you can sometimes take refuge in a religious house. For example in Italy where there are plenty of convents and monasteries, you may well be accommodated in return for a prayer and a donation. In fact, when the Venice Youth Hostel is full—which it usually is in summer—you may well be directed to the nearest monastery or convent.

CHEAP ACCOMMODATION

Outside the western world, it is relatively easy to find accommodation for a matter of a pound or two a night, if you can put up with very basic facilities—often just a bed and chair in the room. Single rooms are usually in short supply, but in many countries it is perfectly acceptable to share a room with several other people. However, women need to be aware that in Muslim countries there will be few rooms open to them, since good Muslim women tend to stay at home, and that where such rooms do exist they will be for women and children, so restful nights are not guaranteed. Women may even have problems in countries which are not nominally Muslim but where the hotel management is. For example the very popular Iqbal Hotel in Nairobi which offers excellent value for money has a manager who sometimes insists on single women paying for two beds rather than letting them share with a man.

When choosing cheap accommodation always check the following before moving in:

- How clean are the sheets?
- How filthy are the toilets?
- Are there mosquito nets (in malarial areas)?
- Do the windows close properly (in malarial areas)?
- Does the door lock properly?
- Is there running water?
- Are there obvious traces of bed-bugs or other creepy-crawlies?
- Is there a working fan (in hot countries)?

Washing facilities

One of the problems with cheap accommodation is that washing facilities usually leave a lot to be desired. However, this is not always a disaster. In other countries visiting public baths is more acceptable than it is in England. In Greece, for example, you may be able to visit a public bath if the facilities in your hotel are poor. In Muslim countries washing carefully is a religious duty, so visitors to Morocco and Turkey for example, can luxuriate in vast **hammams**—public baths—if they do not fancy their hotel showers. Some places, like Fez, make a specific charge for using the baths and issue tickets; in others a tip is required. The baths are single sex and always looked after by a custodian.

Often you are expected to wash modestly and to keep your underwear on; be guided by local occupants. For female travellers, in particular, public baths are a good way of meeting local women who are usually kept at home. In conservative areas hammams may be closed to non-Muslims. They may also be closed on Fridays, the Muslim Sabbath.

Security
You must also watch out for thieves, even in cheap accommodation. This is partly because such places often ignore basic security precautions, but also because in countries where such cheap rooms exist, even the most impoverished traveller is rich by local standards and equipment such as cameras are an ever-present temptation. You may also need to beware of your fellow travellers. This is particularly the case in places like Delhi and Goa with large numbers of penniless junkies. Make sure you take a padlock with you, and that you never leave doors or windows unlocked while you are away.

How to find a cheap room
Cheap accommodation is usually concentrated in certain parts of town, often near railway or bus stations. Guidebooks aimed specifically at budget travellers always identify the particular places to head for if you want to find low-priced rooms. Remember that prices may be cheaper if you are prepared to stay in a nearby village or just outside the centre.

GUEST HOUSES AND BED AND BREAKFAST

In many parts of the world the best alternative to hostels is to find a guest house or private accommodation with the odd room to let. In some countries such as Spain, even this sort of room will be checked for quality by the tourist office and will have a fixed price. Elsewhere arrangements may be more casual, but tourist offices may still be able to give you address lists. In Eastern European countries like Hungary, this type of accommodation represents excellent value for money.

While most accommodation in North America is expensive by budget travellers' standards, there are some bed and breakfast rooms available if you know where to look. The following organisations in the

UK can provide you with directories and can sometimes make advance reservations as well:

Bed and Breakfast in the United States and Canada,
Home Base Holidays,
7 Park Avenue,
London N13 5PG
Tel: (01) 886 8752

Bed and Breakfast USA,
Travel Associations Ltd,
1 Mordan Lane,
London SE13 7NR
Tel: (01) 692 9681

Bed and Breakfast Homes in California,
Pym House,
118 Ebury Street,
London SW1W 9QQ

The American Tourist Office can also supply you with a list of companies based in North America which deal with bed and breakfast accommodation.

CARAVANS AND CAMPERVANS

Caravans are only really a viable option if you want to travel round the UK or to Ireland or Europe, but they are obviously a good idea since they enable you to stay wherever you want with only the cost of hiring a site for the night to take into account once you have made the initial outlay for the van.

The Caravan Club

Regular caravanners should consider joining the **Caravan Club**. Members receive a handbook listing sites throughout the UK. Loans to buy vans are available through Lombard North Central, an information service can help with technical advice and novice caravanners can even go on a training course to build up their confidence. The Caravan Club can arrange tailor-made insurance and offers a roadside repair and recovery service through National Breakdown. The **Red Pennant Service** is available to help with booking ferries and reserving sites overseas. Members also receive *En Route*, the Club magazine which is full of equipment surveys and site news, eight times a year. The **Classified Advertisements** section is an ideal place to look for a secondhand bargain. If you want to sell your own van the minimum charge for advertising is £9.20.

Membership costs £18.00, plus a £3.00 joining fee, and is available from The Caravan Club, East Grinstead House, East Grinstead, West Sussex RH19 1UA (Tel: (0342) 26944).

Campervans overseas

You can also hire a campervan overseas and this is a very popular way of getting round the USA where there are huge distances to cover and accommodation costs are high. You can either wait until you arrive and then book a motorhome or arrange the rental in the UK through a firm like **Caravan Abroad Ltd**, 56 Middle Street, Brockham, Surrey RH3 7HW (Tel: (0737) 842735). To keep costs to a minimum you could consider exploring areas of the Eastern States to take advantage of cheaper fares to New York and Boston. Most travel agents will also be able to supply you with the brochures of companies offering **fly-drive** arrangements including the cost of the flight and the motorhome. Two companies offering such deals are **Globespan**, Suite 40, Odessa Wharf, London SE16 1LU (Tel: (01) 252 1454), and **Jetways**, 93 Newman Street, London W1P 3LE (Tel: (01) 637 5444).

If you do decide to see the States from a van, remember that camp sites cost between USD6 (£3.50) and USD16 (£9.00) per night. For this you will usually receive full hook-up facilities, a picnic table and barbecue stand. Many sites are cheaper and less crowded in May, June, September and October. It helps that petrol is relatively cheap in the States.

HOTELS

While proper hotels are unlikely to offer rock-bottom prices, some are obviously better value for money than others. In particular **chain hotels** like Howard Johnson in the USA are not too outrageously priced, particularly if four people share a double room with two double beds in it.

Cheap times to use hotels

One way of getting a cheaper rate at a hotel is to time your stay for a weekend. Many hotels are full of business travellers all week and virtually empty on Saturdays and Sundays. To encourage extra trade they often offer **discounted weekend rates** which may well include the cost of getting to the hotel or of meals when you arrive.

In any event, try and avoid **peak season** when prices are at their highest. In Europe and the States this usually means avoiding July and August. However in the Caribbean it can mean steering clear of December, January and February; for example Antigua offers discounted rooms to summer guests.

Other cheap ways into hotels

A particular problem for solo travellers is that most hotels levy **single room supplements** because single rooms are few and far between. In cheaper hotels this problem can sometimes be eliminated by sharing with someone else, and in low season some hoteliers may be prepared to waive the charge in order to fill their rooms. Some large hotel chains like the **Sol group** in Spain routinely do away with single supplements during low season. Many tour operators highlight hotels with no single room supplements at the front of their brochures, so always check.

If you do have to pay a single supplement remember that the extra charge does not necessarily reflect the star rating of the hotel. It might be cheaper to stay at a four star hotel with a low single supplement than in a three star with a high one.

If you want to stay at a particular hotel, it is always worth getting its address, either from a travel agency or from a hotel gazetteer or phone book in the library, and writing to ask if they have any **special offers** before you arrive.

Once you have decided to stay in a hotel there are still costs to watch out for:

1. Most hotels have a **check-out** time, often midday. If you overstay this time you risk being charged for another day. Check-out time is usually noted on the back of bedroom doors, but if in doubt, ask. You may be able to negotiate a later time or somewhere to leave your bag after you have vacated the room, but always do this before the time you are due to be out of the room.

2. Avoid using **hotel phones** to make external calls. Their rates are often exorbitant and you may have trouble finding out exactly what they will be until it is too late.

3. Remember that you will be expected to leave a **tip** for the chambermaid if you stay for more than one night.

4. Before requesting **special services** like meals in your room check that you will not be charged for them. Early morning calls are usually free; getting your laundry done is not.

5. Check your bill carefully to ensure **VAT** has only been added to the basic costs and not to service charges as well.

In some countries there are **accommodation passes** which offer discounts to holders. For example, summer visitors to Norway can purchase a **Fjord Pass** from the National Tourist Board, Fred Olsen Lines or the Norwegian State Railways for £5.00. This pass covers two adults and two children under 15 and enables them to stay in hotels for discounted prices of between NOK130 (£11.50) and NOK310 (£27.00).

While it is not essential to book in advance, a central reservations office in Bergen can arrange this if required. Holders of the pass can also take advantage of any other offers the hotels may be featuring during their stay.

Booking

If you intend to stay in a hotel and want to book it in advance, it is usually much cheaper to do this for yourself. Travel agencies only deal with a limited number of hotels—generally upmarket—and make a service charge to cover the cost of telexing or phoning to reserve a room. This charge may be £5.00 or £10.00, but people using British Rail's accommodation reservation service have been paying even more than this.

To make your own booking find the address of the hotel either from a travel agency or from the library. The *Official Hotel and Resorts Guide* and *ABC Worldwide Hotel Guide* are useful sources of addresses. Alternatively, many tourist offices supply graded accommodation lists. If you know the name of the hotel you want, you could even look its address up in an overseas phone book in the reference library.

Some hotels can be booked through **central reservations systems** in the UK. Where this is the case the hotel manuals will include the phone number of the agency so you can phone it directly.

Alternatively you can write to the hotel, preferably in the local language, enclosing an **International Reply Paid Coupon** available from any Post Office for about 60p; or you can phone the hotel directly and make your reservation.

If you are not confident about speaking in another language on the phone, British Telecom offers a **telephone messaging** service. You phone either Freefone BTI or (01) 836 5432 and tell the translators what you need to say. They will then ring the hotel for you and phone you back to confirm the details. There is a minimum charge of £3.50 for fifteen minutes of the translators' time, but this is often cheaper than many agency service charges. You will also be charged for the call at international operator's rates (90p a minute to Western Europe during the day). Translators fluent in all West European languages are available every day. If you need a more esoteric language like Farsi, this can also be arranged but advance notice is required.

SLEEPING ON TRAINS

One way to avoid paying accommodation charges is to take an overnight train. However, if you want to arrive refreshed, sitting up all night may not be a great idea, so you may still need to add the cost of a **sleeping berth** to the price of the train ticket.

Couchettes

On European trains the best option is to pay for a **couchette**, a seat that folds into a bed with blanket and pillow at night. While it is not the last word in luxury, a couchette does allow you to stretch out, and the rocking of the train is likely to ensure a reasonable night's sleep, particularly if you manage to secure one of the top bunks. Few couchette compartments are single sex, but they are often full so women are normally safe. Your sleep is more likely to be disturbed on cross-border routes, and those with lots of stops, by Customs officials and the stopping and starting of the train.

International couchettes—those travelling across more than one country—cost a standard £7.80 (six berth) or £10.00 (four berth). Within individual countries there are various charges. Any main line British Rail station and some branches of Thomas Cook will be able to give you details.

Sleeping cars

In contrast **sleeping cars** are much more costly as the following examples show:

Sample European sleeping car costs	Rail ticket(£)	Sleeper supplement (£)
London to Nice	£90.50	£32.20 (from Calais)
London to Rome	£103.30	£22.50 (from Paris)
London to Madrid	£91.80	£25.80 (from Paris)
London to Moscow	£128.00	£43.40 (from Ostend)

(All fares are for second class, one way journeys)

European **sleeping cars** may be too expensive for rock-bottom budgets, but outside Europe some represent excellent value for money. For example, even a budget traveller should be able to afford a second class berth on the overnight train from Nairobi to Mombasa where carriages come equipped with a fold-down sink and where an attendant comes to make up your bed for you. The Chinese-built Tazara railway running between Dar es Salaam and Kapiri Mpochi in Zambia also offers good value for money. Anyone travelling between Moscow and Leningrad can also take an overnight train and the carriages would be very comfortable were it not for the fact that the heating is turned up to sauna temperatures at all times. However the tea served from a corridor samovar in the morning helps compensate for the heat.

'NO CHOICE' ACCOMMODATION

In Communist countries you may have little or no control over where you stay. There will often be a list of hotels which are allowed to accommodate foreigners and in countries like Ethiopia you risk deportation if you stay anywhere else. Sometimes, as in Burma (Myanmar), the authorities insist that you pay at a central office rather than at the individual hotel to make it harder for you to wriggle out of their control.

The USSR and East Germany are two more countries where you will have to stay where the authorities want you to, while the Chinese also try to restrict foreigners to specified hotels.

HOUSE-SWAPPING

For home-owners, one way to economise on holiday accommodation costs is to swap houses with another family for the duration. In theory, this is also an ideal way to ensure your property is safeguarded while you are away. If the swappers will also look after your pets all the better. The truly affluent may be able to exchange cars too.

There are several ways to arrange a house swap:

House Swap Directories
For between £15.00 and £25.00 you can advertise your own house in one of these directories, and will be sent a copy of it so that you can write to anyone whose home sounds interesting.

E C Bureau
Dunstown
Mintlaw
Aberdeenshire AB4 7UJ
Tel: (077982) 2491

Home Exchange Holidays
35 Marlborough Park
Kempston
Bedford MK42 8AN
Tel: (0234) 50532

Home Interchange
8 Hillside
Farningham
Kent DA4 0DD
Tel: (0322) 864527

Interchange Holidays
6 Blackden Close
Belper
Derby DE5 0DL
Tel: (0773) 824067

Intervac
6 Siddals Lane
Allestree
Derby DE3 2DY
Tel: (0332) 5588931

Worldwide Home Exchange Club
45 Hans Place
London SW1X OJ2
Tel: (01) 589 6055

Embassies
Another possibility is to write to the Embassy of a country you would like to visit. They should be able to tell you addresses of local newspapers where you could place an advertisement for interested house-swappers.

Newspapers and magazines

You could also look in papers like *The Times Educational Supplement* which occasionally have advertisements from people looking for a swap. This has the advantage that the people placing the ads are likely to be similar to those reading them with similar tastes and interests.

If you do decide to try a house-swap, remember the following:

- Check that your insurance will still be valid if you have sub-let your property.
- Confirm in writing with the other family all arrangements about bills, especially phone bills. You can arrange to be billed for a specific period if you let British Telecom know in advance.
- Lock away all valuables.
- Warn the neighbours that strangers will be living in your house so they do not call the police as soon as they see them.

The cost of arranging your swap should not exceed £100 even if you have to try several people before finalising your arrangements. Avoid using an agency to make your arrangements since they will charge you for the privilege.

EMERGENCIES

In an emergency when you really cannot find accommodation in your price range there are several possible options:

- You could try the **police**. Some are more welcoming than others, but in remote places like Suakin in Sudan, it is often standard procedure to sleep on the police station floor.

- In some towns you could also try the **Salvation Army** or its local equivalent. In Reykjavik, for example, the Salvation Army offers the cheapest accommodation after the youth hostels. However, conditions in such hostels are far from luxurious. You may also ask yourself whether you should be taking up space in this sort of accommodation when local people's needs may be far greater. If you *do* need them however, the Salvation Army operates in the following countries:

Antigua, Argentina, Australia, Austria, Bahamas, Bangladesh, Barbados, Belgium, Belize, Bermuda, Bolivia, Brazil, Burma (Myanmar), Canada, Chile, Congo, Costa Rica, Cuba, Curacao, Denmark, Faroe Islands, Fiji, Finland, France, Germany, Ghana, Grenada, Guyana, Haiti, Hong Kong, Iceland, India, Indonesia, Ireland, Italy, Jamaica, Japan, Kenya, Korea, Lesotho, Malawi, Malaysia, Malta, Mexico, Mozambique, The Netherlands, New Zealand, Nigeria, Norway, Pakistan, Panama, Papua New Guinea,

Paraguay, Peru, Philippines, Portugal, Puerto Rico, St Helena, St Kitts, St Lucia, St Vincent, Singapore, South Africa, Spain, Sri Lanka, Surinam, Swaziland, Sweden, Switzerland, Taiwan, Tanzania, Trinidad and Tobago, Uganda, USA, Uruguay, Venezuela, Virgin Islands (US), Zaire, Zambia and Zimbabwe.

Value for money hotels

Looking for cheap accommodation is one area where you may miss out on incredible value if you spend too much time pursuing a bargain. The **Lake Palace Hotel** in Udaipur offers luxury at bargain prices by European standards, while the **Strand Hotel** in Rangoon offers character and excellent meals, once again for much less than any nondescript British chain hotel. They are just two examples of the sort of places it would be a shame to miss. If you can plan and budget carefully, you could bring them within your price range.

TIME-SHARE... A WARNING

Many holidaymakers, especially in Spain, are being approached by touts eager to sell them the delights of 'time-sharing'. This is an arrangement which allows you to buy a share in a house or apartment for a fixed number of weeks in the year in perpetuity, the idea being that you could then stay in your own home for your annual holiday for the rest of your life without ever having to book again. Since you own your share in the property you can also sell it if you get tired of the Costa del Whatever and want to move somewhere else. However, since it is a fairly new development this is probably easier in theory than it is in practice.

Time-sharing is not really for budget travellers, but it's as well to know what it is since the hard-sell tactics of its purveyors have come in for a great deal of criticism. Basically, if you have never given a second's thought to the idea of buying a share in a Spanish villa, refuse all offers of free drinks, meals, and so on, to go and see the properties; and if you do decide to go along leave your cheque book and pen in the hotel and firmly deny the existence of any other way of paying.

14
Cost-Cutting Ways to Eat and Drink Abroad

It is easy to assume that the only way to eat cheaply while travelling is to cook for yourself which, in turn, means buying and carrying cooking equipment. Fortunately there are alternatives for those averse to campfire meals.

EATING OUT ON A BUDGET

Outside Europe, North America, Canada, Australia and New Zealand there are usually staple foods which cost very little to buy in local restaurants. Even within these areas there are cheap options; pasta and pizza are obvious Italian examples, but Greek souvlaki is cheap, nutritious, tasty and ubiquitous and hamburgers can be bought almost anywhere.

The following are examples of ways to eat out abroad without doing your budget too much harm:

- In Maghrebi North Africa the best known staple food is **couscous**, a filling semolina-based dish made with meat. Because it is so well-known, couscous appears on the menus of restaurants catering specifically for the tourist trade. In such places its price is unlikely to be rock-bottom. Scour the back streets however and you can find the same dish in far tastier forms at very realistic prices that would make bothering to cook for yourself look foolish. But there are other even cheaper treats available. **Harira** is a thick, lentil-based soup, delicious with fresh bread or dates and enough for a meal in itself. Then there are various **tajines** which are meat, vegetable or chicken stews in most restaurants. Near the coast you may also find delicious and reasonably-priced fish tajines.

- In Egypt the bargain menu alters. Look out for shops selling **koshari**, a filling bowl of noodles, rice and lentils which sounds awful, tastes gorgeous and costs only pence. **Foul beans** are another good alternative, becoming even tastier as you travel south to Nubia and Sudan.

- In Eastern Africa the staple food is less tasty, consisting of football-sized and shaped wedges of cassava flavoured with vegetable or meat sauce. This **nsima** turns up again in Zambia and Zimbabwe under other names like **sadsa**. If you want to economise you will just have to get used to it; there is nothing much else and what there is is expensive.

- India is a paradise for budget gourmets, especially those with a bottomless appetite for **dahl** and **chapati** in the north, and **rice** and **dhosas** in the south. It is difficult to find the variety of dishes you expect in a UK Indian restaurant, but vegetarians are particularly well catered for and there seem to be few truly expensive meals.

- Thailand is another place where eating out is a delight that will not break the budget. It makes sense to stick to noodle or rice-based dishes and to remember that seafood can be relatively dear. But it is difficult to spend more than a pound on a meal in Thailand, even on a floating restaurant minutes from the Bridge over the River Kwai.

- Hong Kong offers a wide variety of eating opportunities for those on a budget. Firstly there are the **dai pai dong**—street stalls—which sell the widest and cheapest variety of dishes—take care to find one that looks clean. Then there are restaurants selling dim sum lunches, where you choose from a variety of snacks brought round on a trolley.

- Mexico and Central America also offer the opportunity to eat cheaply, provided you stick to rice, tortillas and beans washed down with rather strong coffee.

- Turkey has one of the world's finest cuisines and luckily the cost of living there is sufficiently low to give you plenty of chances to sample it. Carnivores will find the innumerable lamb and fish-based dishes delicious but vegetarians will also discover a wide range of aubergine, pepper and tomato-based items on most menus. Like Greece, Turkey produces marvellous **natural yoghurt**, sometimes used as a chaser for the local aniseed-alcohol, raki. If your tastes run to something less calorific than real Turkish Delight, then there are plenty of cherries and other fruits to round off your meals.

- The Netherlands offers the chance to eat an assortment of tasty sweet and savoury **pancakes** at a reasonable price. Two people could share one sweet and one savoury pancake between them for a grand DFL15.00 (£4.50) which compares very favourably with the cost of two Tourist Menu meals and is likely to be at least as filling.

- Spain is famed for its **paella** and to find a reasonably priced one you will need to turn down the back streets and follow the locals. But if your wallet is feeling the pinch many bars serve up **tapas** with the drinks. These are small, hors d'oeuvre-type dishes which can be meat, fish or vegetable-based. Prices depend on which bar you are in, but a group of you should be able to select half a dozen dishes and share them out to provide an adequate and interesting meal. Occasionally, small tapas—nuts, olives, and slices of salami—are handed out free. The Spanish eat late so there will not be much choice if you turn out at six.

- Italy is the land of pasta, pizza and red wine, all reasonably priced and delicious possibilities for those on a low budget. Italian bread is also wonderful, as are the endless varieties of salami, cheese and olives you can buy to make a filling lunch. If you can afford to splash out occasionally try and sample some of the seafood dishes as well; red mullet and squid make gorgeous main meals, provided you have not made the mistake of filling up on the spaghetti starter first.

- Greece is the land of **souvlaki** or shish kebab which you can pick up cheaply on street stalls to keep the price down. In many tavernas you can also eat **moussakas**—aubergine casseroles—or **dolmades**—stuffed vine leaves—which you can wash down with retsina or ouzo without doing much damage to your bank balance. Be warned that Greek waiters like to serve main courses and starters together; make sure you ask for them separately if you want to avoid tepid moussaka.

Tourist menus

A number of countries offer set **tourist menus**, usually three course meals for a reasonably low price. You'll find such menus in France, Spain, (*Cubierto, Menu Del Dia, Menu De La Casa*), Italy (*Menu Turistico*, Ireland, Denmark (*Dan Menu*) and The Netherlands. These meals may not cost rock-bottom prices, but they are likely to be substantial and often include at least one drink and a dessert, even if only a piece of fruit. In The Netherlands, for example, there are more than five hundred establishments offering a tourist menu at a flat DFL19.50 (£6.00), which includes three courses, but no drink. To encourage high standards the Dutch Tourist Office (VVV) offers an annual Silver Fork award to the restaurant featuring the best tourist menu. There is no catch; you can eat for the same price in Amsterdam's central Damrak as in the suburbs. VVV publishes a leaflet listing all the restaurants involved so you can plan your culinary tour of The Netherlands in advance.

Tips for eating cheaply

Otherwise, eating out in Europe in particular can seem prohibitively expensive. Even so, bear in mind some simple guidelines and you can cut your costs considerably:

- Never eat in a restaurant in the heart of the tourist zone—for example, Grande Place in Brussels, St Mark's Square in Venice,

Sintagma in Athens, the Ramblas in Barcelona. Turn down the side streets instead and prices will drop dramatically.

- Find out whether food is cheaper if eaten standing up—it often is in Portugal and in West Germany's large department stores.

- You may not relish fast food stores in general, but their prices are usually fairly low. There is even a McDonalds in Moscow now.

- Cafés serving 'ethnic' menus are often cheaper than those serving 'local' food. So look for Algerian couscous shops in France, Turkish restaurants in Germany, Indonesian cafés in The Netherlands, and so on.

- If the price of full meals really looks exorbitant, find out what 'snack' foods are available. You can get by perfectly well on **felafel** (fried chickpea) sandwiches in Israel, **tapas** (bar snacks) in Spain, and so on.

- Look for unusual places to eat. In Switzerland, supermarket restaurants sell good value meals, and pavement stalls are often ideal. Station restaurants can also be excellent. If you're in East Berlin this can be a good place to eat and use up the MRK25 (£8.00) you are obliged to exchange for a day's visit. Outside Europe Indian station restaurants also offer excellent cheap food.

- Keep an eye open for 'eat-as-much-as-you-want' menus which are sometimes offered by large hotels. If you are really hungry these can offer a way of stopping the gaps, even if the intitial price looks daunting. The Arrak Hotel in Khartoum is a popular place for overland travellers to fill up.

- If the worst comes to the worst, take a guided tour of a food or drink factory. The Heineken Brewery in Amsterdam is said to offer its visitors liquid refreshment, and Swiss chocolate factories will oblige those whose budgets cannot rise to sweet luxuries.

FOOD SHOPPING ON A BUDGET

The golden rule when shopping abroad, especially outside Europe, is not to buy anything that has been imported. Not only is it absurd to go all the way to Corfu to eat Kellogg's cornflakes but you will pay through the nose for the privilege too. You may eat butter at home, but margarine is fine and half the price abroad. Find out what is popular locally and buy that. Orange juice is fairly cheap in Germany; yoghurt is inexpensive and gorgeous in Greece.

If you have ruled out eating in restaurants on cost grounds, that does not mean you have to eat badly. Throughout most of Europe you can pick up delicious crispy, fresh bread, an endless variety of cheeses and salamis, olives and fruit, particularly oranges, for very reasonable prices. Even in Africa, where choice is sadly limited, bread is usually cheap and far tastier than the cotton-wool Mothers Pride English equivalent. 'La Vache Qui Rit' processed cheese seems to have reached all but the most remote of villages and tastes good even with pitta. Tinned sardines are readily available, so you can stick a tin in your bag for the day when you have to choose between a posh restaurant or starvation. Also remember that any kind of fruit rounds off most meals beautifully. If you ask around in Sudan you can even buy kilo tubs of helva to fill you up and rot your teeth when there's nothing else available.

If you are going on a self-catering holiday to a notoriously expensive area like Scandinavia try and take staple food items like tea, coffee and sugar with you to keep costs down.

DRINKING ON A BUDGET

Again, the golden rule applies—find out what the locals drink and stick to that rather than expensive imported drinks. This is one of the few areas where the budget traveller in Europe is at an advantage, with a never-ending variety of bargain wines to choose from, not to mention the port, sherry, ouzo, and so on. Make sure you take a bottle with you—quite often you can decant litres of wine into your own container at even cheaper prices than when buying it ready-bottled. Take care to ask for 'vin ordinaire' or its local equivalent.

In places in Egypt you can also buy freshly pressed fruit drinks on street stands. Israeli **milk-based drinks** are also usually delicious and far better than an endless flood of Cokes and Fantas. Of course, you need to take great care with what you drink. Water-borne ailments account for much of the world's ill-health, and unboiled water and ice are two of the main culprits, both hard to resist in hot climates.

As a safer alternative to cold drinks you can usually find cheap **tea** outside Europe. In some places you will even be offered tea for nothing. Arab hospitality, even in shops, often extends to cups of free mint tea, while in Burma (Myanmar) you need to buy a cup of sickly tea with milk in order to be given a pot of the delicious China version. **Coffee** is often served in tiny cups and is very strong by British standards. However, it is still a safer option than an iced drink. In any case hot drinks are often more refreshing.

If you know you will have to drink cold drinks en route make sure you have **iodine** (the most effective method) or **sterilising tablets** (Puritabs are one possibility) with you and remember that they need time to take effect. Carry a water bottle with you and fill it up with treated water *before* you get thirsty. If you think you may be forced to drink contaminated water, buy a filter and use that as well. Filters can be bought in YHA Shops and a Filopur model costs £12.95.

15
Seeing the Cities at Minimum Cost

Once you have reached your destination, your transport problems are far from over. Without the luxury of your own car, you still need to be able to get around within the town itself. Hitching in urban areas is notoriously difficult so you will almost certainly have to consider other options.

WALKING

Obviously the cheapest way of getting about is to walk everywhere. However, you will quickly get tired, and may increase your food and drinks bill stoking up the leg muscles.

CYCLING

If you cycle to your destination, you will still have your bike and your transport bills will be non-existent. However, in many towns with a large tourist population you can easily hire a bike. It's usually cheaper to hire it for more than one day. For example in Amsterdam a day's rental averages DFL7 (£2.00), while a week's is roughly DFL30 (£9.00).

Even if you do not want to cycle all the time it can still be the ideal way to do some of your sightseeing. At Luxor, for example, you can hire a bike for the day, slip it onto the ferry to the West Bank and use it to meander round the various ancient monuments. At Pagan in Burma (Myanmar) where hundreds of temples are scattered over a wide area a bicycle is also a cheap and sensible alternative to the horse-and-buggies that ply the main routes.

LOCAL PUBLIC TRANSPORT

In many large towns it is cheaper to buy season, rover or bulk tickets rather than individual ones for each bus or train journey. Sometimes these have to be bought in advance or at a different place from single tickets. Very often tobacconists and newsagents sell bus tickets.

Towns with public transport rover tickets

- **Amsterdam** offers day tickets on the buses, metros and trams for DFL8.50 (£2.50). You can buy these on the buses, metros and trams themselves. However, two day tickets for DFL11.60 (£3.50), three day tickets for DFL14.20 (£4.00) and extra day tickets for DFL2.70 (£0.75) need to be bought in advance at the booth in front of the Central Station or in the Bulldog Café (Leiseplein).

- **Salzburg** has a 24-hour rover ticket valid on all public transport. Tobacconists also sell blocks of five tickets for the buses and trams at a cheaper rate than if bought singly on board. **Vienna** also offers blocks of five tickets for the trams at a reduced price from tobacconists and ticket offices. In addition there is a 72-hour Vienna Rover and a weekly season ticket offering discounted travel on all public transport. In **Innsbruck** a block of ten tickets costs AUS86 (£4.00).
- **Paris** has books of ten Metro tickets on sale for FFR27.50 (£2.50), but there is also a two day rover for about £4.50 and a four day one for about £7.00.
- **Florence, Venice and Rome** all have day rover tickets.
- **Brussels** has a day rover ticket.
- Most **German cities** offer 24-hour City Transport Day tickets.
- **Copenhagen** has a day rover ticket. The Oslo Kortet offers unlimited transport within Oslo for 24, 48 or 72 hours, together with discounts on sightseeing and ski lifts. The 72-hour card also allows one half-price return trip by NSB to and from Oslo and costs NOK130 (£10.50). **Stockholm** has a similar card for 24 or 72 hours. The 72 hour card costs SEK72 (£7.00).
- In **Finland** FIM44 (£6.00) will pay for ten local journeys.
- The **Luxembourg** Billet Reseau offers one day's second class travel on all Luxembourg trains except to the borders for LFR197 (£3.00).
- **Dublin** offers a one day public transport pass for £2.80.
- In Eastern European cities state subsidies guarantee cheap fares, so you can travel round Prague and Moscow for mere pence.

Other tips for using public transport

Quite often on European buses and trams there is no conductor and those with tickets can get into the rear of the bus where they are expected to punch the tickets into a machine to cancel them. It is tempting to skip on and off without paying, but if you are caught by an inspector, expect to have to pay a hefty on-the-spot fine.

Occasionally travelling by public transport is an experience in itself; for example it's worth buying Moscow metro tickets just to view the magnificent individually-designed stations.

Outside Europe, remember that public transport can be horrifically crowded. Trying to board a bus in Cairo in the rush hour is an experience best left to the locals. There will be people hanging onto the doors and windows, and even clinging to the roof. They have been doing that since childhood and it's not a good idea to try and compete with them.

TAXIS

In Europe budget travellers are well advised to steer clear of taxis except in the most desperate circumstances. However, in other parts of the world taxi fares are often cheap enough to consider. Whatever you do, though, *never* take a taxi without agreeing a price with the driver first—it will be no good arguing about it afterwards and meters never seem to work once you have passed beyond the Med.

Of course, there are different ways of defining a 'taxi'. In India, for example, conventional models are cheap enough to hire even for journeys between towns, if you are pushed for time. However, if you widen the definition to include the multitude of rickshaws and three-wheelers you'd be mad to miss out on them. Similarly in Thailand taxi fares are reasonable, and 'tuk-tuk' three-wheeler fares even more so. In Burma (Myanmar) normal taxis will be few and far between, but rickshaws are cheap and omnipresent with unique back and front-facing passenger seats. Once again always agree a price before setting off. This may involve bargaining but you do no-one any favours if you pay too much over the odds, thus creating the expectation of higher fares in the future. Try and keep a sense of proportion, though, or you may find yourself haggling over mere pence. Anyway the drivers are experts; no matter how canny you are, you're bound to pay more than the locals.

Shared taxis

Outside the Western world the idea of the privately hired taxi is also less dominant. Many countries operate a network of shared taxis which ply specific routes, picking up passengers just like buses. Alternatively a group of people can often hire the whole vehicle. Such shared taxis have a variety of local names—'dolmuses' in Turkey, 'matatus' in Kenya. What they have in common is that they are usually reasonably priced, although a little more costly than buses, and always overcrowded.

Where possible avoid taking taxis to and from airports. In such situations the price is bound to be higher than it is in town, simply because the drivers depend on people looking for an easy ride. Occasionally, as at Aswan, there is no alternative apart from walking, cycling or hitching, and you will have to take a taxi. However, it is very unusual to find there really is not a bus or a train. Sometimes the airlines even lay on free or reasonably priced buses to connect with their flights, so always check when making your booking. If you look at the start of each section of the *ABC Guide to World Airways* you will find information about airport buses along with other city details.

OTHER ALTERNATIVES

Occasionally there are other ways of getting round towns. In Venice, for example, you'll want to try the **vaporetti** or water-buses that ply the canals very cheaply. Make sure you keep plenty of small change to pay for them though, or you will end up with pockets full of sweets, plasters, telephone tokens and other forms of 'change'.

In Luxor some hardy souls opt to see the West bank sights by donkey rather than bicycle. In that case you'll need a guide, which is likely to push the price up considerably.

Lots of towns still have horse and carriage transport. Sometimes this is especially laid on for tourists and likely to be costly. But sometimes local people also use the buggies in which case prices will be more reasonable. So **kaleches** in Alexandria and **buggies** in Pagan will not cost you too much provided you barter for the fare beforehand. Sometimes you may think it worth paying a little extra for the experience anyway. Few things can beat clattering around Cracow by night or Marrakesh by day in a horse-drawn carriage.

16
Seeing the Sights
at a Budget Price

When you arrive somewhere new, you probably want to get out and see as much as possible in the time available. Many European tourist offices provide free weekly English language newspapers or magazines full of ideas on what to see and do that are likely to interest their clients. Examples worth looking for include:

- *Brussels Magazine*
- *Amsterdam This Week*
- *Stockholm This Week*
- *Copenhagen This Week*
- *Oslo This Week*
- *What's On in Lisbon*
- *This Week in Rome*
- *The Week in Athens*
- *In Dublin*

Sadly, budgetary restrictions may hamper your sightseeing. However, there are places you can visit either free or at very little cost if you look round carefully and use your imagination.

FACTORIES AND WORKSHOPS

In many places it is extremely easy to arrange free tours round factories or workshops whose owners hope you will end up buying something. Before embarking on such a tour, ask yourself the following questions:

- Are you likely to find the tour interesting? After all, one factory can look much like another. However I have enjoyed visits to a Thai silk factory and umbrella shop, a Dutch clog-maker's and diamond factory and an Egyptian inlaid box workshop, brass foundry and plastic lemon-tree factory. There are bound to be others.

- How much pressure will be put on you to buy? In Morocco any pleasure you might experience from going to see something made is wiped out by the hassle that comes afterwards. Saying 'no' is virtually impossible, so the trip becomes either expensive or ill-tempered or both. You may even find yourself talked into buying something you don't want or that is a great deal less valuable than the salesman would have you believe.

- Are there extra hidden benefits? In many places free refreshments come with the tour. In a Dutch diamond factory this can mean excellent coffee in comfortable surroundings; in Thailand it can mean iced drinks graciously served by a hostess; in Morocco, Turkey or Tunisia it usually means cups of delicious mint tea.

- Is the tour genuinely free? Chiang Mai tour operators in Thailand sometimes throw in a free trip out to the 'umbrella village' at Baw Sang when you book a trek with them. This is a real perk and you will never be asked to pay afterwards. In Sliema in Malta a courtesy 'luqqa' will ferry you across to a glass-blowing factory on Manoel Island where you can look round without any pressure to buy, but in India and many other poor countries, an excursion which starts out as free may end with you feeling morally obliged to pay. You need a thick skin to take full advantage of the freebies.

MUSEUMS AND MONUMENTS

Many people want to visit at least one museum during their stay abroad. In some countries like Morocco and Sudan museum visits are still absurdly cheap. In others they have cottoned on to the potential income and museum addicts soon run up large bills. In Egypt for example, it is horrifically expensive to visit all the sights on Luxor's West Bank if you are not part of a package tour or in possession of an **ISIC card**.

Cheap ways to visit museums

- Find out if there is a day or time when museums are free and visit then. For example, Parisian museums and many West German museums charge half-price on Sundays.

- Buy a **museum pass card**. Dutch Tourist Offices sell a Museum Ticket which gives free entry to all the country's Rijksmuseums and to Amsterdam's municipal museums. It is valid for one year and costs DFL21.00 (£6.00), or DFL8.50 (£2.50) for under-25s and DFL13.50 (£4.00) for senior citizens. Vienna also has a **Sammelkarte** offering discounts at its museums, and Valetta in Malta has a one-day museum pass ticket, giving admission to all state museums for MAL0.50 (£1.00).

- Forge a **student card** or buy one on the black market. This is a popular method in Egypt, but be warned that in Luxor there is a separate ticket booth for student cards and that the custodian records card numbers in a book to stop them being reused.

- Join a **'Friendship' society** which offers free entry in return for an annual subscription.

- Take along a letter from a college or university asserting that you are a student with genuine research needs.

- Check whether any of the museums are free even in towns where there is generally a steep admission charge. For example, in Amsterdam the Peter Stuyvesant collection of modern art is free even if the Rijksmuseum does charge a DFL6.50 (£2.00) entry fee.

Closing days
Watch out for these—there are few things more irritating than travelling some distance to visit a museum, only to find it closed.

National Museum Closing Days
Austria	Monday
France	Tuesday
The Netherlands	Monday
Italy	Monday
Belgium	Monday
West Germany	Monday
Denmark	Monday
Greece	Monday or Tuesday

Many museums will also close over public holidays. The dates of these should be checked in advance with the tourist office to be on the safe side. Before travelling a long distance to see any particular exhibit, it could be worth checking anyway; I have arrived at the Louvre only to find 'Mona Lisa' loaned to New York.

Monuments are usually even more expensive to visit than museums, although you may be admitted at a reduced price if you have an ISIC card. If you do not have such a card but you do have steely nerves and are dressed appropriately you could try infiltrating an organised party and getting counted in on their admission ticket. I have done it at Cairo's Citadel so it is certainly possible!

FREE MUSICAL ENTERTAINMENT

Many European cities offer free street entertainment—you just need to track down the appropriate areas. For example in Paris try outside the Pompidou Centre or in the Tuileries, in Amsterdam stand outside the Central Station on a sunny day, in Madrid try Retiro Park on a Sunday. Collection bags will come round, but there is no obligation to pay if you cannot afford it.

Churches often have free lunch-time concerts. These will be advertised on posters outside the church or in local listings and events magazines. The tourist office may also be able to help.

EXHIBITIONS

Ask at the Tourist Office, look in the local papers or read the free tourist leaflets to find out if the museums or local art galleries are putting on any free exhibitions.

WALKING TOURS AND TREKS

If you cannot afford to take an organised tour, most tourist offices have free street maps available which usually show sights of historic interest that you can walk round. In some cases cheap leaflets which lay out interesting routes are available. For example the Dublin Tourist Office can supply you with a walking map of James Joyce's Dublin.

Trekking

Many travellers want to go trekking while they are away. The cost of doing this is usually low since popular trekking areas are mainly in poorer countries like Nepal and Thailand. Of course it is cheaper to carry your own equipment and to go without a guide. However, if you are a first-timer, think carefully before doing this. Paying a guide or sherpa, especially if you go in a group, is not very expensive and could make the difference between having an enjoyable adventure and an alarming and exhausting one. If you do decide to go it alone, make sure someone knows where you are going and how long you expect to be away.

On the trek your costs are likely to be limited to food, drink and accommodaton for lack of anything else to buy en route. In Thailand, however, allow for small sums spent on **massages** and **opium pipes** in villages along the way.

In Kathmandu in Nepal and Chiang Mai in Thailand there are lots of companies offering organised treks with guides. Usually their prices include the cost of accommodation. Ask other travellers to find the best deals. 'Extras' such as elephant rides and raft trips push prices up considerably.

In Nepal you will need to buy a trekking permit which also increases the cost of the trip.

PARKS

Many European cities have beautiful parks where you can while away sunny afternoons and watch the world go by. Buskers are drawn to the Paris Tuileries, while all sorts of entertainments, including outdoor theatre, jugglers and a boating lake are on offer in Madrid's Retiro Park. Some must be paid for but others are free. Hanging around in the parks—during daylight hours, of course—is a great way to find out what's in fashion and what music is popular. Watch out for gypsies—it will be hard to give them the slip.

CHURCHES AND CATHEDRALS

While many European churches make a charge for visits, at least some parts are usually free to explore. If there is a charge, check to see if there is a time in the week when it is waived. Remember that in countries with a siesta hour churches will often be locked up at the same time. If you are travelling to a particularly remote church, make sure your trip will not coincide with an obscure saint's feast day; I arrived at St Catherine's in Sinai only to find it closed for a Greek Orthodox holiday I had never heard of.

MARKETS

Budget travellers may find wandering along upmarket shopping streets a depressing experience. However, roaming local markets is another matter altogether. Not only are prices lower, but many markets are full of life and colour, a magnet for exotic people and entertainers. Tourist offices will be able to tell you where regular markets take place, but do not forget that others may occur on irregular days and dates, so check in a good guidebook for details.

Interesting markets are not confined to non-European countries. Paris has its flea market, Amsterdam its flower market, Madrid its stamp and book markets and Barcelona its bird market. Particularly exciting markets are in:

Asni, Morocco
Omdurman, Sudan
Chiang Mai, Thailand
Madrid, Spain (the Rastro)

Addis Ababa, Ethiopia (the
    Mercato)
Beersheba, Israel

SIGHTSEEING TRIPS

Most countries with a tourist market offer organised excursions to places of interest, but these can be expensive. Often it is cheaper and more interesting to make arrangements yourself. The exceptions may be when:

- you have limited time to make connections by public transport
- the excursion takes in several places which are far apart
- the excursion takes in places not served by public transport.

Examples of situations where you save a lot by making your own arrangements include:

1. **Day trips to China from Hong Kong**. A day trip to Canton can cost about £80.00, although the hydrofoil crossing is only £3.00.
2. **Danube boat rides** out of Vienna.
3. **Samaria Gorge on Crete**. Roughly half the price if you make your own arrangements.
4. **Excursions to Abu Simbel**. The air fare to and from Abu Simbel in Egypt will set you back more than £50.00 and that is without the taxi fare to the airport. However, every Saturday a ferry leaves from Aswan High Dam and takes four days to make the trip. Take your own food and water and you will save yourself a fortune.

Some excursions take more than a day. For example many people like to take a 'felucca' boat trip along the Nile from Luxor to Aswan or vice versa. Again, it will be cheaper to organise this yourself by negotiating with a boatman rather than buying a package in a local agency. Make sure the price agreed includes food, drink and taxes. There need to be six to eight of you to make this viable.

THEATRES, CINEMAS AND CONCERTS

Before buying theatre tickets, always ask the Tourist Office if there are any discount schemes available. For example in New York tickets for Broadway shows are available at half price, on the day of the performance only, from TKTS ticket outlets. Students can sometimes get discounts on production of their ISIC card, for example in Turkey.

Never buy your tickets from a conventional agency. Almost invariably they charge 10% or 20% commission, although they won't necessarily tell you so. It goes without saying that touts outside popular events like pop concerts charge even more for their 'services'.

LIBRARIES

Even on holiday people sometimes want to read books or newspapers and obviously English versions cost more overseas than they do at home. The longer you are away, the more you may feel you are losing touch. So it is useful to know that the **British Council** has one hundred and twenty libraries overseas. These operate on similar principles to libraries at home and books are catalogued according to the same Dewey decimal system. To borrow from the libraries, you normally need a local sponsor which those on a short trip are unlikely to have. However, you can read in the libraries at no charge and they stock most quality English papers.

British Council offices

The British Council has offices in:

Algeria: Algiers
Australia: Edgecliff, New South Wales
Austria: Vienna
Bahrain: Manama
Bangladesh: Dhaka, Rajshahi and Chittagong
Belgium: Brussels
Botswana: Gaborone
Brazil: Brasilia, Recife, Rio de Janeiro and Sao Paulo
Brunei: Bandar Seri Begawan
Burma (now also known as Myanmar): Rangoon
Cameroon: Yaoundé
Canada: Ontario and Quebec
Chile: Santiago
China: Beijing and Shanghai
Colombia: Bogotá
Cyprus: Nicosia
Czechoslovakia: Prague
Denmark: Copenhagen
Israel: Jerusalem and Tel Aviv
Ecuador: Quito
Egypt: Cairo and Alexandria
Ethiopia: Addis Ababa and Asmara
Finland: Helsinki
Federal Republic of Germany: Cologne, Berlin, Hamburg and Munich
Fiji: Suva
German Democratic Republic: Berlin
France: Paris, Bordeaux, Lille, Lyon and

Marseille
Ghana: Accra and Kumasi
Greece: Athens and Salonica
Hong Kong
Hungary: Budapest
India: New Delhi, Ahmadabad, Bangalore, Bhopal, Hyderabad, Lucknow, Patna, Pune, Ranchi, Trivandrum, Bombay, Calcutta and Madras
Indonesia: Jakarta, Medan and Bandung
Iraq: Baghdad
Italy: Rome, Milan and Naples
Ivory Coast: Abidjan
Japan: Tokyo and Kyoto
Jordan: Amman
Kenya: Nairobi, Kisumu and Mombasa
South Korea: Seoul
Kuwait: Mansouriyah
Lesotho: Maseru
Malawi: Lilongwe and Blantyre
Malaysia: Kuala Lumpur, Sarawak, Sabah and Penang
Mauritius: Rose Hill
Mexico: Mexico City
Morocco: Rabat
Nepal: Kathmandu
Netherlands: Amsterdam
New Zealand: Wellington
Nigeria: Lagos, Enugu, Kaduna and Kano City
Norway: Oslo
Oman: Jibroo and Salalah
Pakistan: Islamabad, Karachi, Lahore and Peshawar

Peru: Lima
Philippines: Metro Manila
Poland: Warsaw
Portugal: Lisbon, Coimbra and Oporto
Qatar: Doha
Romania: Bucharest
Saudi Arabia: Riyadh and Jeddah
Senegal: Dakar
Sierra Leone: Freetown
Singapore
South Africa: Johannesburg and Cape Town
Spain: Madrid, Barcelona, Bilbao, Seville, Valencia, Granada, Palma and Las Palmas
Sri Lanka: Colombo and Kandy
Sudan: Khartoum, Omdurman and El Obeid
Sweden: Stockholm
Tanzania: Dar es Salaam
Thailand: Bangkok and Chiang Mai
Tunisia: Tunis
Turkey: Ankara and Istanbul
Uganda: Kampala
United Arab Emirates: Abu Dhabi and Dubai
USA: Washington DC
USSR: Moscow
Venezuela: Caracas
Yemen: Sana'a
Yugoslavia: Belgrade and Zagreb
Zambia: Lusaka and Ndola
Zimbabwe: Harare

Cultural centres

In many non-European countries there will be French, German and American Cultural Centres as well as the British Council, which may offer free or reduced price film shows and concerts. Find out their addresses and check the noticeboards outside for dates and details.

SAFARIS

Visitors to East Africa are usually keen to go on safari but depressed to discover the prices charged by local agencies. It can be cheaper to assemble a group of people and hire a land-rover to drive yourselves around. Bear in mind that accommodation in the parks may be limited, and expensive—likewise food (especially in Tanzania), although there are sometimes thatched huts or 'bandas' for rent. Do not expect to be allowed to camp in the parks for obvious safety reasons.

If you have to pay for an organised safari look for one that offers 'tented accommodation' and avoid novelties like balloon rides that force the price up.

Those prepared to risk black market transactions in Tanzania and also prepared to stay in village accommodation rather than in the parks may find a safari cheaper there than in Kenya. However, be warned that officials at the park gates inspect your paperwork carefully. If they are suspicious, you could be made to pay again in hard currency or even arrested. To get past them you will have to forge your currency declaration form as well as finding a safe dealer; you may ask yourself whether the ends really justify the means.

HOTELS

Europeans tend to think of hotels only as expensive places to stay. However, in Third World countries they can be positive havens of luxury and good food. If you are really pressed for something to do it may be worth putting on your most presentable clothes and going into a hotel to read their noticeboard. Often you will find there are films showing or cultural events taking place. Usually these are not, strictly speaking, open to members of the public. However, if you keep a low profile you may be able to slip in. In Khartoum, for example, you can sometimes infiltrate video screenings at the Araak or Meridien Hotels.

More expensive hotels usually have swimming pools which you can sometimes use for a small fee. The best ones also have sports complexes with jacuzzis, saunas and gyms which you may be able to use by becoming a temporary member of the sports club or paying a charge for the day. If you fancy a bathe, ask at reception. It probably helps to wear your best clothes while doing so.

If all else fails hotels can be much more comfortable places to while away the evenings than your own lodgings. I can strongly recommend the lounge of the Nile Hilton in Cairo which with its potted plants and ancient Egyptian sculpture makes for much more congenial surroundings than the squalor of the Oxford Hotel on Talaat Harb Street, for some unaccountable reason a favourite with budget travellers.

17
Bargain-hunting
Overseas

You may have many reasons for shopping around, however tight your budget. These include:

- Stocking up on items you need while travelling.
- Collecting souvenirs.
- Planning to sell items for a profit while away.
- Planning to sell items for a profit when you get home again.
- Knowing that a particular item is cheaper or better value than at home.

STOCKING UP WHILE AWAY

It makes sense to buy some things when you reach your destination rather than before you leave home.

Clothing

When going to a country with a flourishing textile industry and a low cost of living, wait until you arrive to kit yourself out. Bazaars in India are full of cheap cotton blouses and the like and in many Far Eastern and African countries you can have clothes run up for you quickly and cheaply. Remember when buying off-the-peg items that Indians, and Asians in general, tend to have smaller builds than Europeans.

Cameras

If you have not already got a camera, consider your route carefully before buying. The same model may cost less if bought in Hong Kong or Singapore, or even in duty-free havens like Abu Dhabi which you may pass through en route to your destination. There may be a problem with Customs duty on your return to the UK, so always keep receipts to prove where you bought the item and how much you paid for it.

If you think you may want to buy a camera abroad, check prices in the UK first so you can recognise a real bargain and not get talked into buying something which costs the same at home. Always ask for an **international warranty card** and a receipt as well. The local Customs and

Excise office should be able to tell you how much tax would be charged on the item you intend to buy.

Miscellaneous items

It also pays to keep an eye open for bargains as you move from place to place and to stock up on what you need where it is cheapest. For example, drivers may want to buy petrol in Andorra where it's cheaper than in France or Spain. Smokers should buy cigarettes and even cigarette papers before arriving in Scandinavia where they cost the earth.

It is never a good idea to carry food-stuffs or plants from one country to another, although some countries are more strict about this than others. For example, the only foods you can import into the USA are Hawaiian pineapples. The Australians actually fumigate the plane before passengers are allowed to leave it; all food imports are prohibited.

SOUVENIRS

One of the fun things about travelling is collecting souvenirs to take home with you. Shops in the UK frequently sell similar items but at grossly inflated prices, with mark-ups of up to 400% being common.

Reasonably priced souvenirs worldwide

Thailand	Cotton bed-spreads, tribal artefacts (Chiang Mai), temple rubbings (Bangkok), paper umbrellas (Baw Sang), silk.
Hong Kong	Made-to-measure clothes, factory-sold clothing.
Burma	Lacquerware (Pagan).
India	Cloth paintings, marble inlaid boxes (Agra), papier-maché work, shawls (Kashmir), cotton clothing.
Morocco	Carpets and carpet belts.
Kenya	Soapstone chess sets (Mombasa), baskets (Nairobi), kangas (coloured cloths).
Tanzania	Masai necklaces (but you may have to barter).
Israel	Rugs, jewellery.
Poland	Inlaid wooden dishes.
USSR	Posters of Lenin, Communist Party badges.
Mexico	Papier-maché money-boxes.
Spain	Earthenware cooking utensils and plant pots.

In general **handicraft items** are good value for money outside the developed world because low labour costs keep the price down. Conversely, in Europe high labour costs make most handicrafts expensive. For example hand-made lace table-cloths from Gozo look appealing, but at roughly £80.00 a time they are hardly a bargain. On the other hand their factory-made equivalents are a positive snip at £8.00 a time.

A NOTE ON BARGAINING

In Europe you will be used to fixed prices, clearly displayed, for most items we buy; but in many parts of the Third World prices are normally arrived at by bargaining. The process is as follows:

1. The shopkeeper suggests a price higher than he expects to get.
2. You decide how much you are prepared to pay.
3. You offer slightly less than this.
4. Bartering begins in earnest.

Some people find this great fun, but never start bartering for something you have no intention of buying. If you cannot talk the price down, it sometimes helps to walk away; certainly you should never let yourself appear too keen to obtain the item in question.

The best places to barter

Bartering can be a pleasure in areas with a small tourist trade. However, there are places—Marrakesh is one of them—where it is a mistake ever to get started. The conventional wisdom is that the shopkeeper will ask twice the real value of the item and that you should offer a half to a third of whatever he suggests. Where there are too many tourists, however, initial offers can be six or seven times the true value, and unless you have a good idea what something *should* cost you stand to get ripped off. One way to avoid this is to visit a fixed price store beforehand—a government workshop, for example—and get an idea of prices. These stores are usually quite expensive, so aim to talk prices down below theirs when you return to your shopkeeper. Never try to barter in a shop displaying a fixed price sign; it is regarded as very poor etiquette.

Bargaining is most common in markets and small shops. At its best in Turkey, Morocco or India it will be a leisurely process, perhaps taking hours, with you and the shopkeeper exchanging pleasantries over a cup of tea in between bursts of haggling. At its worst in the same places it leaves you feeling imprisoned in a shop, with the owner insisting on showing you all sorts of goods you have no desire to buy, while telling you all sorts of tall stories about them at the same time— have you heard the one about the one-humped female and two-humped male camel?

The psychological pressure to buy can be enormous. You are probably so accustomed to self-service in the West that you will feel under considerable obligation to someone who has painstakingly unrolled every carpet in his shop even if you did not ask him to. The longer he can detain you, the greater your feeling of guilt; nor does it help when wads of testimonials from 'satisfied' customers worldwide are dragged out. You cannot always escape by claiming poverty either; the smallest stallholder seems happy to take Access, Mastercard, your father's credit card and so on.

An additional problem is that all this can turn very nasty as well. I have been thrown out of a shop when I suggested returning in a week's time, and have squirmed with embarrassment while a male companion was subjected to interrogation—and abuse—about his sexual prowess under the guise of sales talk. The only answer seems to be to have a very thick skin and a resilience to window-shopping—and to leave your money back at the hotel.

BUYING TO RESELL WHILE AWAY

If you are visiting several countries on a tight budget, remember that it is sometimes possible to buy items cheaply in one country and then resell them elsewhere en route. For example, it often makes sense to buy your duty-free allowance of alcohol and cigarettes to resell even if you do not want to use it yourself. If you buy whisky on the flight from Nepal to India, you will have no trouble selling it to a taxi driver on your way into the city; similarly when you leave Bangkok airport for Rangoon it would be madness not to buy two hundred '555' cigarettes and a bottle of Johnny Walker Red Label first. Even before you leave Rangoon airport you will be beseiged by men offering at least the equivalent of £60.00 for your allowance. If you wait until you reach the town centre, even more astronomical amounts will be offered—even bottles of Coke fetch ten times their cost because of their scarcity. You can even resell your tobacco and alcohol allowance in Turkey. Of course, all such transactions are illegal and should be handled with care.

Specialist items to buy and resell

Not only duty free goods are worth buying to resell. You could, for example, stock up on cosmetics and malaria tablets in Thailand and then sell or exchange them in Burma (Myanmar)—I swapped a tube of malaria tablets and a biro for a Buddhist monk's umbrella. While in Kenya it is worth buying a couple of extra **kangas**—brightly coloured multi-purpose cloths worn by women as skirts or head-dresses—to resell in Tanzania where they are in short supply. Chocolate and flour are also worth taking into Tanzania. Customs officers are on the look out for such imports but are more suspicious of local people than of tourists; they will be more concerned that you might be smuggling currency rather than merchandise.

Universally popular items

Some items have a widespread exchange value. Jeans are popular in Africa and Asia and it may be worth taking a pair with you if only to offload them on arrival—jeans are notoriously hot, sticky and difficult to dry when travelling. Those with familiar names such as Levis and Wranglers are obviously most popular. Even in Eastern bloc countries, jeans are much sought after, but you need to beware of informers if getting involved in what is effectively black market activity.

T-shirts with slogans are also widely popular. Anyone thinking of visiting Morocco, for example, should consider buying a few for resale. Make sure you select suitably macho designs because it is mostly the 'westernised' young men who are after them. Local markets will be a good place to pick these up before you go. Look under 'Textile Printers' in *Yellow Pages* for the addresses and phone numbers of companies who will print designs to order on T-shirts.

Swapping items often makes more sense than actually selling them. For example good sunglasses are popular with Moroccan men but since they are very poor, they are unlikely to offer what you paid for them. However, shopkeepers may be happy to swap them for souvenirs that you would regard as having a similar value.

BUYING TO SELL ON YOUR RETURN HOME

You may be tempted to buy goods abroad that are scarce and potentially valuable back home; but remember that you really need to know what you are doing. After all, a Turkish carpet may seem a bargain in Istanbul, but it would be difficult to smuggle home and will attract Customs duty that will bump up its actual price. Unless you actually know someone beforehand who will buy it from you for a good price, remember that shops want to make a profit and are unlikely to offer you much for it. Unless you're an expert you may get caught out over the quality of your purchase; Moroccan carpet-sellers are marvellous at spinning the most unlikely stories about rugs that actually started life in Spanish factories.

The same applies to buying jewels to resell. It may seem temptingly easy to smuggle these, but unless you are an expert you stand to be duped by someone with a good sales patter.

However if you have a local crafts market where you can get a stall for a reasonable price it may be worth bringing or sending back saleable quantities of small items like bangles, pictures, baskets and so on. Your library should have a copy of the *Markets Year Book*, a World Fair's publication listing addresses, phone numbers and features of markets throughout the UK.

Whatever you do, do not be tempted to smuggle **drugs** or **gold**. Most countries have hefty penalties for drug offences—including the death penalty in Malaysia—and two English women are currently languishing in Kathmandu jail for gold running. Be wary of anyone asking you to carry anything through Customs for them—particularly into Malaysia or out of Turkey or any other country with a known drugs trade—and remember that airport security is getting tighter as the threat of terrorism increases, so the likelihood of getting caught is also increasing. No matter how much the item to be smuggled is worth, it just is not worth it.

BUYING TO SAVE MONEY AT HOME

Because different countries have different tax rates and different popular products, some travellers go abroad partly to do their shopping at a cheaper price. This applies especially to people on day trips to the European Channel ports. Particular bargains include:

- Wines.
- Lager-type beers bought in large quantities—a local supermarket may even be prepared to buy these from you for resale.
- Olive oil.
- Hand-made chocolates.

Not surprisingly, the best prices are usually found in hypermarkets, but they are more or less the same from one port to another. If the reason for your trip is bargain hunting, do not travel to France on a Monday, when most shops are closed.

Taking a car across the Channel pushes up the price, but makes it possible to buy more on one trip. However, there are car parks at the UK ports and at garages in Dover and Folkestone (£1.50–£4.00 per day), so you could leave your car there ready to load up as soon as you get off the ferry again.

Tax exemptions

At the moment, international travellers can always take advantage of tax exemptions on limited amounts of alcohol, perfumes, tobacco products and miscellaneous goods. Within the EC these allowances are now under reconsideration. Obviously, using these allowances is one way in which budget travellers can keep their costs down.

Normally duty-free allowances are only available when you are leaving a country. However at Reykjavik and Singapore passengers can buy duty-free goods on arrival. Sometimes, particularly at Third World airports, duty-free items can only be paid for in hard currency. This is the case at Tel Aviv and Rangoon airports, so you need to keep some currency until you leave in order to take advantage of your allowance. In a few places like Malta you can pay for duty-free goods inside the country and then pick them up at the airport when you leave.

What you are allowed to bring into the UK duty-free

Goods obtained duty- and tax-free in the EC (ie in a duty-free shop) or duty- and tax-free on a ship or aircraft, or goods bought outside the EC.

Goods obtained duty- and tax-paid in the EC (ie in local shops).

Alcohol

2 litres of still table wine
plus
1 litre over 22% vol (eg spirits and strong liqueurs)
or
2 litres not over 22% vol (eg low strength liqueurs or fortified or sparkling wines)
or
A further 2 litres of still table wine

5 litres of still table wine
plus
1½ litres over 22% vol (eg spirits and strong liqueurs)
or
3 litres not over 22% vol (eg low strength liqueurs or fortified or sparkling wines)
or
A further 3 litres of still table wine

Perfume

50 grams (60cc or 2 fl oz)

75 grams (90cc or 3 fl oz)

Eau de Toilette

250cc (9 fl oz)

375cc (13 fl oz)

Tobacco

200 cigarettes
or
100 cigarillos
or
50 cigars
or
250 grams of tobacco

300 cigarettes
or
150 cigarillos
or
75 cigars
or
400 grams of tobacco

Other Goods

£32 worth (but no more than 50 litres of beer or 25 mechanical lighters)

£250 worth (but no more than 50 litres of beer or 25 mechanical lighters).

(Fortified wines include port, sherry, vermouth and madeira. A cigarillo is a cigar weighing less than 50 grams.)

Additional rules for duty-free shopping

• Nobody under 17 is entitled to a tobacco or drinks allowance.

- No-one is permitted to mix their duty-free and duty-paid allowances within the same allowance bands. So you can mix spirits with still table wine and buy one duty-free and the other duty-paid because they appear in different allowance bands. You can also mix spirits and sparkling wine if you take half the amount shown of each; but they must both be either duty-free or duty-paid, not a combination of the two.

- You are also allowed to mix your main duty-free table wine allowance with an extra two litres duty-free or three litres duty-paid since they appear in different allowance bands.

- You can take half your tobacco allowance as cigarettes and half as cigars as long as they are both duty-free or both duty-paid.

- If you buy more drink, tobacco, lighters, perfume or eau de toilette than your allowance the duty due can amount to more than what you originally paid for the items.

For further information on allowances contact HM Customs and Excise, Dorset House, Stamford Street, London SE1 9PJ. (Tel: (01) 928 0533), or any Customs and Excise office (addresses in the phone book).

Where to buy duty-free

Deciding whether to use the duty-free facilities on board ships and planes and at ports and airports may depend on prices within the country you are visiting. Sometimes it will be cheaper to buy duty-paid goods in local shops rather than waiting for your duty-free allowance. In Greece, Spain and Italy local drink and cigarettes may be cheaper than their duty-free equivalents.

Some countries offer particularly good duty-free prices. For example, alcohol is particularly cheap in Gibraltar—but compare prices in different shops before buying. Perfume is especially cheap in the Channel Islands.

Countries where it makes particular sense to buy your duty-free allowance include:

Austria	Norway
Belgium	Portugal
Denmark	Sweden
Ireland	Switzerland
The Netherlands	USA

However, remember that some airports put mark-ups of up to 200% on duty-free goods, so they are not always the 'bargain' which you anticipated. Basically, you need to have a good idea of costs at home in order to compare airport prices realistically. It may be cheaper if you buy what you want on the plane home, but the range of goods available will be more limited.

There are also a few duty-free havens in the world. These include Kos and Rhodes (Greece), Eilat (Israel), Singapore, Hong Kong and the Canary Island ports. Many of the Caribbean islands also offer extensive tax-free shopping facilities. To take advantage of your tax exemption in Israel your purchase must be worth over USD50.00(£29.00) and be paid for in hard currency. You must also allow the receipt to be sealed up with the goods when you buy them. Although you pay tax at the time of purchase, it will be refunded either when you leave the country or when you return home. You will also receive a 5% discount on the purchase price.

It is always worth finding out if you are eligible for a tax rebate as a non-resident. In Canada, for example, you could claim back the 9% sales tax on purchases of CAD500 (£246) or more if you can prove that you are non-resident.

The European Community
In 1992 the European Community will become a reality with far fewer border formalities for EC citizens than at present. One result of this is likely to be the abolition of duty-free purchases within the EC. However you will continue to be able to bring in items duty-free from further afield.

18
Steering Clear of Other Incidental Costs

FINES

Budget travellers can least afford to fritter money away on petty fines. However, without the aid of a guide they are likely to slip up as they make their way around, and in many countries venial crimes incur on-the-spot fines which are tricky to evade. Here are some of the pitfalls:

Public Transport Fines

In many countries ticket inspectors can fine anyone they catch on buses and trains without a valid ticket. Pleading ignorance or lack of language *may* get you out of trouble, but on the whole it is better to play safe. In Amsterdam anyone using public transport without an appropriate ticket is liable to an on-the-spot DFL26 (£7.50) fine. In Czechoslovakia, losing your seat reservation coupon can also result in an instant penalty of several pounds in hard currency. In France, you are expected to punch your railway ticket into a machine on the platform to validate it; failure to do so may mean having to pay again.

Driving fines

Similarly, in many countries police and traffic wardens can impose instant fines on anyone breaking the highway laws. Places where this can happen include Malta, Hungary and France where the police demand a deposit from offenders until their fine is worked out; usually this comes to the same amount as the deposit which can be quite a lot. Penalties which could attract on-the-spot fines include crossing white lines, ignoring traffic lights, running out of petrol on a motorway and overloading your car.

Visa Fines

Overstaying your visa or contravening its conditions in other ways can also lead to on-the-spot fines, usually when you try to leave the country. For example, anyone overstaying a Guatemalan visa will be charged USD10.00 (£6.00) for each extra day when they leave the country.

Reporting To The Police

In many countries, temporary residents have to register with the local police. In Europe this chore is done for you by your hotelier, which explains why you are so frequently expected to hand over your passport on arrival. In some cases however, you are expected to register yourself and the fine for failing to do so can be quite steep. For example, visitors to Egypt are expected to register within seven days of arrival, so make sure you do.

Italian Fiscal Receipts

In Italy most restaurants, hotels and other sales outlets are expected to issue numbered receipts showing the charge they have made, including VAT. In the event of a spot check, both proprietor and consumer are liable for an on-the-spot fine if this hasn't been done. So take care that you get a receipt for everything you pay for.

EXCISE AND IMPORT DUTIES

Excise duty

Excise duty may not be a fine but it *is* another extra cost budget travellers will want to avoid. Duty is payable on any goods you import into a country above the stated duty-free amounts. These vary with every country, but usually cover quantities of alcohol, cigarettes, perfume, cameras and other goods you can bring in. You can find out the precise amounts for every country in the world by looking in the *ABC Guide to International Travel*.

Import duty

In the UK, excise duty is levied on anything you import which exceeds the duty-free allowances (see **Bargain-Hunting Overseas**). VAT is then charged both on the extra amount and on the excise duty. In addition, you may have to pay **import duty** on goods, especially if they were bought in non-EC countries. This duty is charged as a percentage of the amount by which the price you paid exceeds your allowance. VAT is levied, once again, on this amount and on the excess. The percentage you pay varies according to the item in question and where it was bought. For example, 12% duty might be charged on a Hong Kong calculator while a Swiss watch would not attract any import duty at all.

If you know that what you want to buy abroad will be subject to UK duty, consult the **Customs Tariff** in a reference library or at a Tax Office to find out how much you may have to pay.

SALES TAXES AND SERVICE CHARGES

In the UK, we are used to the price shown on an item being the price we pay for it. Sometimes VAT is charged separately, for example on electrical goods, and in restaurants service charges are not always included in the total.

In other countries, taxes are often not included in the price and you are expected to know about them as a customer. For example, in the USA most prices need tax added to them. In Cyprus, restaurants normally add 13% to the bill for tax and service charges. In Agadir, expect to find a hefty 30% added to most meal bills. Even in EC countries the price inclusive of VAT is not always shown. For guidance the following rates of VAT apply:

	Standard Rate %	Increased or Luxury Rate %
Belgium	19	25/33
Denmark	22	22
France	18/6	33/33
Germany (West)	14	14
Greece	18	36
Ireland	25	25
Italy	18	38
Luxembourg	12	12
Netherlands	20	20
Portugal	16/12	30/21
Spain	12	33
UK	15	15

(After 1992 it is likely that VAT rates will be standardised throughout the Community.)

Tipping

Incidentally tipping, which is so widespread in England, is not always expected elsewhere. For example the Swiss do not expect tips, nor do the Austrians or Singaporeans unless it is for exceptional service, and in most Eastern bloc countries tipping would be out of place. Conversely in other countries even higher tips are expected. For example in Guatemala the recommended amount is 20% of the charge. In America, taxi drivers expect 20%, restaurants look for 15% and porters want 50 cents per bag. On a cruise you could be expected to leave tips amounting to USD5 (£3.00) a day, so always check before you leave home.

AIRPORT TAXES

Some of the nastiest 'extra' expenses sprung on travellers are airport taxes, either on domestic or international flights. In some cases these charges are collected by the ticket-issuing agent as for the USA and Canada, so there is no risk of a surprise. However in other cases, the tax must be paid at the check-in desk on departure. Furthermore, some governments require the tax to be paid in **hard currency** rather than local money.

Passengers in transit and infants under two are usually exempt from airport taxes, while children under 12 occasionally pay half price. The tax is often reduced if you are flying to an adjacent or politically affiliated country.

It's vital to check whether you will have to pay a tax before turning up at the airport, especially if it must be paid in hard currency. The following chart indicates where taxes are levied and their approximate amount. Check the latest edition of the *ABC Guide To International Travel* for up-to-date costs.

Airports which levy taxes

For translation of IATA currency codes see **Appendix 4**

Country	Airport	Departure Tax	Domestic Tax	International Tax
Afghanistan		AFG200		
Albania		LEK30		
Angola			AKZ80	AKZ400
Anguilla		ECD10		
Antigua			ECD10	ECD15
Argentina			ARA1	ARA8
				ARA2.5
				(to Uruguay)
Aruba		USD9		
Australia		AUD20		
Bahamas		BHD2		
Bangladesh			BDT10	BDT200
Barbados		BDD16		
Belgium	Brussels	BFR300		
	Antwerp	BFR115		
Belize		BZD20		
Benin		CFA2,500		
Bermuda		BED10		
Bolivia			BOB2	BOB16
Brazil		various amounts		
British Virgin Islands		USD5		
Bulgaria		LEV3 (departing to Libya)		
Burma (Myanmar)		BUR15 (if ticket bought in Burma)		
Burundi		FRB1,100		
Cayman Islands		CID6		
Central African Republic			CFA2,500	CFA4,200
Chad			CFA2,500	CFA4,200
Chile	Santiago	USD12.50		
China		RMB15		

Country	Airport	Departure Tax	Domestic Tax	International Tax
Colombia			COP325 USD7 (to San Andres or Leticia)	USD15
Comoro Islands			AFR500	AFR5,000
Congo	Brazzaville		CFA500	
Cook Islands		NZD20 (children aged 2-12 pay half)		
Costa Rica		CRC313 CRC63 (for stays of less than 48 hours)		
Dominica		ECD15		
Dominican Republic				USD10
Ecuador				USD20
El Salvador			-	SAC45
Equatorial Guinea			CFA425	CFA2,250
Fiji				FID10
Gambia		UKL7		
Grenada				ECD25
Guinea-Bissau				USD12 USD8 (to rest of West Africa
Guinea Republic			GNF100	GNF200 GNF150 (to rest of Africa)
Guyana			GYD50	
Haiti	USD15			
Honduras		USD10 (business arrival tax) USD2.5 (other arrival tax)		
Hong Kong				HKD120
India		INR50 (to Pakistan, Nepal, Bangladesh, Sri Lanka, Afghanistan, Maldives, Thailand, Singapore) INR 100 (everywhere else)		
Indonesia	Jakarta/ Denpasar		RPA2,000	RPA9,000
	Others		RPA600-1800	RPA2,000-8,000
Iran				IRI5,000
Iraq		IRD2		
Israel	Tel Aviv	USD7 (to Egypt) USD10 (to other places)		
	Eilat/ Jerusalem	USD5		

Country	Airport	Departure Tax	Domestic Tax	International Tax
Israel	Rafiah	NIS22.10		
	Nitzana	NIS5.50		
	Taba	NIS12.80		
Jamaica				JAD40
Japan	Narita			JME2,000
Jordan				JOD7
Kenya				USD10
Kiribati Republic				AUD5
Korea (South)				WON5,000
Laos				USD5
Lebanon				LEL150
Lesotho				LSL10
Liberia				LID10
Libya				LBD5
Madagascar				FMG1,500
Malawi				USD10
Malaysia			RGT3	RGT15
				RGT5 (to Singapore/ Brunei)
Maldives				MVR50
Mali			CFA500	CFA2,500
				CFA1,500 (to the rest of Africa)
Mauritania			MOG270	MOG860
				MOG560 (to the rest of Africa)
Mexico			MEP3,500	USD10
Mozambique			MZM800	MZM1,600
Nauru		AUD10		
Nepal			NER10-30	NER200
Netherlands Antilles			AFL5	AFL9-10
New Zealand				NZD2
Nicaragua				USD10
Nigeria			NGN5	NGN50
Niue		NZD10		
Norfolk Islands		AUD10		
Oman				R103
Pakistan			PAR10	PAR100
Panama				BAL15
Papua New Guinea				NGK10
Paraguay				GUA1,200
Peru	Lima			USD10
	Arequipa/Cuzco			USD2
Philippines			PHP10	PHP200
Rwanda				FRR800
				FRR250 (to Burundi, Tanzania, Uganda, Zaire)

Country	Airport	Departure Tax	Domestic Tax	International Tax
St Kitts & Nevis		ECD13.50		
St Lucia				ECD20
				ECD10
				(to the rest of the Caribbean)
St Vincent		ECD14		
Western Samoa		SAT20		
Senegal			CFA2,000	CFA5,000
				CFA4,000
				(to the rest of Africa)
Sierra Leone				USD10
Singapore				SID12
				SID5
				(to Brunei/ Malaysia)
Solomon Islands				SBD20
Sri Lanka	Colombo	SLR200		
	Others	SLR2.50-5		
Sudan			SUL15	SUL40
Surinam		SFL30		
Syria				SYL10
				SYL5
				(to other Arab states)
Taiwan				NTD300
Tanzania		USD10		
Thailand			BHT20	BHT150
Tonga				TOD5
Trinidad & Tobago				TTD20
Tunisia			TUD0.305	
Turkey	Istanbul	USD10		
	Others	USD7		
Turks & Caicos		USD10		
Tuvalu				AUD10
Uganda		USD10		
Uruguay				USD4.50
				USD2.50
				(to Buenos Aires)
Vanuatu			VUV200	VUV1,000
Venezuela				VBO497
Yemen (North)			YEM20	YEM75
Yemen (South)				DYD1.45
Yugoslavia			YUD1,500	YUD4,000
Zaire			ZAI200	USD12
Zambia			ZMK20	USD10
Zimbabwe				USD10

PORT TAXES

You cannot always avoid taxes by travelling by ship since some ports have their own charges. For example, people departing from the British Virgin Islands will be charged USD4 (£2.00). Cruise passengers should always check whether these are included in the cost of their trip.

MISCELLANEOUS TAXES

Budget travellers need to remember that governments can tax anything that takes their fancy, you can be caught unawares by sudden demands. For example, travellers to the New Valley oases of Egypt (Bahariya), Farafra and Dakhla) may be startled to find there is a New Valley Tax specially for visiting these areas, and hotel guests in Antigua will find 6% added to all their bills to help pay for the development of tourist facilities. So *never* run your funds down to zero.

EXCESS BAGGAGE CHARGES

Another extra charge to watch out for is the exorbitant one levied by the airlines on passengers whose baggage exceeds the free allowance—generally twenty kilogrammes for economy class, but check with the airlines at the time of booking. This charge is calculated as 1% of the first class fare per excess kilogramme regardless of the class travelled.

If you think your baggage could be overweight, weigh it before arriving at the airport. Then look round for someone who has very little luggage and ask if they would be prepared to carry some of yours through for you. You may have problems convincing anyone, however, because airline passengers are constantly cautioned against carrying packages for drug couriers.

Alternatively, decide which items are least valuable and post them home instead. Airmail is quick and costly but freighting goods by sea does not cost very much provided you are prepared to wait up to six months for their arrival.

What can you take on a plane in addition to the free baggage allowance?

- Handbag.
- Overcoat.
- Blanket.
- Umbrella or walking stick.
- Camera.
- Binoculars.
- Book for reading during flight.
- Crutches or collapsible wheelchair.

Sometimes you can also carry a pair of skis at no extra charge—check with the carrier at the time of booking. Children up to the age of 12 have the same baggage allowance as adults on international flights. However infants paying only 10% of the fare have no free baggage allowance, although you are allowed to carry baby food and so on onto the plane without charge.

19

Working Your Keep

If your funds are limited, an obvious way to make them last is to look for work abroad. There are lots of opportunities in the following areas:

- Tourism—hotels, bars, ski resorts, and so on.
- Fruit-picking.
- Teaching English.
- Au pairing.
- Factory work.
- Agricultural work.

Jobs in the EC

Outside Europe you usually require a work permit to find a job legally and these are increasingly hard to come by except through very restricted channels—see examples below for the USA, Canada and Australia. However one advantage of EC membership is that British citizens have freedom of movement within the Community. So although you may need to obtain a residency permit in some countries, you are free to look for work in France, Italy, Greece, Belgium, Denmark, Ireland, West Germany, Gibraltar, Luxembourg and The Netherlands. You will soon also be able to look for work in Spain and Portugal legally.

If you would like to find full-time work in another EC country, can speak the language and have relevant qualifications then you should ask for form **ES13** from a local Jobcentre. When you have filled in your requirements, this can be forwarded to other member countries whose employment services are linked up through the SEDOC central computer.

SEDOC

SEDOC – The European System for the International Clearing of Vacancies and Applications for Employment – helps people find jobs in EC countries. The addresses of SEDOC offices in other EC countries appear in Caroline Jackson's useful booklet *A Student's Guide to Europe*. If you are already in another EC country, you can apply directly to these offices for help in finding work.

If you have been unemployed in the UK for at least one month and wish to look for work in another member state, ask your unemployment benefit office to get you form **E303** from the DSS Overseas Branch. This authorises you to receive your benefit for up to three months in the other EC state while you look for work. To qualify, you must sign on for work there no later than seven days after you were last registered as being available for work in the UK. If you have still not found work at the end of the three months, you will have to return to the UK to continue to claim benefit. Before you accept any job abroad, make sure you know all of the following:

1. Name and address of employer and address where you would work.
2. What job you would do.
3. Details of your work and of any related duties.
4. The normal period of notice to be given by yourself or by the employer.
5. Whether the contract is open-ended or fixed term. If fixed, for how long.
6. Whether there is a trial period and if so, for how long.
7. How many and what hours you are expected to work.
8. How much overtime you would be able or be expected to work.
9. Normal gross earnings, overtime rates, special rates for night, Sunday and holiday work, whether pay is on piece rates and whether there are any bonuses.
10. How often and how you are paid, and whether the employer keeps a week or month in hand, and for how long.
11. What would happen if the job fell through.
12. What you would be paid if there was short-time working for any reason.
13. What holiday pay you get and whether the firm closes for set holidays.
14. Arrangements for sick leave and sick pay.
15. Pension arrangements, if applicable.
16. Whether accommodation is provided and on what terms.
17. Whether your employer would pay your fares at the start and end of the contract, and whether they would pay your fare home if the contract ended early for any reason.
18. Whether you need to have a medical, and at whose expense.

WORKING HOLIDAY SUGGESTIONS

Israeli Kibbutzim/Moshavim

Scattered the length and breadth of Israel are about 250 **kibbutzim** which are mainly agricultural settlements where people lead a communal existence. Most kibbutzim welcome overseas visitors for periods of a month or more to help with their work, especially the harvesting of crops ranging from bananas to dates and grapes. In return for their labour, visitors receive bed and board and a small sum of money for extras. On some kibbutzim even cigarettes and toiletries are supplied free.

Volunteers normally work eight hours a day for six days a week and may need to start work as early as four in the morning, so it is not a soft option. In addition those assigned to the factory, cowshed or poultry house may have to work shifts. Generally speaking you will not be expected to do the same work throughout your stay.

Kibbutzim accept visitors aged between 18 and 32 who are in sound health and have passed a recent medical.

There are several ways to find work on a kibbutz—perhaps the cheapest is to make your own way to Israel and approach one of the **kibbutz** offices in Tel Aviv to find a placement. However in summer there is a great demand for places and it may be safer to make arrangements before leaving home, in which case you should try one of the following organisations:

Project 67
36 Great Russell Street
London WC1B 3PP
Tel: (01) 636 1262

Worldwide Student Travel
37/38 Store Street
London WC1E 7BZ
Tel: (01) 636 6357
(Moshav only)

Kibbutz Representatives
1A Accommodation Road
London NW11 8EP
Tel: (01) 458 9235
(Kibbutz only)

Gil Travel Ltd
65 Gloucester Place
London W1 3PE
Tel: (01) 935 1701
Moshav only)

If you *do* decide to try your luck when you arrive, remember that officials at Tel Aviv's Ben Gurion airport are making it very difficult for people arriving on one-way tickets and will expect to see evidence that you can support yourself during your stay.

You will not make your fortune on a kibbutz. However, it does offer an opportunity to stay for an extended period abroad at little cost. Often your kibbutz will organise trips to the Dead Sea and other popular sights, and on your days off you can explore the countryside easily because Israel is so small.

Moshavim are collectively organised but privately owned farms which also require outside help with work. There are nearly 1,000 moshavim in Israel, some of them organised around individual families, some of them rather more communal. Overseas visitors are usually attached to individual families with whom they live and eat. One difference from a kibbutz is that you are paid more than just pocket money.

On a moshav you can expect to work for at least seven hours a day for six days a week, or for eight hours a days for five days a week. The work can be tough and the pay is low. On the other hand, you should be able to save most of it to finance the next stage of your travels.

Agencies in the UK also handle enquiries about moshavim (see the addresses above). Once again, you must be physically fit and between 21 and 32.

Israeli archaeological digs

Anyone with archaeological interests who is over 18 and fit for hard physical work in hot sun can also apply to work on an Israeli dig. Although most of the work is manual, people with experience in pottery-drawing and so on may be able to make use of their skills as well. Normally, you are expected to work for two weeks but can buy a charter air ticket valid for up to a month or an open-dated yearly return which costs an additional £30.00. Each year there are a number of different sites to choose from, and each will have different UK departure dates and costs. Further details are available from Project 67, 36 Great Russell Street, London WC1B 3PP (Tel: (01) 636 1262).

Other archaeological opportunities

Apart from the regular digs in Israel, there are usually other digs overseas that require extra help. To find out about these, you could subscribe to *Archaeology Abroad* which costs £3.50 for an annual subscription from 31-34 Gordon Square, London WC1H 0PY, which is published three times a year and which summarises the possibilities. You are more likely to be accepted on an overseas dig if you have had archeaological experience in the UK first. To find out about UK digs contact The Council For British Archaeology, 112 Kennington Road, London SE11 6RE, which publishes *British Archaeological News* listing all the current opportunities.

USA: Camp America and Bunacamp

Across the USA there are about 12,000 summer camps which look after children aged 8 to 14 from the months of June to August. These camps are always keen to recruit summer staff for nine weeks at a time, and placements are arranged by two organisations, **Camp America** and **Bunacamp**. In return they offer:

- board and lodging for nine weeks
- free transport to the USA and back
- help in getting a visitor's J-1 work visa
- six weeks' free time for independent travel at the end of the placement
- orientation and accommodation in New York on arrival

- help in case of any emergency
- pocket money of USD100 (£58.00) to USD450 (£262) depending on age and experience.

Since travelling in the USA is relatively expensive, and getting a work permit notoriously difficult, this can be a sensible way for anyone over 18, or 19½ for Bunacamp, and under 35 to spend time there, but you must be certified physically fit by a doctor, and have a suitable skill to teach at the camp. Preference tends to go to people with sporty interests and to teachers.

People are also needed to do maintenance and other manual work in Camp America camps. If you do not think you are cut out for constant work with children, you could apply to work in the kitchens, do the driving, and so on. You would still be employed on the same conditions but there is a better chance of being accepted on this programme. Pocket money is paid at a flat rate of USD300 (£176.00) per person.

KAMP

Bunacamp has a similar kitchen and maintenance programme, **KAMP**, but it is only open to full-time students on degree or Higher National Diploma courses in academic subjects at tertiary level. The minimum salary they pay for the nine-week period is USD450 (£261.00) but KAMP participants have to pay a £55.00 registration fee on top of the £40.00 BUNAC insurance premium. KAMP participants are, in effect, loaned their fare to the States which is repaid by the camp on completion of the work contract. Because of this you will be asked to provide a **guarantor**, normally a close relative.

Companion schemes

Through Camp America you can also apply to be placed in a family as a '**companion**' to their children. Once again, pocket money is paid at a flat rate of USD300 (£176.00) and preference tends to go to holders of driving licences. Places are very limited on this scheme.

Camp America is at:
American Institute for Foreign Study (UK) Ltd,
37A Queens Gate,
London SW7 5HR
Tel: (01) 589 3223

Their deadline for applications is 31st May each year, and applicants are required to arrange a local interview and pay a good faith deposit of £25.00.

Bunacamp is at:
232 Vauxhall Bridge Road,
London SW1V 1AU
Tel: (01) 630 0344

Once again you must arrange your own local interview. There is also a £2.00 fee to register with **BUNAC** (The British Universities North America Club).

Au Pair in America programme

For those with a year to spare, there is now a legal scheme for au pairing in the USA for people aged between 18 and 25. Conditions are standard, with a nine hour day, five and a half days a week. In return au pairs receive USD100 (£58.00) a week pocket money, their return fare to the States and the all important J visa.

Those interested in this possibility should write to:

Au Pair In America,
Dept CA,
37 Queens Gate,
London SW7 5HR
Tel: (01) 581 2730

Work America and Work Canada programmes

If you are a student, another possible way to spend the summer in the States is to apply through **BUNAC** for a working visa for any job you can find, for example, bar or restaurant work. In this case, you must either have someone who is prepared to sponsor you while you look for work in the States, or have arranged a job before you leave the UK. The scheme only allows you to stay in America between 1st June and 19th October. Once again, you must be registered as a full-time tertiary level student on an advanced course, and a member of BUNAC. Final year and foreign students may have trouble being accepted for a visa unless they have irrefutable proof of their intention to return to the UK at the end of their placement.

Those wishing to use this scheme must pay a £52.00 registration fee. In addition they must be able to pay the cost of a charter fare to the USA; BUNAC can loan students half the air fare, but this has to be repaid from their earnings.

A similar scheme applies to students wanting to find work in Canada for no longer than six months in the summer. In this case, those without a guaranteed job or a Canadian sponsor may still be accepted, provided they can show a letter from a bank confirming that they have ordered at least CAD1,000 (£493.00) in travellers cheques. However, the rules are such that although students between school and college may be accepted, final year students will not be. In addition, everyone applying through this scheme must have a medical with a designated doctor at a cost of about £50.00. Once again BUNAC can help by advancing half the air fare to be repaid from what you earn. Anyone who wants to work in Canadian summer camps should apply through Bunacamp, while those wanting to work as tobacco pickers should apply to the Canadian High Commission, 38 Grosvenor Street, London W1X 0AA (Tel: (01) 409 2071).

If you are interested in either of these schemes, apply to BUNAC, 232 Vauxhall Bridge Road, London SW1V 1AU (Tel: (01) 630 0344) for further information.

Icelandic Fish Processing Factories

If you have a high tolerance for low temperatures and a liking for the quiet life, you might consider looking for work in an Icelandic fish processing factory. In theory, these jobs can be arranged from the UK by applying to The Icelandic Freezing Plant Corps, Estate Road, No 2, South Humberside Industrial Estate, Grimsby, South Humberside DN13 2TG (Tel: (0472) 44181). In practice, few British travellers find work this way; the majority arrive in Iceland as tourists and then approach Reykjavik offices for placement. The best time of year for seeking work is January and February and if you are lucky a firm will pay your plane fare to the village where your factory is situated. Work in the factories can be very dull and conditions in workers' hostels spartan. Most work is paid on piece rates and even with overtime you are unlikely to make your fortune. It could be an interesting experience nonetheless.

Officially you need a work permit to take a factory job, but provided you do not outstay the three month visitor's permit, many employers will turn a blind eye to this requirement. However, it does mean Immigration officials will be interested in seeing your return ticket, and funds to support yourself in a very expensive country; nor is it easy to take large sums of money out with you legally.

Norwegian Farm Working Guest programme

English or German speakers aged between 18 and 30 with between one and three months to spare can apply to be accepted into a Norwegian farming family as a working guest, helping out both with household tasks and on the farm. You will be expected to work 35 hours a week for bed, board and a small amount of pocket money. Placements are made by the **Norwegian Youth Council (LNU)**, Rolf Hofmogst 18, 0655 Oslo 6 (Tel: 010-47-2-02670043), to whom you send two photographs, a medical certificate and a registration fee of NOK250 (£22.00) before April each year. These jobs are only available from May to September.

If you would prefer to wait until you get to Norway before finding work, you may be able to earn more money, particularly if you can drive a tractor, and are prepared to work long hours. Much of the work will be fruit and vegetable harvesting or haymaking.

Au pairing

If you are going abroad for long periods of time, you may consider taking domestic work in a private home as one way of finding out about local life and learning the language at low cost. The drawbacks to this kind of work are obvious; depending on your employer, you can end up working long hours with little time off at very tedious chores. However you will receive bed, board and pocket money in return for your efforts, and, if you are lucky with your family, you may even have a good time into the bargain.

To find an au pair placement you could do one of the following:

- Approach an **employment agency** such as the UK and Overseas Domestic and Au Pair Agency, Suite 29, Kent House, 87 Regent Street, London W1R 7HF; (Tel: (01) 439 6354). The Federation of Recruitment and Employment Services, 10 Belgrave Square, London SW1X 8PH (Tel: (01) 235 6616), supplies a list of agencies which might be able to help you in return for an SAE and a 34p stamp. Many agencies also advertise in *The Lady* magazine. Expect to pay a placement fee of perhaps £40.00 to the agency.
- Look in *The Lady* for people advertising for au pairs, nannies and cooks or place your own ad. A whole section is devoted to overseas vacancies and you will find anything here, although the majority of ads are for European vacancies. Many of them ask for qualifications and references. *The Lady* is a weekly publication available from newsagents. To advertise in it, write to the Classified Advertisement Dept, *The Lady*, 39-40 Bedford Street, London WC2E 9ER.

Always check the conditions very carefully before accepting and try and get the following details in writing:

- How many hours you will have to work each day or week.
- How many days off you will get each month.
- How many children you will have to look after, and their ages.
- What housework you will be expected to do.
- Whether you will be expected to drive.
- Whether you will be expected to babysit regularly.
- How much you will be paid.
- What accommodation will be provided for you and whether it will be self-contained.
- Whether your fares to and from the placement will be paid.
- How much holiday you will be allowed.

Grape-picking

Traditionally, students have often looked for work helping with the **French grape harvest** between mid-September and mid-October. Once again, the work is hard—especially for the first few days—and poorly paid with long hours, but there is plenty of good wine to make up for the aches and pains. You might be able to arrange work in advance through **Vacation Work International**, 9 Park End Street, Oxford OX1 1HJ (Tel: (0865) 241978) but they charge a registration fee. Instead, you could look for the addresses of winegrowers in French telephone directories in the library—look under '*Viticulteurs*' or '*Producteurs Négociants*'—and write to them directly, enclosing an International Reply-Paid Coupon for an answer. You can also get useful addresses from the **Centre d'Information et de Documentation Jeunesse (CIDJ)**, Travaux Saisonniers Agricole, 101 Quai Branly, 75740 Paris Cedex 15.

If you are prepared to arrive in France and then look for work you could either visit village farms on the off-chance and ask to be taken on (in which case, start asking round early in the season, ie in August), or you could visit the French equivalent of our Jobcentres, the **Agence Nationale pour l'Emploi (ANPE)**, and ask about farmers who are specifically looking for help.

Grape-picking is also possible in West Germany from mid-October to mid-November. People who speak fluent German should be able to find work by asking around, but it is possible to arrange a placement beforehand through **Concordia**, 8 Brunswick Place, Hove, East Sussex BN3 1ET (Tel: (0273) 772086) if you are prepared to pay a fee.

Teaching English as a foreign language (TEFL)

One great asset that English speakers have when it comes to looking for work overseas is that there is a great demand for people to teach the language, whether in Europe or further afield. While it is not essential to have a teaching qualification if you are prepared to arrive in a town and ask around for work, it definitely helps if you want to find employment before you leave home and if you want to secure the best paid posts. If you have a degree or teaching certificate tuck a photocopy of it in your bag. If you have an **RSA TEFL qualification** so much the better, and if you are serious about finding teaching work it would be worth investing about £400 before you leave to take a month-long intensive course. The Royal Society of Arts, 8 John Adam Street, London WC2N 8EY (Tel: (01) 930 5115), will supply you with a list of approved centres around the country.

Finding TEFL jobs

To find work before you leave, consult *The Guardian Education Supplement* on Tuesdays or *The Times Educational Supplement* on Fridays. You could also write to **The British Council**, 65 Davies Street, London W1Y 2AA (Tel: (01) 499 8011), although they only normally want well-qualified experienced teachers prepared to accept a two or three year contract.

Once you are abroad, visit the **British consulate** to see if there are any adverts for English teachers. A local office of the British Council (addresses available from 65 Davies Street, see above) might also be able to help. Ask other travellers as well; in areas like Bangkok, they may be the best source of tips.

English language teachers are particularly often required in Spain, Italy, Turkey, Egypt, Sudan (one year posts available each August—contact the Sudan Cultural Centre, 31 Rutland Gate, London SW7 1PG), Brazil, Mexico, Peru, Hong Kong, Singapore, Thailand and Japan.

Teaching in Japan

Of the countries which welcome English teachers, Japan is possibly the most expensive. Teaching English there may, therefore, be one of the few ways through which you can get there as a budget traveller. It is easy to arrive in Japan on a tourist visa and then find work privately.

However, if you want to arrange work before you leave, or to be able to stay for a longer period, you need to apply for a **teaching visa**. First of all you need to find a potential employer, and then send proof of their sponsorship and a copy of your qualifications to the Japanese Embassy. Processing the visa can take several months. Teaching visas can only be obtained outside Japan, so if you find work and then want to change your status, you may have to leave Japan, perhaps for South Korea, and then reapply for a permit.

Teaching jobs are not always very well paid and Japan's cost of living is high. However, you can easily supplement your income with **private tuition**. The best times to look for teaching jobs are February and September, although *The Japan Times* always has adverts for teachers in its Monday editions. While you are looking for work, you may be able to stay in a hostel for foreigners—look for adverts in *The Tokyo Journal*—but if you find a regular job, your employer may be able to help you find accommodation.

Workcamps

In many countries, there are voluntary workcamps during the summer which provide an opportunity not only to carry out some useful task but also to stay abroad at little cost for two to four weeks and meet other people at the same time. What you have to do in the camps depends on where you are, and some are much harder work than others. Typical projects might involve building a children's adventure playground or a facility for the disabled. There are lots of camps in France and Morocco and you do not always have to speak a local language to join in.

If you would like to participate in a workcamp you need to make arrangements in the UK. The *International Directory of Voluntary*

Work (Vacation Work) lists the addresses of organisations arranging workcamps. The Quaker Workcamps are particularly popular but competition for places is fierce. You can contact them at Friends House, Euston Road, London NW1 2BJ (Tel: (01) 387 3601). International Voluntary Service (IVS), 53 Regent Road, Leicester LE1 6YL (Tel: (0533) 541862) may also be able to offer you a place. You will have to pay your fare to the camp and a registration fee to the organisation placing you; but in return for thirty to forty hours' work a week you will receive free board and lodging.

Couriers

Readers of *The Guardian* and *The Times* will be familiar with the ads placed by camping companies, especially those based in the south of France, looking for couriers for the summer period. Once again, for those prepared to put up with long hours for very little money, this is one way of spending several months out of the UK at little cost. The work mainly involves setting up the camps at the start of the season and then maintaining them over the next few months.

Advertisements are also sometimes placed by long-haul overland companies like **Exodus**, **Top Deck**, **Tracks** and **Contiki** who want drivers, cooks, couriers and mechanics. Since these are often jobs requiring a lot of responsibility, those accepted are usually over 26, single and experienced drivers or travellers. Acceptance of one of these jobs usually entails attending a training course at your own expense. The cost is normally returned when you complete your contract. If you are interested, pick up the brochures of any of the long-haul companies and get in touch with them directly.

Ski resort work

Skiing holidays are notoriously expensive. One way to cut the costs is to find work in one of the resorts, preferably of the sort that leaves you enough time to get in plenty of skiing yourself. Obviously if you are an expert skier you could hope to find work as a ski instructor. For most people the type of work available will be more menial; hotel and bar work, ski technician jobs—fitting boots and skis, catering, and so on.

A very popular option is to apply for work as a chalet girl through companies like **Ski Supertravel, John Morgan, Small World** and **Bladon Lines** which accommodate their clients in chalets with a live-in cook or housekeeper. For these jobs you need to be able to deal with group catering and the normal demands put upon any resort representative or courier. In a few cases cordon bleu standards are required; usually ordinary cooking skills are adequate.

There are several ways to find work in a ski resort:

- Pick up the brochures of ski tour operators from any agency and write to the Personnel Department for advice. *The St James Press Holiday Guide* (Winter edition) lists all the companies and where they operate.

- Apply to the specialist agency **Jobs In The Alps** (PO Box 388, London SW1X 8LX) before the end of September. However, if they do manage to place you, you will have to pay them an agency fee throughout the season.

- Apply for a job on the spot, preferably in the first fortnight of September. It helps to speak the appropriate language but, with perseverance, you should find something.

Australian working holiday visas

These are available for periods of up to one year to single people or childless couples between 18 and 25 (in exceptional circumstances people between 25 and 30 may be accepted) who want to visit Australia and work during their stay. The application form states that the scheme is intended to let you undertake work as an incidental part of your visit and that you should not normally work for more than three months in any one job.

To get a visa you need to show that you have a substantial amount of money (about £1,500 for a six month stay and £2,000 for a year-long visit) in the bank so that you will be able to support yourself while finding work. If you do not actually have this amount of money, you may be able to borrow it for long enough to have your application processed, but you will need to supply an explanation of your sudden wealth.

Applicants in South Wales and Southern England should write to the Australian High Commission, Australia House, The Strand, London WC2B 4LA. Those in North Wales and Northern England should write to the Australian Consulate, Chatsworth House, Lever Street, Manchester M1 2D1. Those in Scotland, Northern Ireland, Northumbria and Tyne and Wear should write to the Australian Consulate, 2nd Floor, Hobart House, 80 Hanover Street, Edinburgh EH2 2DL.

Once you have a working visa, you should not have problems with Immigration; on the other hand, if you arrive in Australia on an ordinary tourist visa, Immigration will want to see a return ticket home again and sufficient funds to support yourself.

Finding work in Australia once you have arrived is not particularly difficult. You could try a branch of the **Commonwealth Employment Service** (CES), the Australian version of our Jobcentres, for advice. There are also private employment agencies—some, like Kelly Girl, with branches in the UK; and hotel and bar work can be found simply by asking around.

While in Australia, you might like to try your hand at some of the more unusual forms of work like grape-picking, tobacco-picking, working on a sheep farm or mining. Even if you do not have a working holiday visa you should have no difficulty finding work.

Nicaraguan work brigades

For those with ideological commitments, the Nicaraguan Solidarity Campaign organises **international work brigades** to pick coffee or work on reafforestation projects. Coffee-picking goes on from November to March, while the reafforestation work is carried out in June, July and August. Travel arrangements are organised in co-operation with Progressive Tours and everyone has the chance to spend one or two weeks looking round Nicaragua at the end of their stint. Work brigades are not cheap because you must pay £850-£900 for your air fare, board, and so on. However, the Nicaraguan Solidarity Campaign supplies those applying for work with a leaflet suggesting ways of raising the fare from sponsorship. The leaflet emphasises that the work is hard, the weather hot and the accommodation basic, but points out that there have even been volunteers in their seventies.

To apply for a placement write to NSC Brigades, 23 Bevenden Street, London N1 6BH, enclosing an SAE. Applications for brigades before Christmas should be made by mid-June, those for after Christmas by the end of July.

Voluntary Services Overseas (VSO)

If you are prepared to commit yourself to two years overseas on local salaries then VSO could be for you. Nowadays most applicants have specific qualifications that make them useful in the host country. Volunteers are particularly needed in the following fields: agriculture, forestry, fisheries, education, librarianship, health, business, commerce, technical trades, crafts, engineering, community and social development. You can usually indicate an area where you would like to work, but VSO does not operate worldwide—for example, it does not have a programme in India. Recruitment takes place three times a year. Contact VSO at 9 Belgrave Square, London SW1X 8PW (Tel: (01) 235 5191).

Voluntary agencies

Other voluntary agencies that you could approach to find an overseas placement include:

Oxfam, Oxfam House, 274 Banbury Road, Oxford OX2 7DZ (Tel: (0865) 56777).
CIIR, 22 Coleman Fields, London N1 7AF (Tel: (01) 354 0883).
Tear Fund, 100 Church Road, Teddington, Middlesex TW11 8QE (Tel: (01) 997 9144).

UNAIS, 3 Whitehall Court, London SW1A 2EL (Tel: (01) 930 0679).

Project Trust, Breacachadh Castle, Isle of Coll, Argyll PA78 5TB (Tel: (087) 93357). For people aged 17½ to 19.

Gap Activity Projects, 7 Kings Road, Reading (Tel: (0734) 5945914). For people aged 17½ + between school and university.

Christians Abroad, 11 Carteret Street, London SW1H 9DL (Tel: (01) 222 2165).

British Council of Churches, Youth Unit Section, 2 Eaton Gate, London SW1 (Tel: (01) 730 9611).

Concordia (Youth Service Volunteers), Brunswick Place, Hove, Sussex BN3 1ET (Tel: (0273) 772086).

United Nations Association, Wales, The Welsh Centre for International Affairs, Temple Of Peace, Cathays Park. Cardiff (Tel: (0222) 28549).

International Voluntary Service, 3 Belvoir Street, Leicester LE1 6SL (Tel: 0533) 541862).

Missions To Seamen, St Michael Paternoster Royal, College Hill, London ECAR 2RL (Tel: (01) 248 7442). For British seamen.

VMM, Shenley Lane, London Colney, St Albans, Herts AL2 1AR (Tel: (0727) 24853).

United Nations Volunteers, Palais Des Nations, 1211 Geneva 10, Switzerland (Tel: (010) 4122 985850).

British Executive Service Overseas, 10 Belgrave Square, London SW1X 8PW (Tel: (01) 235 0991). For retired executives.

EC Young Workers Exchange programme

This scheme is open to people aged 18 to 28 who are nationals of an EC member state and employed or registered unemployed, and who would otherwise have only limited opportunities to travel. To make it possible for them to do so the programme pays 75% of their transport costs, as well as all accommodation costs.

Short-term schemes of three weeks to three months offer a programme of meetings and visits to find out about a particular local industry or profession. Long-term schemes involve six months' practical work experience, with two month's language tuition provided beforehand to enable participants to get as much as possible out of their visit.

For more details write to Nick Wood, Intercultural Educational Programmes, Seymour Mews House, Seymour Mews, London W1H 9PE (Tel: (01) 486 5101).

Working as an 'Assistant'

Foreign language students and graduates can also look for work in EC schools. In particular, people aged 18 to 20 with A-level French can go to work, under supervision, as **assistants** in French schools. In return they usually receive free board, subsidised meals and a small allowance.

This work is very popular, and you need to apply by June of the year preceding the one in which you want to work at the latest.

People between 20 and 30 who are either studying modern languages or have completed a course within the previous two years can apply for short-term placements in schools elsewhere.

To find out more about these schemes write to The Central Bureau, Seymour Mews House, Seymour Mews, London W1H 9PE (Tel: (01) 486 5101).

Normal employment outside the EC

There are a few places left in the world, including Hong Kong and South Africa where you can still look for work without much trouble. Start your hunt as you would at home, through newspapers and agencies.

Casual work

Even if you do not go abroad with the intention of working to finance your trip, there may be occasions when shortage of cash forces you to look for ways to make money. If so, try all the usual sources of casual work—farms, factories, hotels, bars, building sites and so on. However, it you have a particular talent, you might be able to turn it to profit instead. For example, if you can play the guitar, accordion or flute or if you have a good singing voice or dancing ability, you might be able to pick up cash **busking** at beach resorts or in European town centres. Obviously, you risk being moved on by the police but probably not before you have made the price of a few drinks.

If you are artistic, you might also be able to turn your hand to a spot of pavement art in city centres. You could even try making and selling small craft items like jewellery, using locally-produced shells, gems, and so on.

Other ways to make money

In normal circumstances it is probably better not to resort to selling blood. However, in an emergency it is worth knowing that you can do so in Spain, Italy, Greece, West Germany and the USA. As the AIDS epidemic takes a grip, though, it would be crazy to try selling blood in anything other than the most hygienic circumstances. As an alternative, men can sometimes sell sperm to sperm banks in the UK, USA and Israel. Women may also be able to find work in topless bars.

If you are faced with penury, remember that you may be able to raise money by selling some of your belongings, particularly outside Europe. I held an ad hoc auction in a Khartoum market once; it did not make me a fortune but it certainly lightened my luggage, raised the cost of a few meals and caused much amusement into the bargain.

Whatever you do, try to keep your dignity. Countries with real beggars to support can do without foreigners joining them, and although you can certainly raise funds by scavenging for abandoned bottles which offer refunds, you may well be doing some child out of their livelihood.

THE WINSTON CHURCHILL MEMORIAL TRUST

The **Winston Churchill Memorial Trust** provides approximately 100 travelling fellowships every year to UK citizens of any age who propose a study project related to their trade, profession or interests and which requires a period of about eight weeks spent abroad. Each year, awards are made in approximately a dozen categories, such as urban renewal, marketing and retailing, or the maintenance and renewal of woodlands and forests. These categories are announced in the summer and all applications must have been received by October of the same year. The categories offered change each year to give everybody a chance. The Trustees of the scheme emphasise that no educational or professional qualifications are required, but that candidates need to show that they will make effective use of what they have learnt when they return to the UK.

For further information, contact The Winston Churchill Memorial Trust, 15 Queens Gate Terrace, London SW7 5PR (Tel: (01) 584 9315).

INCOME TAX

Many countries now operate a **Pay As You Earn (PAYE)** system of collecting tax, which is based on the assumption that what you earn each month is a twelfth of what you will earn in the year as a whole. So if you only work for part of any tax year you will pay out more in tax than you should do, and can reclaim the surplus as a **rebate**. However, usually you will have to wait until the end of the current tax year for your rebate. If you have worked for a while in one country and are then moving on, let the local tax office know that you do not propose to earn any more in that year.

Obviously, this applies in the UK too. If you only work for a few months and then give up your job to go travelling, you may well be eligible for a rebate on some of the tax you have already paid. The UK tax year runs from April to April, and rebates are often only available at the end of the period.

20
Turning Your Travels
Into Hard Cash

There are several ways to recoup some or all of the costs of your trip on your return to the UK. These include:

- Selling items bought abroad (see **Bargain-Hunting Overseas**).
- Selling your photographs.
- Selling stories to magazines or newspapers.
- Giving lectures.

PHOTOGRAPHY

If you want to sell pictures of your travels, you will need to plan ahead since there are few markets for ordinary holiday snapshots.

Equipment

In the first place you need to invest in reasonable photographic equipment; a **35 mm camera with ultra-violet filter**, **wide angle lens** and **zoom lens** is the minimum required. Bear in mind the sort of climatic conditions you will be dealing with. If it will be very humid buy **silica gel** to put in with your films and lenses to protect them against mould. Silica gel is available from chemists but comes in large packs, so buy it beforehand and repackage according to your needs. If it will be very sunny make sure you have suitable filters for your lenses. If it will be very dusty take lots of plastic bags to wrap your cameras in to protect them. You should also buy a lead-lined bag to protect your films from airport X-ray machines if you will be flying.

Cost of equipment	*Approximate price*
35 mm camera	£170.00
Wide angle lens (Vivitar)	£45.00
Zoom lens (Vivitar 70–210 mm)	£93.00
Silica gel (500 grams)	£3.50
Lead bag	£8.00
Filters	£4.00

To these basic costs you will also need to add the price of cases to protect the camera body and lenses. A thick neck strap is also worth considering.

Restrictions on photography

If your photography is intended to be more commercial than commemorative, you will need to bear in mind certain inconvenient facts. In some countries you actually need a **permit** to take pictures, although this may be issued for free. Sudan is one country where you must sign a form promising not to take any unflattering pictures before you will be allowed to use your cameras. In Muslim countries taking pictures of women—or indeed taking pictures of any people—may not be advisable, and in many countries you will be expected to pay for the pictures you take. In Marrakesh, for example, the colourful water-sellers expect payment for posing, and in Tanzania the Masai make a good living from passing photographers. Of course, there are no set fees for these pictures but you can easily find out the going rate from other travellers.

There is no market for colour print photos in the UK; if you want to sell your pictures you need to take either good quality black and white prints or colour slides. Ideally you should carry two cameras, one loaded with colour film, the other with black and white.

Developing film

Obviously, if you want to take pictures with a view to selling them, you need to buy plenty of film which can bump up your costs. It will also be expensive to develop the films when you get home, unless you have a dark-room and can do your own developing. It's easy to learn how to develop black and white film; colour is a different matter altogether and best left to the professionals.

The cheapest developing services are usually offered by mail order firms like **Bonusprint**, 20 Wellacre Road, Kenton, Middlesex HA3 0BN (Tel: (01) 953 9911) and **Truprint**, Argyle Way, Stevenage, Herts SG1 2AR (Tel: (08894) 5100). During the summer their purpose-designed envelopes are usually available at Post Offices. Surprisingly few films go astray in the post. If yours does, it's worth knowing that the Small Claims Court has awarded compensation, ruling that disclaimers of liability on the envelopes in effect form an unfair contract term. Obviously, these companies deal mainly with holiday snapshots. For more professional services consult a guide like the *Freelance Photographers Market Handbook*.

Perhaps even more surprisingly few films posted from overseas get lost. If you are away for a long time, you may think it worth sending your pictures home rather than risk them being damaged by prolonged exposure to humidity, airport X-ray machines and potential luggage thieves. As airport security is tightened so even hold baggage is likely to be X-rayed so it may be safer to get films developed before posting. However, always check on the standard of developing before committing yourself; black and white films are sometimes wrecked by unprofessional machine-developing overseas.

Selling your photos

If you are serious about financing your trip in this way, then you need to do some advance research. Consider the sort of magazines or newspapers that might be interested in your pictures and then study the type of photographs they use. Do they want scenery shots or pictures featuring people? Some magazines provide detailed information for intending contributors. For example Wexas, publishers of *The Traveller*, require at least thirty colour transparencies and twenty black and white photos to be submitted with each feature article sent in for consideration. They even go so far as to suggest that Kodachrome film is preferable to Ektachrome and which colours and contrasts are most acceptable.

Travel magazines are one obvious market for your pictures, but most magazines and newspapers have a travel section which may be another possibility. If you have some particularly suitable pictures you could also try some of the main tour operators to see if they would buy the pictures for their brochures. The addresses of all ABTA tour operators are published in the *TTG Travel Trade Directory*. Look up the name of the company in an alphabetical listing first to find out which town it is based in. Then look in a second alphabetical listing for each town to find the full address.

If you have taken a large number of good quality transparencies you could also try approaching an agency, although they would charge 50% commission on arrangements they make for the use of the pictures. Agency addresses are included in *The Freelance Photographers Market Handbook*. One agency that is particularly interested in travel pictures is the James Davis Worldwide Photographic Travel Library, 30 Hengistbury Road, New Milton, Hants BH25 7LU (Tel: (0425) 610328).

If you have never taken commercial pictures before, don't bank on selling your photos since you will be competing against professionals. It's probably wiser to think of photography as one possible way of recouping a little of the money you paid out.

WRITING ARTICLES

You may not want to pay for and carry all the equipment needed to become a travel photographer, but anyone with a good grasp of English can try writing articles about their travels. For this the only equipment needed is a pen, a notebook and an eye for detail.

Again, you need to have thought about the possibilities before you set out. Buy the magazines or newspapers you think you could write for and analyse what they publish very carefully. Unromantic as this may seem, you need to sit down and count the words in the articles, study the type of titles they like, think about whether the articles are anecdotal or factual, and so on. You probably won't get very far if you submit a marvellous 5,000-word serious account of your travels to a paper that uses 1,000-word witty stories.

There are innumerable possible markets for travel articles, but remember that you will be competing against professionals when you submit your stories to national newspapers and magazines. A better bet may be to try one of the London freebies which specialises in advertising travel products, particularly:

1. *TNT*, Ross Stokes (Editor), 52 Earls Court Road, London W8 6EJ (Tel: (01) 937 3985).
2. *Trailfinder*, Linda Zeff (Editor), 14 Oxford Gardens, London N20 9AG (Tel: (01) 445 3192).
3. *LAW*, Paul Jollands (Editor), 5 Mallow Street, London EC1Y 8QR (Tel: (01) 253 1680).
4. *Southern Cross*, Tim Grimwade (Editor), 121 Warwick Road, London SW5 9EZ (Tel: (01) 244 6529).

Your local paper may also be interested in articles concentrating on what a local resident has been up to abroad. In fact, it may be worth contacting them before you leave in case some angles would be more marketable than others. Of course, there are also plenty of specialist publications which might be interested in your trip. A cycling magazine, for example, might buy your story about how you pedalled across the Sahara, while a magazine for walkers might be interested in the precise details of one of your treks. The names, addresses and editorial requirements of most publications can be found in either *Willing's Press Guide* (your library will have a copy) or in *The Writer's and Artist's Year Book*.

If you want to write for publication, you will need to take plenty of notes while away and make sure you have all the details to fill out your articles. It helps to draft them during the actual journey, or at least to think through the themes carefully. There is nothing more infuriating than sitting down to write about that lovely meal you ate at such and such a place, only to discover you do not remember its name or precise address.

Even if you don't want to become an expert photographer, your articles are likely to be more marketable if you can submit appropriate pictures with them. So try to invest in a 35 mm automatic camera at the very least, and get used to taking slides or black and white pictures.

LECTURES

If you are good at speaking in front of people, you might also consider talking about your travels when you get back. Obviously, you are more likely to be in demand if you've travelled further afield than Paris or Majorca, although even these offer possibilities if you can find an original approach.

There are several ways to find venues for lectures. In the first place you could contact your Local Education Authority and see whether you might be able to fit a talk into their evening class programme. There may be other local organisers of evening classes, like a Workers Educational Association group, to contact as well.

Alternatively you could contact a local university or polytechnic. Some of these have geography or exploration societies which are always looking for speakers.

There is also the **Globetrotters Club** which meets in London once a month. There you will be speaking to experienced travellers and standards are usually very high. However, it is a good way to get to know other travellers. Contact Globetrotters via BCM Roving, London WC1N 3XX.

If you want to give talks when you return home, once again you should consider taking decent photography equipment with you, since all the best travel talks incorporate slides or film.

You are unlikely to make your fortune giving lectures. LEAs pay proper rates, but often you will only be offered your expenses or a meal. So if your sole motive for speaking would be to make money, make sure you find out about the pay first.

Making money from your trip – your tax position

The information given in this chapter is based on the assumption that you are hoping to make incidental money from your travels. If you go into travel photography or writing more seriously, you can off-set some of the costs against tax. In that case, make sure you keep all your receipts, and itemise your expenses as you go along. You will need to register yourself as self-employed and present your accounts once a year. You should also keep the drafts and published copies of your articles to show to the Inland Revenue Inspectors, should they want proof of your business status.

21
Turning Problems Into Cash Bonuses

Low budget travellers may be particularly interested in ways of making money out of travel problems. This is sometimes possible when you are booked on a flight that turns out to be full, or when something in the holiday you paid for does not match up to your expectations.

BUMPING

Bumping is what happens when passengers arrive to check in for a flight only to find that it is overbooked and there are no seats available, even if they hold confirmed reservations.

Airlines are aware that a proportion of passengers who reserve seats on a flight may not turn up, and they don't charge them. However, to cover the costs of these 'no-shows' they do overbook flights as a matter of routine—so if everyone *does* show up, there isn't enough space available. If you fly on a non-IATA airline there is an even worse risk of being bumped without compensation.

Airline compensation procedures

European airlines have a voluntary **code of conduct** to deal with this situation. On an international flight if they cannot get you to your destination within four hours of your scheduled flight arrival time on one of their planes or on another airline, you are entitled to compensation amounting to half the one-way fare, up to a maximum of £150. If you were booked on a domestic flight, compensation is due if they cannot get you to your destination within two hours of the expected time. The airline should also provide you with appropriate meals and accommodation free of charge.

However if the delay has serious consequences—for example, if it causes you to miss connecting flights—you can refuse to accept this compensation and sue the airline. If that is what you decide to do, then do not sign any forms accepting compensation under the code of conduct.

Most American airlines ask for volunteers to be bumped from overbooked flights. In return they are given cash compensation or a free ticket. However, if not enough people come forward the airlines are obliged to offer compensation of up to USD400 (£233). BA and KLM have started a similar system of asking for volunteers in Europe. With luck the idea will spread.

Even if you are bumped from a charter flight you should receive compensation, so don't let yourself be fobbed off with excuses.

Inevitably if you are bumped from a smaller Third World carrier, you can expect a harder battle for compensation. It is worth a try and perseverance has been known to bring results, but don't bank on it.

WHEN YOUR HOLIDAY DOESN'T MEET EXPECTATIONS

When you book a package holiday, a contract is formed between you and the tour operator. The operator is obliged to provide the holiday as described in the brochure, and to a reasonable standard bearing in mind the cost. If you are dissatisfied with your holiday in some specific way and cannot resolve the difficulty at the resort, write to the operator and explain what went wrong. If you are offered compensation which you regard as inadequate, write again. If you are sent a cheque for a sum less than you think reasonable, do not bank it.

If you are still not satisfied, you can ask **ABTA** (The Association of British Travel Agents) to attempt **conciliation** for you. If you are still unhappy, you can then appeal through ABTA for independent **arbitration** providing you are not claiming more than £1,000 per head or £5,000 per booking form. Finally you can make a claim through the County Court.

Claiming compensation

A *Holiday Which?* survey on this subject concluded that it was worth suggesting how much compensation you expected, since people who specified an amount often received it. They broke down what you could claim for under the following headings:

- **Loss of value**. The difference between the value of the holiday you booked and the one you received.
- **Loss of enjoyment**. Compensation for disappointment.
- **Expenses**. Refund of reasonable expenses incurred as a result of the holiday's deficiencies, for example for extra meals bought away from your hotel because the restaurant was closed.

The survey also suggested persevering with claims, since those who held out longest seemed to be awarded the most. County Court settlements were usually for the largest sums, although the magistrates were less consistent in their decisions than the ABTA arbitrators. ABTA is at 55-7 Newman Street, London W1P 4AH (Tel: (01) 637 2444).

The EC is currently studying tour operators' liability and has talked of making operators responsible for every aspect of the holidays advertised in their brochures. This has particularly significant implications for long-haul operators, especially at the budget end of the market (Intasun started programmes to Goa, Bangkok and Acapulco in 1989). They hope the changes will be restricted to European holidays. If the changes are approved they should be publicised in the papers, so keep your eyes peeled.

Lost baggage

With more and more people flying round the world each year, an increasing number of bags fail to arrive with their owners at their destination. The majority turn up eventually, although you may have been greatly inconvenienced in the meantime. The **Warsaw Convention** defines permanent loss as occurring if the bag has not shown up after three weeks. The airlines should then pay you USD20 (£11.62) per kilogramme of lost baggage. Even if you had been carrying baggage weighing the normal maximum twenty kilos you would only receive £232.55, a sum unlikely to cover the cost of replacing everything, so make sure you take out adequate insurance.

If you arrive at your destination and your bag is obviously lost somewhere en route, the airline should provide you with USD50 (£29.00) to pay for replacement clothing for the first three days. However some Far Eastern airlines will lend you emergency clothing packs instead of handing over money. Again, if the airline which has lost your bag is from an impoverished Third World country, do not hold out too much hope of extracting on-the-spot cash.

Delayed departure

The last two summers have brought the problem of delayed flight departures into prominence as some people waited more than a day for their holiday to get off the ground. If your flight is delayed, the compensation you can claim varies depending on which company you booked with, what insurance you took out and how you paid for the holiday.

Budget travellers do not usually pay for their flights with American Express or Diners Club cards. However, if you can do so, there are definite advantages. If you use one of these cards to pay for a scheduled flight which is delayed by up to four hours, you can use your card to buy food and drink worth up to £100 in airport restaurants to see you through the wait. If you miss a connection as a result of the delay and have to wait another four hours, you can buy more meals on the card and use it to pay for accommodation worth up to £100. These costs are covered by the card companies' insurance, and you will not be billed for the money spent provided all of it has been charged to the card.

Package holidaymakers on charter flights would only be as lucky as the small print in the front of the tour operator's brochure. Intasun guarantees to compensate passengers for delays of over twelve hours and allows them to cancel at little or no cost if the delay continues, but usually compensation is only available to people who have taken out insurance with a 'delayed departure' policy. Few people profit from hanging around at Gatwick.

22
Miscellaneous
Money Saving Tips

CARDS

To make sure you save money whenever possible, try to leave Britain with as many of the following cards as possible:

International Student Identity Card (ISIC)

Available from student unions and STA Travel and Campus Travel offices throughout the country for a charge of £4.00, ISIC cards are invaluable for getting discounts on flights, buses, trains, and so on. They also qualify their holders for **reduced entry charges** at many worldwide museums and art galleries. For example, in Egypt there is an entirely separate ticket booth at Luxor for ISIC cardholders to obtain reduced price entry to the Valleys of the Kings, Queens and Nobles.

Because ISIC cards are so useful, there is a flourishing black market supplying them to non-students. Athens is one town where you may be able to pick up a card for a small fee.

To get an ISIC card, you need proof of the educational establishment you are attending and two passport-sized photographs, signed on the reverse. Since the card will be stamped by the union to validate it, forgery is not as easy as many people seem to think. It's also worth knowing that the colour of the cards changes yearly. If you will be away for a long time, you may also need a letter of identification from your college as subsidiary proof of student status.

Example of discounts available to ISIC cardholders
- 50% off Egyptian train fares
- Camping for about 50p a night in Hungary
- Discounts on Greek inter-island ferries
- 50% off Danish museum and art gallery entry fees
- Reduced price entry to some Turkish and Parisian cinemas

Youth International Educational Exchange Card (YIEE):

If you are under 26 but not a student you could buy a YIEE card which looks very like an ISIC card. This also bears a passport-sized photograph and brings some of the same travel discounts as an ISIC card. The card comes with a booklet listing the various discounts available around the world. However, in practice some places listed, like Toledo in Spain, do not recognise it while other places which are not listed do, so it is always worth asking.

A YIEE card costs £3.50 and can be obtained from the Central Bureau of Educational Visits and Exchanges, Seymour Mews House, Seymour Mews, London W1H 9PE, or from STA Travel and Campus Travel offices.

Youth Hostels Association Card

If you are a UK citizen, over 26 and cannot get a student card it may be worth joining the YHA even if you don't intend to use hostels, since the YHA card is occasionally accepted as proof of eligibility for youth fares, for example in parts of Egypt. Non-UK residents can buy an International Youth Hostels Federation (IYHF) card from STA Travel offices for £6.00.

British Rail Cards

Even though you are travelling outside the UK, it may still be worth taking your British Rail discount cards with you. The Senior Citizens and Family Railcards bring discounts in Europe as well, provided they are topped up with European cards. (see **Special Deals For Special People**.)

DEALING WITH BEGGARS AND UNSOLICITED GUIDES

Beggars

Many travellers in Third World countries are shocked by the poverty and overwhelmed by the problem of deciding how to deal with beggars who surround them on the streets, at tourist sights and even on public transport. Try to keep the problem in perspective. Although tourists are an inevitable target for beggars since they are automatically deemed to be, and are, wealthy compared with the locals, some travellers develop a paranoid suspicion that they are being picked on, when a quick look round should reassure them that beggars try everybody, and have to in countries where there are few welfare services.

The best thing to do is decide on a strategy and stick to it so that each encounter does not present a new dilemma. If you want to give to beggars, keep plenty of small change. Do not give a large note to one person; in the first place it's unfair, and in the second you will attract attention and a crowd of other hopefuls. Since it is difficult to select the most worthy cases, and there are horrific stories of children being mutilated on purpose to make them more attractive as beggars, you may prefer not to give at all. If you do make such a decision, you'll need to develop a very thick skin to ignore some of the most appalling sights. When you come home again, you might like to help in a more organised, long-term way by donating to one of the charities working to improve conditions in the world's poorest countries.

Unsolicited guides

Different from the beggars but even trickier to handle are the unsolicited 'guides' and 'friends' who throng Third World towns with large tourist trades. Of course, there are plenty of people who will genuinely want to befriend you and practise their English, but there are just as many who want to make money out of you, honestly or otherwise. If anyone offers to show you around make sure you discuss terms first, however embarrassing that may seem. Try and have a cup of tea with them before going anywhere so you have a chance to assess their honesty. Too many tourists have been led into the warren-like medinas of Morocco, only to have their guide refuse to show them the way back unless they pay more. There are also *klong* boatmen in Bangkok who will waft you far from shore and then refuse to return you until you have handed over an enormous sum. Be particularly wary when you first arrive somewhere and are still getting your bearings; it is easy to be swept away on a wave of euphoria at your new surroundings, at which point you are easy prey for the unscrupulous.

The chances are that you will not want a guide at all, particularly if you have got a good guidebook, but if you do want one it may be best to ask the tourist office to arrange for an official one: their prices may be higher but they usually speak better English and know more about the sights, and since they have a proper income and employer, they should be less tempted to rip you off by taking you on a tour of the shops where they earn commission.

Choosing the right guide

However, in some places it is virtually impossible to escape the offers and the harassment can take on nightmarish proportions. It may help to remind yourself that it is usually borne of poverty and lack of alternative employment, but unless you want your trip to turn into a series of arguments, it may be best to bow to the inevitable and set out to choose someone before they choose you. Many people find younger boys more amenable and less threatening than their older brothers. Others will place more emphasis on finding someone with a good grasp of their language. Once you have found someone reliable, stick with them through your trip. For the price of an extra tip at the end you should be protected against further harassment and may actually end up making a real friend.

Unfortunately, you still need to be careful even of people who say they do not want money. Beware of going anywhere with a group of strangers unless someone knows where you will be and what time you should be back. Be particularly cautious if drugs, however soft, are on offer; few countries smile on them and some 'friends' will ship you to the police if you take what they offer. Avoid taking valuables with you until you get to know people well: there have been many instances of travellers fed doped food or drink and then robbed while they were asleep. At the very least, you may come under pressure to give things away that you would rather hang on to.

Women and guides

It goes without saying that women need to be even more cautious about who they trust than men do. Sadly, they may also have to accept that they can make things harder for themselves by trying to swim against the tide. For example, a lone woman in Morocco is in for a very rough ride; however much she may prefer travelling alone, she will be better off pairing up with someone else to help with the hustlers.

Despite these warnings, there would be little point in going abroad if you avoided all contact with local people for fear of being swindled. Some of the happiest times I have had when travelling have been when I have been befriended by someone. It just pays to be careful.

BRIBERY AND CORRUPTION

For most westerners, offering someone a bribe is hardly an everyday occurence; but in the Third World there are situations where you will make very little headway unless you accept that this is the norm.

Frequently the question of bribes arises at borders (see **Cutting The Cost Of The Paperwork**) where Immigration officials sometimes require sweeteners to let you through. When approaching a known dodgy border, some travellers advise inserting a banknote in your passport. Although it may almost seem like inviting trouble, and might cause difficulties if the official turns out to be straight, you could always claim you had forgotten where you put the money; with luck, they might turn a blind eye anyway. However, it may not just be those with the entry stamps you have to contend with. At the border between Tanzania and Zambia, for example, Customs officials on the Tanzanian side who come aboard the trains sometimes want bribes to turn a blind eye to illegal currency exchanges, while on the Zambian side the official responsible for checking cholera certificates has been known to expect a 'gift' even when they are in order. In such situations, it is wise to pay up rather than risk prosecution for breaking the law or being ejected from the train in the middle of nowhere.

Occasionally, you may get the impression that a supposedly overbooked bus or train, or an apparently full hotel might have space after all if you offered more than the normal price. Depending on how much time and energy you have to spare, it might be best to regard this as tipping rather than bribery and just get on with it.

Bribery and the police

The trickiest situations to handle are those involving the police. If they stop you, you will have to decide whether you really are in trouble or whether they're just after extra cash. You might try a line such as 'in our country we have a system of on-the-spot fines. Do you have something similar here?', but bear in mind that an honest cop could be very upset if offered a bribe. In that case, if you weren't in trouble beforehand, you very soon would be.

The difficulty with all of these situations is that few people, even the most corrupt, come straight out with their demands. Usually, you have nothing more to go on than body language and pregnant pauses. However, since some officials are notorious for liking to make people sweat, even these can be deceptive. Offering a bribe is almost always an offence, so you stand to land yourself in trouble if you make a mistake; on the other hand, if you don't, you could face a night in an unsalubrious cell with a court case and fine to follow. If you are reluctant to offer a bribe, you could try name-dropping or claiming to be a journalist or someone else with influence. But if you do decide to come up with the money, do not make it too much in case you are labelled wealthy and a soft touch. Probably the only thing you can do to protect yourself is to read the latest guidebooks and ask other travellers, who may know more about local expectations. If in doubt, err on the side of caution.

COLLECTING YOUR MAIL

If you intend to be away for any length of time, friends may need to be able to contact you. In most parts of the world, mail will be held at central post offices for you to collect. Sometimes you will need to show a passport or other means of identification and occasionally a small charge will be levied. Never assume that parcels sent 'Post Restante' to poorer parts of the world will stay untouched until you come to collect them.

'Poste Restante'

Different post offices handle 'Poste Restante' mail with varying degrees of efficiency. However, even the most conscientious are sometimes baffled by non-local names; so to ensure your mail is correctly pigeon-holed, ask everyone to address it according to the following format:

P. YALE
Poste Restante
Main Post Office (Lista de Correos in South America; PTT in French-
    speaking countries)
Street
Town
Country

If you are sure a letter should be there but clerks tell you it isn't, ask them to check under your initials as well as your surname before despairing.

Holders of American Express travellers cheques have the bonus of being able to use American Express offices worldwide as mailing addresses. When you call to collect your mail, you will be asked to show your cheques, or credit card, but will not usually be charged. On the whole less mail seems to go astray this way, so it is a definite perk of using their services.

Do not expect mail to be kept indefinitely. In most cases it will be returned to its sender if you have not collected it after a month.

GENERAL TIPS

In Italy, beware of charges to use the beach. Elsewhere be warned that you are usually expected to pay for deckchairs, parasols, and so on.

Several countries have **entertainment** or **leisure cards** which offer discounts on transport and entrance fees. Visitors to The Netherlands, for example, can buy the Holland Leisure Card, valid for one year and costing £6.00. Before buying such a card, however, always check exactly what is on offer—if you are not planning to visit any of the attractions using the scheme, then you are unlikely to recoup your costs. The Copenhagen Card costs DKR60 (£5.00) for one day, DKR110 (9.00) for two days and DKR150 (£12.50) for three days, and offers discounts on museum entrance fees and buses and trams.

There are also sometimes special discount arrangements for foreigners. For example, in Yugoslavia you can use your foreign currency to buy dinar cheques which offer 10% discounts in tourist shops.

Public lavatories are often quite expensive to use and frequently far from hygienic, especially outside Europe. Your best bet is to smarten up and stride confidently into the downstairs toilets of a luxury hotel. If challenged you can always claim sudden ill-health.

Remember that if you need to make long-distance phone calls for information in the UK, calls made between 0900 and 1300 (Mondays to Fridays) are charged at peak rates. Between 0800 and 0900, and between 1300 and 1800 (Mondays to Fridays) calls are charged at standard rates. The cheapest rate applies from 1800 in the evening and all weekend. If you don't need an answer quickly, it is often cheaper to write.

Leaving home – a final checklist

Finally, it doesn't matter how carefully you budgeted for your holiday if you come back to find your house burgled. Much of the cost may be recoverable through insurance, but there are usually incidental costs which you have to pay yourself. Ideally you will already have installed locks on your windows and doors or a burglar alarm, but even if you haven't you can reduce the likelihood of a burglary by taking the following simple precautions:

- Cancel milk, papers and other regular deliveries.

- Leave a key with a trusted neighbour who can pull curtains and turn on lights in the evenings, so it looks as if you are home.

- Ask someone to push all mail, including free newspapers, right through your letterbox every day.

- Look for a house-sitter who will take care of things in your absence in return for a reduced or non-existent rent. It is better to ask a friend—perhaps someone from another town who would be glad of a break—rather than use an agency who will charge for finding somebody. If you are going to be away for a long time, and own your own home, you could consider sub-letting it, particularly if it's in London where there's a considerable demand for flats to let to business travellers. If you do do this, bear in mind that it is a major undertaking, best arranged with an estate agent who can act as manager in your absence in return for a fee. Make an inventory of everything you own and inform the utilities, your insurance company and the building society if you have a mortgage. Do not expect to make a huge profit from such an arrangement but it is one way to pay the bills while you're away.

- Don't forget to turn off the gas, water and electricity if your home is going to be empty to guard against fire, flood and other expensive accidents in your absence.

TRAVELLING THROUGH WAR ZONES AND AREAS OF HOSTILITY

Sadly, many parts of the world which would otherwise be attractive to travellers are either completely closed to them or difficult and dangerous to visit. The situation can change overnight, so it is vital to keep up with the news and to check with the relevant embassies before travelling. For example as this book was going to press Burma (Myanmar) was closed and then reopened to travellers as a result of rioting, while China was reopened to tourists for the first time since the massacre in Beijing. Tibet has also been on and off itineraries at regular intervals, depending on the state of internal politics. Large parts of northern Sri Lanka have also been closed to tourists as the Tamil Tigers struggled for an independent Tamil state. Finally, the situation in Eastern Europe is changing on an almost daily basis, and may well continue to do so for some time to come.

If you do travel to a war zone or area of tension, or find yourself caught up in one because trouble breaks out after you arrive, it is important to bear in mind the likely impact this will have on your budget.

The additional cost of travelling through a war zone

First of all, if you want to travel between areas which are hostile to each other you may have to pay more for visas and may even have to pay bribes at borders to be allowed to cross. In some cases, you may also need to buy a second passport (see **Cutting The Cost Of The Paperwork**). Some insurance companies are reluctant to cover anyone whose itinerary looks likely to result in a bill, so if you are travelling to a war zone you may have to pay higher premiums; some companies will not insure you at all. Endsleigh Insurance is valid for all countries.

Once inside the country the state of hostilities may mean you have to pay more for transport and accommodation for the sake of safety. Remember that your itinerary may be curtailed by military considerations, and that you may also have to pay for permits to go to areas the authorities would prefer you not to visit.

Hostilities can have varying effects on your plans. In 1984, I visited Sudan just after civil war broke out between north and south. Although I had planned to travel overland to Kenya this proved impossible, and after an extended stay of two months while I tried to find a way out, I eventually resorted to paying a hefty, unplanned air fare to leave the country. The flight took me to Kampala which was also in a state of tension, with a curfew at 1930 every day and shots audible in the streets. I was still able to stay in cheap accommodation there and could use the train to continue my journey. However, plans to visit some of the remoter game parks had to be abandoned since it sounded just too dangerous.

So if your budget really is rock-bottom, stick only to those countries which are peaceful and have stable governments. Otherwise you risk having to pay more than you originally intended for something which may be very different from what you wanted.

Some potential trouble-spots around the world

The Middle East	Lebanon, Israel (especially the West Bank and Gaza Strip), Kurdish areas of Syria, Libya, Iran, Iraq
West Africa	Senegal and Mauritania
Central Africa	Sudan, Chad, Ethiopia (Eritrea and Tigre)
Southern Africa	South Africa, Namibia, Mozambique
Indian Subcontinent	Sri Lanka, Kashmir border areas between India and Pakistan, Burma (Myanmar), Afghanistan, Nepal
The Far East	Cambodia, Laos, Vietnam, North Korea, the border areas between China and Tibet, Thai border areas
Europe	Northern Ireland, Basque areas of Spain, Eastern Europe, Cyprus
Central America	Guatemala, El Salvador, Nicaragua
South America	Argentina, Chile, Peru

23
Special Deals
for Special People

Most of this book has dealt with the needs of able-bodied adults in the 18 to 60 age range. However there are, of course, travellers both older and younger than this and people with disabilities who may also want to see the world at a reasonable cost. Some women travellers may have special needs that can affect their budgets, while those who are happy to travel as a group can often make financial gains from doing so.

INFANTS AND CHILDREN

In the travel world, an **infant** is usually defined as anyone under the age of 2; any older and they become a **child**.

Children travelling by air

As far as most scheduled airlines are concerned, infants are usually carried at 10% of the normal fare, although they are not allocated a seat and have no free baggage allowance. Where there is more than one infant the second is normally treated as a child and charged accordingly.

However on holiday charter flights the first infant is usually carried free. The only payment you will have to make will be a nominal sum—perhaps £15.00 paid directly to the hotelier for use of a cot and for the child's food.

Children over 2 and under 12 pay 50% of scheduled air fares and have their own seat and baggage allowance. On discount fares like APEXes they may be charged more, perhaps 67% of the full adult fare.

Discounted holidays for children

Most tour operators offer discounted holidays for children under 11 or 12. People who book as soon as the brochure is published may even be able to take advantage of a limited number of free holidays for children. However, these are not usually in the high season which, of course, coincides with school holidays. The conditions attached to the discounts vary from company to company. In most cases, the child must be sharing a room with two full fee-paying adults. However a few companies offer discounts for single parent families too, so read the front of each brochure carefully. Two companies which specialise in holidays for one parent families are **Better Life Holidays**, 1 Effingham

254

Street, Ramsgate, Kent CT1 9AT (Tel: (0843) 589855) and **Value Vacations**, Gullivers House, 56 Goswell Road, London EC1M 7AD (Tel: (01) 253 1122).

Children travelling on trains

British Rail carries infants under 5 free and charges half fares for anyone under 15. On the continent, railways regard children under 4 as infants and carry them free. Children aged 4 to 11 generally pay half fare, but check with continental rail agents for precise details.

There is also a **British Rail Family Railcard** which costs £15.00 and is valid for one year. It entitles adults to either half price or one third off standard class tickets. Children travel for £1.00 each. Up to four adults and four children—not necessarily related—can use the same card, provided they travel together. The card can be extended to offer discounts on the Continent by paying a further £5.00 for a **Rail Europ Family Card**, permitting up to eight people living at the same address to benefit from reduced price rail travel. At any one time at least three people, one of whom must be an adult, must travel together. The first adult pays the full fare while others pay reduced prices. Children aged 5 to 11 pay half the adult reduced fare and children aged 4 pay even less.

Children travelling by coach and ferry

As usual, there are no hard and fast rules about bus and coach reductions. However, in the UK National Express carries one infant under 5 and accompanied by an adult free. Children between 5 and 16 pay discounted fares depending on their route.

Most UK-based ferry companies carry children under 4 free and children up to 14 at considerably reduced prices. Sally Line carries the first child aged up to 14 free even on peak price sailings. Hoverspeed also offers family fares with an inclusive price for a car containing up to two adults and two children.

Travel documents for children

Children under the age of 16 can travel on one or both of their parents' passports. After that they must hold their own travel documentation. Where visas are required to enter a country, children and infants must usually have these too. Sadly there are rarely discounts available.

A few insurance companies offer reduced premiums for children, but this is by no means standard and you will need to shop around.

Where adults are required to be vaccinated before they can be admitted to a country, children too will need to be injected. Once again they will have to pay as much as their parents for this. Infants under 1 are not expected to be vaccinated against yellow fever.

YOUNG PEOPLE

Air Fares

Although in most cases passengers become adults as far as the airlines are concerned as soon as they reach 12, nevertheless there are some special youth and student fares available.

In most cases student fares are only offered to people studying abroad and travelling to and from their place of study. With the great increase in the number of 'seat-only' charter fares available, there are fewer and fewer occasions when these fares represent the best value for money. However, if you are studying abroad, check with your travel agent.

Youth fares for people under 22 or 25 are more widely available especially to the Middle East. Again, they do not automatically represent the best value for money but could still be worth checking out. Once overseas, if you do have to fly you may find a youth fare offers a good deal, so always ask if one is available. The **Youth Fare India** offers 25% discount on all domestic air fares within India for up to 120 days to people aged between 12 and 30. However, since it must be paid for in dollars, it only offers a real bargain when the dollar is weak.

Rail fares

The railways are more generous to youthful travellers. For those over 16 and under 24 it's worth investing £16.00 in a **Young Persons Railcard**, for which you will also need two passport-sized photos and evidence of your age, and which is available from main British Rail stations, rail agents and student travel offices. These permit you to travel anywhere in the UK for two thirds of the applicable standard class single, return, saver return, day return or rail rover ticket for one year, although there is often a £3.00 single or £6.00 minimum return fare. Mature students in full-time education can also use these railcards which offer additional benefits like half-price membership of the YHA and discounts on Inter-Rail Cards; benefits vary from year to year so always check the latest British Rail leaflet.

Although the Young Persons Railcard is not valid in Europe, there are many discount rail options for those under 26 (see **Travelling Around Without Busting Your Budget**).

Bus fares

Discounts on bus fares are, as usual, more haphazard. However National Express offers a **Student Coachcard** costing £3.90 which gives those in full-time education 33% off usual fares for a year. These cards are available at student travel offices and National Express and Scottish Citylink agencies. Alternatively, they can be ordered by post although you must then send proof of your student status with the application form.

SENIOR CITIZENS

As people live longer and stay healthy for longer, more of them are choosing to travel in retirement. This trend has also been encouraged by the increasing number of early retirements with golden hand-shakes.

The travel world usually regards anyone over 60 as a senior citizen but, as with child discounts, it's always worth checking whether there are special offers available to anyone over 55.

Rail fares

Unfortunately, airlines are not in the habit of offering discounts to senior citizens, but the railways are much more generous. Anyone over 60, even if they are not resident in the UK, is eligible for a **British Rail Senior Citizen Card** offering one third off standard or first class single, return, saver return, day return and rail rover tickets. The card costs £15.00, is valid for one year and is available from main British Rail Stations and rail agents, on production of proof of age. Furthermore, for an extra £5.00 you can buy a **Rail Europ Senior Card** which offers discounts of up to 50% on railways in Belgium, France, Finland, Greece, Luxembourg, The Netherlands, Portugal, Ireland, Spain and most of Switzerland, and up to 30% on railways in Austria, Denmark, West Germany, Hungary, Italy, Norway, Sweden and Yugoslavia.

Within the UK, National Express offers discounted coach fares to men and women over 60. The amount will depend on the route.

Several tour operators now recognise older clients as a special category and cater for them accordingly. The best known of these is probably **Saga Holidays**, PO Box 65, 119 Sandgate Hill, Sandgate, Folkestone, Kent CT20 3SG (Tel: (0303) 47000). In particular some companies offer long-stay package deals, allowing retired people to spend up to three months of the winter soaking up the sun in somewhere like the Costa del Sol. The price of these deals is very low, so that it can work out considerably cheaper to winter in Spain than in England, if your heating bills are taken into account. For example, long-stay holidays booked through Intasun's Golden Days programme start at £1.95 per day. Contact ILG Travel Ltd, PO Box 228, Bromley, Kent BR1 1LA; (Tel: (01) 290 1900 for a brochure).

Travel documents

If you are thinking of a long-stay holiday, remember that most tourist visas are only valid for three months initially. If you plan to stay longer you may need to pay for an extension.

Some insurance policies exclude 'elderly' travellers, so find out whether there is an upper age limit for cover before taking out a policy. If you have particular medical problems, check that they are not excluded by contacting the insurance company directly. Age Concern produces fact sheets for elderly holidaymakers and offers insurance through a subsidiary company, **Age Concern Insurance Services**, 202 Tooting High Street, London SW17 0SF (Tel: (01) 672 2212). Neither ABTA's Travel Guard nor the AA's Five Star policy has an upper age limit.

DISABLED TRAVELLERS

Air Fares
While scheduled and charter airlines are happy to make special arrangements for disabled clients and will provide wheelchair assistance on request, they do not go as far as offering any discounted fares. RADAR (see below) publishes a guide to the general accessibility of air travel for disabled people.

Rail fares
Once again, the railways do better. The **British Rail Disabled Person's Railcard** offers one third reductions on standard class single, return and saver return tickets and half fares on day returns. Anyone who is registered as blind, partially sighted, deaf and without speech or in receipt of an attendance or mobility allowance or any other disability pension is eligible for a card. A companion travelling with them will also be entitled to the discounts and no charge is made for accompanying guide-dogs. Even disabled travellers without railcards are entitled to some discounted fares, as listed in the leaflet **British Rail and Disabled Travellers**. The Disabled Person's Railcard costs £12.00 and entitles its holder to further discounts on Motorail, shipping services, and so on, for one year.

Useful contacts for disabled people
The **Royal Association for Disability and Rehabilitation (RADAR)** is an organisation devoted to the needs of the disabled. It publishes several useful books, a monthly *Bulletin*, and *Contact*, a quarterly journal, which contains information on many topics including holidays. There is also a *Holiday Fact Sheet* giving the addresses of associations which can help with holiday information for the disabled. The RADAR publication *Holidays And Travel Abroad...A Guide For Disabled People* gives details on travel to more than 40 countries with information about transport, accommodation, tour operators and useful contacts. These can all be obtained by writing to 25 Mortimer Street, London W1N 8AB (Tel: (01) 637 5400).

Another useful source of advice is the **Holiday Care Service**, 2 Old Bank Chambers, Station Road, Horley, Surrey RH6 9HW (Tel: (0293) 774535).

Insurance

Disabled holidaymakers need to be particularly careful when arranging insurance cover. Both RADAR and the Holiday Care Service can advise you, but always check the details of your disability with the insurance company directly. It may help to get a letter from your doctor confirming that you are not travelling against his or her advice. **Mondial** and **Europ Assistance** are two companies worth trying, but if you fail to get insurance through the usual channels, Campbell Irvine Ltd, 48 Earls Court Road, London W8 6EJ (Tel: (01) 937 6981) has a scheme for the physically disabled. Not only will it provide you with a new escort if your own is unavailable, but it will also find another airline or hotel to accommodate you if the one you booked with cannot deal with your wheelchair. **The Traveller's Medical Service**, Golden Square, Petworth, West Sussex GU28 OAP, has a policy which covers the expenses of flying a friend, relative or nurse out to join you and accommodating them if necessary. If you are a member of the **Disabled Drivers' Association**, they will be able to help with motoring insurance abroad. The address is 18 Creekside, London SE8 3D2 (Tel: (01) 692 7141). Those with a mental disability need to be even more careful with insurance since many policies exclude all claims arising from mental illness, including depression or anxiety.

Medical arrangements

If you have specific medical needs, such as access to a kidney dialysis machine, contact the embassy of the country you plan to visit before you go, to find out the nearest hospital to where you plan to stay which has a machine. If they are unable to help you, the Foreign Office here may know the answer. Once you have found out, let the company insuring you know so that you can be rushed there in an emergency.

It's worth noting that the **Youth Exchange Centre** has a special fund to help organise international educational visits for the young disabled. They can be contacted at Seymour Mews House, Seymour Mews, London W1H 9PE (Tel: (01) 486 5101).

Any disabled person, or family with a disabled person, can approach their local DSS office and ask to join one of the holidays they organise for the disabled. Alternatively, they can ask for financial help to make their own holiday arrangements.

WOMEN TRAVELLERS

Of course, women can take advantage of all the special deals mentioned above. However, they often end up paying more for their travels than men do. This is particularly the case in parts of the world where dormitory accommodation is the norm and yet women may not share with men—primarily Muslim countries. In such places, women frequently have to pay for an expensive double room since singles are almost non-existent. Since much cheap accommodation is also found in seedier parts of town, women may also be forced to move upmarket simply to feel safe.

Travel documents

Usually women can obtain insurance cover on the same terms as men. However, if you are seven months pregnant most companies will refuse to cover you, so always check before committing yourself to travel.

As a woman, you may also have difficulty in obtaining a visa for some Muslim countries, particularly if you are travellling alone; expect such problems if you want to visit Saudi Arabia or Libya.

Separate arrangements for women

It's worth bearing in mind that in some Third World countries where women are kept apart from men, there may be separate queues, often shorter, for women. This is sometimes the case in Indian railway stations, but it can even apply in shops in Egypt. The item bought may cost the same but at least it will take less time and hassle to obtain it. It is also worth asking if there are separate sections of buses or trains for women. On the Tazara railway, for example, there are separate sleeping compartments which help to ensure undisturbed nights. However, in other parts of the world such as Afghanistan women often end up travelling on the roofs of buses—in which case it's wiser to emphasise the fact that you are foreign rather than the fact that you are a woman.

Although some women are confident about travelling alone, others worry about the risk of harassment. Consequently more women take up places on escorted overland trips, where they will be protected by being part of a group. Since these excursions are usually more expensive than going it alone, once again they end up paying extra.

There *can* be financial advantages to being female inasmuch as people will often offer hospitality, and even cash, to women when they might feel embarrassed about doing the same for a man. I have met women travellers who were living on virtually nothing since they assumed they would always find men willing to pay for their meals, accommodation and so on. However, all such offers need to be considered carefully. Frequently they come with an unspoken price tag which you may not want to pay.

GROUP TRAVEL

If you are travelling as part of a group of ten or more people, always find out whether there are discounts available. Although there are some group fares on scheduled airlines, these will not always work out cheaper than taking a charter, particularly if the charter company offers a group reduction.

British Rail offers 25% price reductions on all standard class tickets, including Savers, to groups of ten or more people travelling to and from their destination together on the same group ticket. Those aged 16 and 17 are given a 25% discount off the child fare. Those under 4 travel free as usual but are not included as members of the group in terms of the numbers needed to qualify. Except on short journeys and during rush hours, British Rail will reserve seats for all group members included in the ticket charge.

Most tour operators also offer discounts for groups of at least ten people. Normally they must all be travelling together to the same destination for the same length of time to qualify, but conditions vary, so read the front or back of the relevant brochure carefully. There are normally bigger reductions available if you travel in the low season. Sometimes you may qualify for one completely free place for your group leader, although they may still have to pay room or board supplements and the insurance premium.

SPECIAL DIETS

If you have a special diet, whether for reasons of health, religion or conscience, this needs to be taken into account when you make your travel plans. Obviously it helps to holiday in countries where such diets are familiar.

Vegetarians

Vegetarians should be in their element in India and many parts of the Far East; spoilt for choice, they will have no difficulty finding suitable meals at reasonable prices too. Conversely, if they visit countries like Sudan where lamb may be all that is on offer, they will have a hard time of it and may end up paying through the nose for everything they eat.

You can find vegetarian restaurants in most parts of Europe, although some are quite expensive. **Canterbury Travel**, 249 Streatfield Road, Kenton, Middlesex HA3 9BY (Tel: (01) 204 4111), offers tailor-made vegetarian holidays in Austria but they are not particularly cheap. Package holiday hotels vary in their ability to deal with vegetarians. Your best bet may be self-catering or opting for hotels with buffet-style meals which are more likely to have suitable dishes. Contact The Vegetarian Society at 53 Marloes Road, London W8 6LA (Tel: (01) 937 7739) for more information.

Religious diets

Those who eat **kosher** are guaranteed suitable arrangements in Israel or in places with large Jewish populations like parts of north London and New York. Elsewhere, the easiest way to manage may be to become a temporary vegetarian. **Halal** meals are available throughout most of the Middle East and parts of the Indian subcontinent. Elsewhere such diets may be hard to come by and expensive.

Airlines are getting better at providing special meals. Provided you let them know at least 48 hours beforehand, the larger ones should be able to provide at least the following special meals at no extra charge:

Jewish (Kosher/Kedassia), vegetarian (all types), Muslim, diabetic, fat-free, low-calorie, salt-free, gluten-free and low-sodium.

In general, if you have special needs of any kind it is vital to let everyone involved know as soon as possible so that appropriate arrangements can be made. Tell your travel agent if you want a groundfloor room and check that they mark this as a 'special request' on the booking form even if it cannot be guaranteed. Let the airline know if you will need a wheelchair, assistance at the airport, a special meal or a bassinet for your baby. Consult your insurance company about anything that is worrying you before you leave home. The more people who know about the situation the more likely you are to end up with what you need.

COLLEGE STAFF

If you work in a third-level educational establishment it's worth knowing that you are eligible for a **Campus Travel College Staff Card** which will enable you to take advantage of some of the charter flights and other bargains usually restricted to students. Cards are available from Campus Travel offices on production of proof of your employment in a college, polytechnic or university and a passport-sized photograph.

Appendix 1
Worldwide Tourist Offices and Consulate Addresses in the UK

Country	Tourist Office	UK Consulate
Afghanistan		31 Princes Gate, London SW7 1PT. Tel: (01) 589 8891.
Albania	c/o Albturist, Regent Holidays, 13 Small Street, Bristol. Tel: (0272) 211711.	131 Rue de la Pompe, Paris 16, France. Tel: 010-331-553-51-32.
Algeria	6 Hyde Park Gate, London SW7 5EW. Tel: (01) 584 5152.	6 Hyde Park Gate, London SW7 5EW. Tel: (01) 221 7800.
Andorra	63 Westover Road, London SW18 2RF. Tel: (01) 874 4806.	63 Westover Road, London SW18 2RF. Tel: (01) 874 4806.
Angola	34 Percy Street, London W1P 9FQ. Tel: (01) 637 1945.	87 Jermyn Street, London SW1Y 6JD. Tel: (01) 839 5743.
Antigua & Barbuda	Antigua House, 15 Thayer Street, London W1M 5DL. Tel: (01) 486 7073.	Eastern Caribbean High Commission, 10 Kensington Court, London W8 5DL. Tel: (01) 937 9522.
Argentina	c/o Brazilian Embassy, 111 Cadogan Gardens, London SW3 1RQ. Tel: (01) 730 7173.	50-53 Hans Place, London SW1X 0LB. Tel: (01) 584 1701.
Australia	4th Floor, Heathcoat House, 20 Savile Row, London W1X 1AE. Tel: (01) 434 4371.	Australia House, Strand, London WC2B 4LA. Tel: (01) 379 4334.

Austria	18 Belgrave Mews West, London SW1X 8HU. Tel: (01) 235 3731.	18 Belgrave Mews West, London SW1X 8HU. Tel: (01) 235 3731.
Bahamas	23 Old Bond Street, London W1X 4PQ.	10 Chesterfield Street, London W1X 8AH. Tel: (01) 408 4988.
Bahrain	98 Gloucester Road, London SW7 4AU. Tel: (01) 370 5132.	98 Gloucester Road, London SW7 4AU. Tel: (01) 370 5132.
Bangladesh	28 Queens Gate, London SW7 5JA. Tel: (01) 584 0081.	28 Queens Gate, London SW7 5JA. Tel: (01) 584 0081.
Barbados	263 Tottenham Court Road, London W1P 9AA. Tel: (01) 636 9448.	263 Tottenham Court Road, London W1P 9AA. Tel: (01) 636 9448.
Belgium	Premier House, 2 Gaytor Road, Harrow, Middx HA1 2XU. Tel: (01) 861 3300	103 Eaton Square, London SW1W 9AB. Tel: (01) 235 5422.
Belize	West India Committee, 48 Albermarle Street, London W1X 4AR. Tel: (01) 629 6355.	15 Thayer Street, London W1M 3LD. Tel: (01) 486 7073
Benin	125-9 High Street, Edgware, Middlesex HA8 7HS. Tel: (01) 951 1234.	125-9 High Street, Edgware, Middlesex HA8 7HS. Tel: (01) 951 1234.
Bermuda	9-10 Savile Row, London W1X 2BL. Tel: (01) 734 9822.	6 Burnstall Street, London SW3 3ST. Tel: (01) 734 8813/4.
Bolivia	106 Eaton Square, London SW1W 9AD. Tel: (01) 235 4255.	106 Eaton Square, London SW1W 9AD. Tel: (01) 235 4255.
Botswana	6 Stratford Place, London W1N 9AE. Tel: (01) 499 0031.	6 Stratford Place, London W1N 9AE. Tel: (01) 499 0031.
Brazil	15 Berkeley Street, London W1 5AE. Tel: (01) 499 0877.	6 Deanery Street, London W1Y 5LH. Tel: (01) 499 7441.
British Virgin Islands	48 Albemarle Street, London W1X 4AR. Tel: (01) 629 6355.	26 Hockerill Street, Bishops Stortford CM23 2DW. Tel: (0279) 54969.

Bulgaria	18 Princes Street, London W1R 7RE. Tel: (01) 499 6988.	186-8 Queens Gate, London SW7 5HL. Tel: (01) 584 9400.
Burkina Faso	150 Buckingham Palace Road, London SW1W 9SA. Tel: (01) 730 8141.	150 Buckingham Palace Road, London SW1W 9SA. Tel: (01) 730 8141.
Burma (Myanmar)	19a Charles Street London W1X 8ER. Tel: (01) 499 8841.	19a Charles Street, London W1X 8ER. Tel: (01) 499 8841.
Burundi		Square Marie-Louise 46, 1040 Brussels, Belgium. Tel: 010-322-230-4535.
Cameroon	84 Holland Park, London W11 3SB. Tel: (01) 727 0771.	84 Holland Park, London W11 3SB. Tel: (01) 727 0771.
Canada	Canada House, Trafalgar Square London SW1Y 5BJ. Tel: (01) 629 9492.	Macdonald House, 38 Grosvenor Street, London W1X 0AA. Tel: (01) 629 9492.
Cape Verde Islands		Avenida do Restello 33, 1400 Lisbon, Portugal. Tel: 010-3511 613400.
Cayman Islands	Hambleton House, 17B Curzon Street, London W1Y 7FE. Tel: (01) 493 5161.	Hambleton House, 17B Curzon Street, London W1Y 7FE. Tel: (01) 493 5161.
Central African Republic		20 Boulevard de Montmorency, 75016 Paris, France. Tel: 010-331-4224-42-56.
Chad		65 Rue Belles Feuilles, 75016 Paris, France. Tel: 010-331-4553-36-75.
Chile	12 Devonshire Street, London W1N 2DS. Tel: (01) 580 6392.	12 Devonshire Street, London W1N 2DS. Tel: (01) 580 6392.
China	4 Glentworth Street, London NW1 5PG. Tel: (01) 935 9427.	31 Portland Place, London W1N 3AG. Tel: (01) 636 1835.

Colombia	Suite 10, 140 Park Lane, London W1Y 3DF. Tel: (01) 493 4565.	Suite 10, 140 Park Lane, London W1Y 3DF. Tel: (01) 493 4565.
Congo		37 bis Rue Paul Valery, 75016 Paris, France. Tel: 010 331-500-60-57.
Cuba	167 High Holborn, London WC1V 6PA. Tel: (01) 240 2488.	15 Grape Street, London WC2H 8DR. Tel: (01) 836 7618.
Cyprus	213 Regent Street, London W1R 8DA. Tel: (01) 734 9822.	93 Park Street, London W1Y 4ET. Tel: (01) 499 8272.
Czechoslovakia	17-9 Old Bond Street, London W1X 3DA. Tel: (01) 734 9822.	28 Kensington Palace Gardens, London W8 4QY. Tel: (01) 727 3966.
Denmark	Sceptre House, 169-73 Regent Street, London W1R 8PY. Tel: (01) 734 2637.	55 Sloane Street, London SW1X 9SR. Tel: (01) 235 1255.
Djibouti		Ambassade de Djibouti, 26 Rue Emile Menier, 75016 Paris, France. Tel: 010-331-47-27-4922.
Dominica	1 Collingham Gardens London SW5 0HW. Tel: (01) 370 5194.	1 Collingham Gardens, London SW5 0HW. Tel: (01) 370 5194.
Dominican Republic	6 Queens Mansions, London W6 7EB. Tel: (01) 602 1885.	Flat 2, 103 Lexham Gardens, London W8 6JN. Tel: (01) 370 3231.
Eastern Caribbean (Montserrat, St Lucia, St Kitts, Nevis, St Vincent, the Grenadines)	15b Thayer Street, London W1M 5LS. Tel: (01) 486 9119.	10 Kensington Court, London W8 5DL. Tel: (01) 937 9522.
Ecuador		3 Hans Crescent, London SW1X 0LN. Tel: (01) 584 2648.
Egypt	168 Piccadilly, London W1Y 9DE. Tel: (01) 493 5282.	19 Kensington Palace Gardens Mews, London W8 4QL. Tel: (01) 229 8818.

El Salvador	Flat 9, Welbeck House, 62 Welbeck Street, London W1M 7HB.	Flat 9, Welbeck House, 62 Welbeck Street, London W1M 7HB. Tel: (01) 486 8182.
Equatorial Guinea		6 Rue Alfred de Vigny 20, 75008 Paris, France. Tel: 010-331-47-66-4433.
Ethiopia	17 Princes Gate, London SW7 1PZ. Tel: (01) 589 7212.	17 Princes Gate, London SW7 1PZ. Tel: (01) 589 7212.
Fiji	52-4 High Holborn, London WC1V 6RL. Tel: (01) 242 3131.	34 Hyde Park Gate, London SW7 5BN. Tel: (01) 584 3661.
Finland	66 Haymarket, London SW1Y 4RF. Tel: (01) 839 4048.	38 Chesham Place, London SW1X 8HW. Tel: (01) 235 9531.
France	178 Piccadilly, London W1V 0AL. Tel: (01) 491 7622.	College House, 29-31 Wrights Lane, London W8 5SH. Tel: (01) 937 1202.
Gabon	48 Kensington Court, London W8 5DB. Tel: (01) 937 5282.	48 Kensington Court, London W8 5DB. Tel: (01) 937 5285.
Gambia	57 Kensington Court, London W8 5DG. Tel: (01) 937 6316.	57 Kensington Court, London W8 5DG. Tel: (01) 937 6316.
East Germany	c/o Berolina Travel, 20 Conduit Street, London W1R 9TD. Tel: (01) 629 1664.	34 Belgrave Square, London SW1X 8Q2. Tel: (01) 235 4465.
West Germany	Nightingale House, 65 Curzon Street, London W1Y 7PE. Tel: (01) 495 3990.	23 Belgrave Square, London SW1X 8PZ. Tel: (01) 235 5033.
Ghana	13 Belgrave Square, London SW1X 8AR. Tel: (01) 285 4142.	38 Queens Gate, London SW7 5HR. Tel: (01) 584 6311.
Gibraltar	Arundel Great Court, 179 The Strand, London WC2R 1EH. Tel: (01) 836 0777.	Arundel Great Court, 179 The Strand, London WC2R 1EH. Tel: (01) 836 0777.

Greece	195-7 Regent Street, London W1R 8DL. Tel: (01) 734 5997.	1a Holland Park, London W11 3TP. Tel: (01) 727 8040.
Grenada	1 Collingham Gardens, London SW5 0HW. Tel: (01) 373 7808.	1 Collingham Gardens, London SW5 0HW. Tel: (01) 373 7808.
Guatemala		13 Fawcett Street, London SW10 9HN. Tel: (01) 351 3042.
Guinea-Bissau		Rua de Alcolena 17, 1400 Lisbon, Portugal. Tel: 010-3511-615371.
Guinea Republic		24 Rue Emile Menier, 751016 Paris, France. Tel: 010-331-553-7225.
Guyana	3 Palace Court, Bayswater Road, London W2 4LP. Tel: (01) 229 7684.	3 Palace Court, Bayswater Road, London W2 4LP. Tel: (01) 229 7684.
Haiti	55 Park Lane, London W1Y 3LB. Tel: (01) 409 3115.	33 Abbots House, St Mary Abbots Terrace, London W14 8NU. Tel: (01) 602 3194.
Honduras	47 Manchester Street, London W1M 5PB. Tel: (01) 486 3380.	47 Manchester Street, London W1M 5PB. Tel: (01) 486 3380.
Hong Kong	125 Pall Mall, London SW1Y 5EA. Tel: (01) 930 4775.	6 Grafton Street, London W1X 3LB. Tel: (01) 499 9821.
Hungary	c/o Danube Travel, 6 Conduit Street, London W1R 9TG. Tel: (01) 493 0263.	35b Eaton Place, London SW1X 8BY. Tel: (01) 235 2664.
Iceland	c/o Icelandair, 73 Grosvenor Street, London W1X 9DD. Tel: (01) 499 9971.	1 Eaton Terrace, London SW1W 8EY. Tel: (01) 730 5131.
India	7 Cork Street, London W1X 2AB. Tel: (01) 437 3677.	India House, Aldwych, WC2B 4NA. Tel: (01) 836 8484.
Indonesia	70/1 New Bond Street, London W1Y 9DE. Tel: (01) 629 0862.	157 Edgware Road, London W2 2HR. Tel: (01) 499 7661.

Iran		50 Kensington Gardens, London W8 5DD. Tel: (01) 937 5225.
Iraq	c/o Iraqi Airways, 4 Lower Regent Street, London SW1. Tel: (01) 930 1155.	21 Queens Gate, London SW7 5JG. Tel: (01) 584 7141.
Ireland	Ireland House, 150/1 New Bond Street, London W1Y 0AQ. Tel: (01) 497 3201.	17 Grosvenor Place, London SW1X 7HR. Tel: (01) 235 7171.
Israel	18 Great Marlborough Street, London W1V 1AF. Tel: (01) 434 3651.	15 Old Court Place, London W8 4QB. Tel: (01) 937 8050.
Italy	1 Princes Street, London W1A 7RA. Tel: (01) 408 1254.	38 Eaton Place, London SW1X 8AN. Tel: (01) 235 9371.
Ivory Coast		2 Upper Belgrave Street, London SW1X 8BJ. Tel: (01) 235 6991.
Jamaica	Jamaica House, 50 St James Street, London SW1A 1JT. Tel: (01) 493 3647.	50 St James Street, London SW1A 1JT. Tel: (01) 499 8600.
Japan	167 Regent Street, London W1R 7FD. Tel: (01) 734 9638.	46 Grosvenor Street, London W1X 0BA. Tel: (01) 493 6030.
Jordan	217 Regent Street, London W1 3DD. Tel: (01) 437 9465.	6 Upper Phillimore Gardens, London W8 7HB. Tel: (01) 937 3685.
Kenya	13 New Burlington Street, London W1X 1FH. Tel: (01) 839 4477.	45 Portland Place, London W1N 4AS. Tel: (01) 636 2371.
South Korea	Vogue House, 1 Hanover Square, London W1R 9RD. Tel: (01) 408 1591.	4 Palace Gate, London W8 5NF. Tel: (01) 581 3330.
Kuwait	46 Queens Gate, London SW7 5HR. Tel: (01) 589 4533.	46 Queens Gate, London SW7 5HR. Tel: (01) 589 4533.
Laos		5 Palace Green, London W8 4QA. Tel: (01) 937 9519.

Lebanon	90 Piccadilly, London W1V 9PA. Tel: (01) 409 2031.	15 Palace Garden Mews, London W8 4RB. Tel: (01) 727 6696.
Lesotho	10 Collingham Road, London SW5 0NR. Tel: (01) 373 8581.	10 Collingham Road, London SW5 0NR. Tel: (01) 373 8581.
Liberia	Pembridge Place, London W2 4XB. Tel: (01) 221 1036.	21 Princes Gate, London SW7 1QB. Tel: (01) 589 9405.
Luxembourg	36-7 Piccadilly, London W1V 9PA. Tel: (01) 434 2800.	27 Wilton Crescent, London SW1X 8SD. Tel: (01) 235 6961.
Malawi	52 High Holborn, London WC1V 6RL. Tel: (01) 409 2031.	33 Grosvenor Street, London W1X 0DE. Tel: (01) 491 4172.
Malaysia	57 Trafalgar Square, London WC2 5DJ. Tel: (01) 930 7932.	45 Belgrave Square, London SW1X 8QT. Tel: (01) 235 8033.
Mali		487 Avenue Molière, B0160, Brussels, Belgium. Tel: 010-322-345-7589.
Malta	Suite 207, College House, London W8 5SH. Tel: (01) 938 1140.	Suite 207, College House, Wrights Lane, London W8 5SH. Tel: (01) 938 1140.
Mauritius	23 Ramillies Place, London W1A 3BF. Tel: (01) 439 4461.	32/3 Elvaston Place, London SW7 5NW. Tel: (01) 581 0294.
Mauritania		89 Rue de Cherche Midi, 75006 Paris, France. Tel: 010-331-548-2388.
Mexico	60-1 Trafalgar Square, London WC2N 5DS. Tel: (01) 734 1058.	8 Halkin Street, London SW1X 7DW. Tel: (01) 235 6393.
Monaco		4 Audley Square, London W1Y 5DR. Tel: (01) 629 0734.
Mongolia	7 Kensington Court, London. Tel: (01) 937 0150.	7 Kensington Court, London W8 5DL. Tel: (01) 937 0150.

Morocco	174 Regent Street, London W1R 6HB. Tel: (01) 437 0073/4.	49 Queens Gate Gardens, London SW7 5NE. Tel: (01) 581 5001.
Mozambique		Avenue de Berna no. 7, 1000 Lisbon, Portugal. Tel: 010-3511-771747.
Nepal	12a Kensington Palace Gardens, London W8 4QU. Tel: (01) 229 6231.	12a Kensington Palace Gardens, London W8 4QU. Tel: (01) 229 6231.
Netherlands	143 New Bond Street, London W1Y 0QS. Tel: (01) 499 9367.	38 Hyde Park Gate, London SW7 5DP. Tel: (01) 584 5040.
New Zealand	New Zealand House, 80 Haymarket, London SW1Y 4QT. Tel: (01) 930 8422.	
Nicaragua	8 Gloucester Road, London SW7 4PP. Tel: (01) 584 4365.	8 Gloucester Road, London SW7 4PP. Tel: (01) 584 4635.
Niger		154 Rue de Longchamps, 75116 Paris, France. Tel: 010-331-504-8060.
Nigeria	9 Northumberland Avenue, London WC2N 5BX. Tel: (01) 839 1244.	56-7 Fleet Street, London EC4Y 1JU. Tel: (01) 353 3776.
Norway	20 Pall Mall, London SW1Y 5NE. Tel: (01) 839 6255.	25 Belgrave Square, London SW1X 8QD. Tel: (01) 235 7151.
Oman	44a Montpelier Square, London SW7 5DN. Tel: (01) 584 6782.	44a Montpelier Square, London SW7 5DN. Tel: (01) 584 6782.
Pakistan	35 Lowndes Square, London SW1X 9JN. Tel: (01) 235 2044.	35 Lowndes Square, London SW1X 9JN. Tel: (01) 235 2044.
Panama	24 Tudor Street, London EC4Y 0AY. Tel: (01) 353 4792.	24 Tudor Street, London EC4Y 0AY. Tel: (01) 353 4792.
Papua New Guinea	14 Waterloo Place, London SW1R 4AR. Tel: (01) 930 0922.	14 Waterloo Place, London SW1R 4AR. Tel: (01) 930 0922.

Paraguay	Braemer Lodge, Cornwall Gardens, London SW7 4AW. Tel: (01) 937 1253.	Braemer Lodge, Cornwall Gardens, London SW7 4AW. Tel: (01) 937 1253.
Peru	52 Sloane Street, London SW1X 9SP. Tel: (01) 235 6867.	52 Sloane Street, London SW1X 9SP. Tel: (01) 235 6867.
Philippines	199 Piccadilly, London W1V 9LE. Tel: (01) 439 3481.	1 Cumberland House, Kensington High Street, London W8 4QE. Tel: (01) 937 3646.
Poland	Polorbis Travel, 82 Mortimer Street, London W1N 7DE. Tel: (01) 637 4971.	73 New Cavendish Street, London W1N 7RB. Tel: (01) 636 4533.
Portugal	New Bond Street House, 1-5 New Bond Street, London W1Y 0NP. Tel: (01) 493 3873.	3rd Floor, Silver City House, 62 Brompton Road, London SW3 1BJ. Tel: (01) 581 8722.
Qatar	115 Queens Gate, London SW7 5LP. Tel: (01) 581 8611.	115 Queens Gate, London SW7 5LP. Tel: (01) 581 8611.
Romania	77-81 Gloucester Place, London W1H 3PG. Tel: (01) 935 8590.	4 Palace Green, London W8 4QD. Tel: (01) 937 9667.
Rwanda		Avenue De Fleurs 1, B-1150, Brussels, Belgium. Tel: 010-322-763-0702.
Sao Tome		Avenue Brugmann 42, 1060 Brussels, Belgium. Tel: 010-322-347-5375.
Saudi Arabia	30 Belgrave Square, London SW1X 8QB. Tel: (01) 235 0303.	30 Belgrave Square, London SW1X 8QB. Tel: (01) 235 0303.
Senegal	11 Phillimore Gardens, London W8 7OG. Tel: (01) 937 0925.	11 Phillimore Gardens, London W8 7OG. Tel: (01) 937 0925.
Seychelles	50 Conduit Street, London W1A 4PE. Tel: (01) 439 9699.	PO Box 4PE, 50 Conduit Street, London W1A 4PE. Tel: (01) 439 9699.

Sierra Leone	33 Portland Place, London W1N 3AG. Tel: (01) 636 6483.	33 Portland Place, London W1N 3AG. Tel: (01) 636 6483.
Singapore	33 Heddon Street, London W1V 9LE. Tel: (01) 437 0033.	5 Chesham Street, London SW1X 8ND. Tel: (01) 235 9067.
Somalia	60 Portland Place, London W1N 8DG. Tel: (01) 580 7148.	60 Portland Place, London W1N 3DG. Tel: (01) 580 7148.
South Africa	Regency House, 1-4 Warwick Street, London W1R 5WB. Tel: (01) 439 9661.	South Africa House, Trafalgar Square, London WC2N 5DP. Tel: (01) 839 2211.
Spain	57-8 St James Street, London SW1A 1LD. Tel: (01) 499 0901.	20 Draycott Place, London SW3 2RZ. Tel: (01) 581 5921.
Sri Lanka	52 High Holborn, London WC1V 6RL. Tel: (01) 405 1194.	13 Hyde Park Gardens, London W2 2LU. Tel: (01) 262 1841.
Sudan	308 Regent Street, London W1R 5AL. Tel: (01) 631 1785.	3-5 Cleveland Row, St James, London SW1A 1DD. Tel: (01) 839 8080.
Swaziland	58 Pont Street, London SW1X 0AE. Tel: (01) 581 4976.	58 Pont Street, London SW1X 0AE. Tel: (01) 581 4976.
Sweden	3 Cork Street, London W1X 1HA. Tel: (01) 437 5816.	11 Montagu Place, London W1H 2AL. Tel: (01) 724 2101.
Switzerland	Swiss Centre, 1 New Coventry Street, London W1V 8EE. Tel: (01) 734 1921.	16-18 Montagu Place, London W1H 2BQ. Tel: (01) 723 0701.
Syria	134 North End House. Fitzjames Avenue, London W14 OR2. Tel: (01) 602 2469.	8 Belgrave Square, London SW1X 8PH. Tel: (01) 245 9012.
Taiwan	4th Floor, Dorland House, 14-16 Regent Street, London SW1Y 4PH. Tel: (01) 930 5767.	4th Floor, Dorland House, 14-16 Regent Street, London SW1Y 4PH. Tel: (01) 930 5767.

Tanzania	77 South Audley Street, London W1Y 5TA. Tel: (01) 499 7727.	43 Hertford Street, London W1Y 7TF. Tel: (01) 499 8951.
Thailand	9 Stafford Street, London W1X 3FE. Tel: (01) 499 7679.	29-30 Queens Gate, London SW7 5JB. Tel: (01) 589 2857.
Togo	30 Sloane Street, London SW1X 9NE. Tel: (01) 235 0147.	20 Wellington Court, 116 Knightsbridge, London SW1 7PJ. Tel: (01) 584 1948.
Tonga	New Zealand House, 12th Floor, Haymarket, London SW1Y 4TE. Tel: (01) 839 3287.	New Zealand House, 12th Floor, Haymarket, London SW1Y 4TE. Tel: (01) 839 3287.
Trinidad & Tobago	20 Lower Regent Street, London SW1Y 4PH. Tel: (01) 839 7155.	42 Belgrave Square, London SW1X 8NT. Tel: (01) 245 9351.
Tunisia	7a Stafford Street, London W1X 3PG. Tel: (01) 499 2234.	29 Princes Gate, London SW7 1QG. Tel: (01) 584 8117.
Turkey	1st Floor, 170-3 Piccadilly, London W1V 9DD. Tel: (01) 734 8681.	Rutland Lodge, Rutland Gardens, London SW7 1BW. Tel: (01) 589 0360.
Turks & Caicos	West India Committee, 48 Albemarle Street, London W1X 4AR. Tel: (01) 629 6355.	West India Committee, 48 Albemarle Street, London W1X 4AR. Tel: (01) 629 6355.
Uganda	Uganda House, 58-9 Trafalgar Square, London WC2N 5DX. Tel: (01) 839 5783.	Uganda House, 58-9 Trafalgar Square, London WC2N 5DX. Tel: (01) 839 5783.
UAE	48 Princes Gate, London SW7 2QA. Tel: (01) 589 3434.	48 Princes Gate, London SW7 2QA. Tel: (01) 589 3434.
USSR	Intourist, 319 Marsh Wall, Isle of Dogs, London E14 9FJ. Tel: (01) 538 8600.	5 Kensington Palace Gardens, London W8 4QS. Tel: (01) 229 3215.
USA	22 Sackville Street, London W1X 1DE. Tel: (01) 439 7744.	Visa Branch, 5 Upper Grosvenor Street, London W1A 2JB. Tel: (01) 499 3443.

US Virgin Islands	25 Bedford Square, London WC1B 3HG. Tel: (01) 637 8481.	
Uruguay	48 Lennox Gardens, London SW1X 0DL. Tel: (01) 589 8835.	48 Lennox Gardens, London SW1X 0DL. Tel: (01) 589 8835.
Venezuela	1 Cromwell Road, London SW7 2HR. Tel: (01) 584 4206.	56 Grafton Way, Bello Lodge, London W1P 5LB. Tel: (01) 387 6727.
Vietnam	12-4 Victoria Road, London W8 5RD. Tel: (01) 937 1912.	12-4 Victoria Road, London W8 5RD. Tel: (01) 937 1912.
Yemen Arab Republic	Yemen Airways, 5-6 Cork Street, London W1X 1PB. Tel: (01) 434 3926.	41 South Street, London W1Y 5PD. Tel: (01) 629 9905.
Yemen People's Democratic Republic	57 Cromwell Road, London SW7 2ED. Tel: (01) 584 6607.	57 Cromwell Road, London SW7 2ED. Tel: (01) 584 6607.
Yugoslavia	143 Regent Street, London W1R 7LB. Tel: (01) 493 1188.	7 Lexham Gardens, London W8 5JU. Tel: (01) 370 6105.
Zaire	26 Chesham Place, London SW1X 8HH. Tel: (01) 235 6137.	26 Chesham Place, London SW1X 8HH. Tel: (01) 235 6137.
Zambia	163 Piccadilly, London W1V 9DE. Tel: (01) 493 0848.	2 Palace Gate, London W8 5NG. Tel: (01) 589 6655.
Zimbabwe	Colette House, 52-5 Piccadilly, London W1V 9AA. Tel: (01) 629 3955.	Colette House, 52-5 Piccadilly, London W1V 9AA. Tel: (01) 629 3955.

Appendix 2
Budget Travel Guidebooks

While there are hundreds of guidebooks on the market, the following are probably most suitable for independent travellers on tight budgets.

LONELY PLANET GUIDEBOOKS

Shoestring Guides

South-East Asia	Brunei, Burma (Myanmar), Hong Kong, Indonesia, Macau, Malaysia, Papua New Guinea, Philippines, Singapore, Thailand.
West Asia	Afghanistan, Bangladesh, Bhutan, India, Iran, Maldives, Nepal, Turkey, Pakistan, Sri Lanka, Middle East.
North-East Asia	China, Hong Kong, Japan, Korea, Macau, Taiwan.
South America	The USA–Mexico border to Tierra del Fuego.
Africa	

Travel Survival Kits:

Alaska, Australia, Baja California, Bali and Lombok, Bangladesh, Burma (Myanmar), Canada, Chile and Easter Island, China, Colombia, East Africa, Ecuador and the Galapagos Islands, Egypt and Sudan, Fiji, Hong Kong, Macau and Canton, India, Indonesia, Japan, Jordan and Syria, Kashmir, Ladakh and Zaskar, Kenya, Korea and Taiwan, Mexico, Malaysia, Singapore and Brunei, New Zealand, Pakistan, Papua New Guinea, Peru, Philippines, Rarotonga and the Cook Islands, Sri Lanka, Thailand, Tahiti and French Polynesia, Tibet, Turkey, West Africa, Yemen.

Other Lonely Planet Publications:

Bushwalking in Papua New Guinea	Travel with Children
Ecuador and the Galapagos Islands	Trekking in the Indian Himalaya
Kathmandu and the Kingdom of Nepal	Trekking in the Nepal Himalaya
	Tramping in New Zealand

Phrasebooks for: China, Indonesia, Nepal, Papua New Guinea, Sri Lanka, Thailand, Tibet.

ROUGH GUIDES

Amsterdam and Holland
Brittany and Normandy
China
Crete
Eastern Europe
France
Greece
Hungary
Kenya
Mexico

Morocco
New York
Paris
Peru
Portugal
Scandinavia
Spain
Tunisia
Yugoslavia

BRADT PUBLICATIONS

These are aimed mainly at walkers and backpackers.

Backpacker's Africa: West and Central
Backpacker's Africa: East and South
Guide to Madagascar
Guide to Mauritius
No Frills Guide to Sudan
Zimbabwe and Botswana
Backpacking in Chile and Argentina

Backpacking in Mexico and Central
  America
Backpacking in Peru and Bolivia
Backpacking in Venezuela, Colombia
  and Ecuador
Backpacker's Greece
South American River Trips
  (2 volumes)

Contact Bradt Publications, 41 Nortoft Road, Chalfont St Peter, Buckinghamshire SL9 0LA (Tel: (02407) 3478) for up-to-date price list.

FROMMER PUBLICATIONS

$-A-Day Series

Australia on $25 a Day
Eastern Europe on $25 a Day
England on $30 a Day
Europe on $30 a Day
Greece on $30 a Day
Hawaii on $50 a Day
India on $25 a Day
Ireland on $30 a Day
Israel on $30 and $35 a Day

Mexico on $20 a Day
New York on $50 a Day
New Zealand on $40 a Day
Scandinavia on $50 a Day
Scotland and Wales on $40 a Day
South America on $30 a Day
Spain and Morocco on $40 a Day
Turkey on $25 a Day
Washington DC and Historic Virginia
  on $40 a Day

Dollarwise Guides

Alaska
Austria and Hungary
Belgium, Holland and Luxembourg
Bermuda and the Bahamas
California and Las Vegas
Canada
Caribbean

Japan and Hong Kong
Mid-Atlantic States
New England
New York State
Northwest (USA)
Portugal, Madeira and the Azores
Skiing in Europe

Cruises (Alaska, Caribbean, Mexico, Hawaii, Panama, Canada, USA)
Egypt
England and Scotland
Florida
France
Germany
Italy

Skiing USA (East)
Skiing USA (West)
South Pacific
Southeast and New Orleans
Southwest (USA)
Switzerland and Liechtenstein
Texas

LET'S GO BUDGET GUIDES

California and Hawaii
Europe
France
Great Britain and Ireland
Greece
Israel and Egypt

Italy
Mexico
Pacific and Northwest USA, Western Canada and Alaska
Spain, Morocco and Portugal
USA

FODOR'S GREAT TRAVEL VALUE SERIES

This is a series aimed at the budget traveller and includes such titles as *Mexico* and *Europe*. Prices range between approximately £6.95 and £10.95.

Appendix 3
Further Reading

How to plan your trip cheaply
C Dodwell, *An Explorer's Handbook* (Hodder and Stoughton)
J Hatt, *The Tropical Traveller* (Pan)
M Shales, *The Traveller's Handbook* (Wexas)

Regional Guides

Europe
S Calder, *Traveller's Europe Survival Kit* (Vacation Work)
F & B Delthil, *Good Value Guide to Paris* (Aurum)
M Dubin, *Greece On Foot* (Cardec)
C Evans, *On Foot Through Europe* series (Quill)
M Turner, *Pauper's Paris* (Pan)
Also
Collins Independent Guides, such as *Spain* by H Debelius
Youth Hostel Association Guides to the Benelux countries, Switzerland,
    Denmark, Spain and Portugal, West Germany and Norway.

Africa
K Naylor, *Africa: The Nile Route* (Lascelles)

South America
A Greenberg, *Brazil On Your Own* (Harrap Columbus)
The South American Handbook (Trade and Travel Publications)

North America
M Turner, *Pauper's New York* (Pan)

Asia
J D Bisignani, *Japan Handbook* (Moon Publications)
B Dalton, *Indonesia Handbook* (Moon Publications)
S Griffith, *Traveller's Survival Kit to the East* (Vacation Work)
D Jenkins, *Student Guide to Asia* (AUS)

Middle East
H Greenberg, *Israel on Your Own* (Harrap Columbus)

Bargain travel spots
W Newlands, *Where To Go* (Associated Magazines Ltd)

When to find a bargain
R Hicks and F Schultz, *The Out-Of-Season Holiday Guide* (Helm)

Carrying money the cheap way
W Ellington, *Travel Money* (Rosters)

Guarding against calamities
The Guide To Caravan Insurance (The Caravan Insurance Centre, Bakers of Cheltenham, Molloy House, Parabola Road, Cheltenham, Gloucestershire GL50 3AH (Tel: (0242) 528844)). A summary leaflet published for free.
Holiday Insurance (The Association of British Insurers, Aldermary House, Queen Street, London EC4N 1TT (Tel: (01) 248 4477)). A summary leaflet published for free.

Kitting yourself out for your trip
K Ward, *Discovering Backpacking* (Shire)

Keeping safe and well on a budget
Dr R Dawood, *How To Stay Healthy Abroad* (Oxford Paperbacks)
C Mooney, *Healthy Holiday Guide* (Headway Publications)
Dr A C Turner, *The Traveller's Health Guide* (Lascelles)
Well Away, The British Medical Journal's Guide for travellers. Available from The Publishing Department, BMJ, Tavistock Square, London WC1H 9JR.
While You're Away: The Traveller's Guide to Health. Leaflet SA41 published for free by The Department of Health Leaflets Unit, PO Box 21, Stanmore, HA7 1AY (Tel: (0800) 555777).

How to choose the best value package deal
The Dollarwise Guide to Cruises (Frommer)
C France, *Macmillan and Silk Cut Ski Resort Guide* (Macmillan)
C and P Foreht, *Dollarwise Guide to Skiing Europe* (Frommer)
C Gill, *The Good Skiing Guide* (The Consumers Association and Hodder and Stoughton)
The Good Resort Guide (Pickfords)
C Leocha and W Walker, *Ski Europe* (World Leisure)
G McDonald and K Wood, *Holiday Coastal Spain* (Fontana)
G McDonald and K Wood, *Holiday Greece* (Fontana)
G McDonald and K Wood, *Holiday Portugal* (Fontana)
G McDonald and K Wood, *Holiday Turkey* (Fontana)
G McDonald and K Wood, *Holiday Yugoslavia* (Fontana)
R Mead, *European Ski Resort Guide* (Batsford)
Travelmate (Berlitz and W H Smith). A series of guidebooks.

How to reach your destination without busting your budget
AA Camping and Caravanning Guide (AA)

F Barrett, *Daily Telegraph Consumer's Guide to Air Fares* (Daily Telegraph Publications)

D Brydon, *Africa Overland: A Route And Planning Guide* (Lascelles)

S Calder, *Europe: A Manual For Hitchhikers* (Vacation Work)

C Evans, *On Foot Through Europe* series (Quill)

G Ferguson, *Europe by Eurail*

K Libura, *Autoroutes To The Sun* (Le Guide)

G McDonald and K Wood, *Europe By Train* (Fontana)

G McDonald and K Wood, *Round The World Air Guide* (Fontana)

RAC Camping and Caravanning Guide: Europe (RAC)

RAC Continental Motoring Guide (RAC)

R Strauss, *Trans-Siberian Rail Guide* (Bradt)

R Van der Plas, *Bicycle Touring Manual* (Bicycle Books)

K Welsh, *Hitch-Hiker's Guide to Europe* (Fontana)

K and T Whitehill, *Europe By Bike* (The Mountaineers)

Travelling around without busting your budget
AA Traveller's Guide To Europe (AA)

B Coo, *Scenic Rail Guides To Western Canada, Central And Atlantic Canada*

N Crane, *Cycling In Europe* (Pan)

L Demery, *Japan By Rail*

G Ferguson, *Europe By Eurail*

I Fistell, *America By Train*

P Fraenkal, *Overland* (David and Charles)

S Madron, *Cycling In France* (G Philip)

G McDonald and K Wood, *Europe By Train* (Fontana)

R Neillands, *Walking Through France* (Collins)

H Phillips, *Caravanning Through France* (Michelin)

T Plant, *Train Journeys In Viking Lands*

R Strauss, *Trans-Siberian Rail Guide* (Bradt)

Staying away for next to nothing
Bed And Breakfast (North America) (Fodor)

The Best Bed And Breakfast USA And Canada (UKHM Publcations)

Camping And Caravanning In Europe (AA Publications)

Camping And Caravanning In France (Michelin)

Caravan And Camp In France (Mirador)

Sarah Lloyd, *An Indian Attachment* (Futura)

H Rubinstein, *The Good Hotel Guide* (CA/Hodder and Stoughton)

Cost-cutting ways to eat and drink abroad
V Harris, *Edible Italy* (Ebury Press)
F Kynacopoulos and T Salmon, *Self-Catering In Greece* (Croom Helm)
C and C Stewart, *Self-Catering In Spain* (Croom Helm)
A Williams, *Self-Catering In The Alps* (Croom Helm)
C Wright, *Self-Catering In Portugal* (Croom Helm)

Seeing the cities at minimum cost
Thomas Cook Railpass Guide (Thomas Cook)

Bargain-hunting overseas
A Shopper's Guide To The Caribbean (Frommer)

Working your keep
J Bedford, *Kibbutz Volunteer* (Vacation Work). Lists all the kibbutzim
    with details of their crop.
Directory Of Work And Study In Developing Countries (Vacation Work)
Susan Griffith, *Work Your Way Around The World* (Vacation Work)
Susan Griffith And Sharon Legg, *Au Pair And Nanny's Guide To
    Working Abroad* (Vacation Work)
International Directory Of Voluntary Work (Vacation Work)
C Jackson, *A Student's Guide To Europe* (Conservatives In The
    European Parliament, available free from 2 Queen Annes Gate,
    London SW1H 9AA (Tel: (01) 222 0411))
R Jones, *How To Get A Job Abroad* (Northcote House)
R Jones, *How To Teach Abroad* (Northcote House)
David Leppard, *Directory Of Jobs And Careers Abroad* (Vacation
    Work)
V Pybus and C James, *Working In Ski Resort Europe* (Vacation Work)
H Sewell, *Volunteer Work* (Central Bureau For Educational Visits And
    Exchanges)
Summer Employment Directory Of The USA (Writers Digest Books)
Time Between (Careers Research And Advisory Centre, Bateman Street,
    Cambridge CB2 1LZ)
D Woodworth, *Summer Jobs Abroad* (Vacation Work)

Turning your travels into hard cash
M Campbell, *Writing About Travel* (A&C Black)
Freelance Photographer's Market Handbook (BFP Books)
J Hedgecoe, *Practical Landscape Photography* (Ebury Press)
D and S Kirkpatrick, *Improve Your Holiday Photography* (Hare
    Fountain Books)
C Semenzato, *Photographing Places* (Century Publishing)
L P Zobel, *The Travel Writer's Handbook* (Writer's Digest Books)

Special deals for special people

AA Traveller's Guide For The Disabled (AA)

M Davies, N Jansz, L Longrigg and L Montefiore, *Half The Earth: Women's Experiences Of Travel Worldwide* (Pandora/RKP)

Family Travel (Including Baby Travel) (St John's Wood Press)

Dr D Haslan, *Travelling With Children* (Futura)

Holidays And Travel Abroad (RADAR)

Holidays For Disabled People (RADAR)

Hyde, Pook and York, *Holidays With Kids* (Piatkus)

The International Travel Guide (Vegetarian Society). Covers most places from Argentina to Zimbabwe.

D and M Lees, *Travel In Retirement* (Helm)

M and G Moss, *The Handbook For Women Travellers* (Piatkus)

A Sangster, *The Vegetarian Traveller* (Thorsons). Deals mainly with Europe.

M Wheeler, *Travel With Children* (Lonely Planet)

Also

Berlitz produce a series of travel books in large print.

Appendix 4
IATA Currency Codes

IATA codes have been used to identify currencies around the world throughout the text. A list of codes appears below:

ADH	United Arab Emirates Dirham		Caledonia, French Polynesia)	FOR	Hungarian Forint
AFG	Afghanistan Afghani	CHP	Chilean Peso	FRB	Burundi Franc
AFL	Netherlands Antilles Guilder	CID	Cayman Islands Dollar	HKD	Hong Kong Dollar
				IKR	Icelandic Krona
AFR	Comoro Islands Franc, Togo Franc	CKR	Czechoslovakian Koruna	INR	Indian Rupee
				IRD	Iraqi Dinar
		COP	Colombian Peso	IRI	Iranian Rial
AKZ	Angolan Kwanza	COR	Nicaraguan Cordoba	IRL	Irish Punt
ALD	Algerian Dinar	CRC	Costa Rican Colon	JAD	Jamaican Dollar
ARA	Argentinian Austral	CVE	Cape Verde Escudo	JOD	Jordanian Dinar
ARI	Saudi Arabian Riyal	CYL	Cyprus Pound	JYE	Japanese Yen
AUD	Australian Dollar	DFL	Dutch Guilder	KES	Kenyan Shilling
AUS	Austrian Schilling	DFR	Djibouti Franc	KIP	Laotian Kip
BAL	Panamanian Balboa	DKK	Danish Krone	KUD	Kuwaiti Dinar
BDD	Barbados Dollar	DMK	West German Mark	LBD	Libyan Dinar
BDT	Bangladeshi Taka	DOP	Dominican Republc Peso Oro	LEK	Albanian Quindarke
BED	Bermudan Dollar			LEL	Lebanese Pound
BFR	Belgian Franc	DRA	Greek Drachma	LEM	Honduran Lempira
BHD	Bahraini Dollar	DYD	South Yemeni Dinar	LEU	Romanian Leu
BHT	Thai Baht	ECD	East Caribbean Dollar (used in Dominica, Grenada, Montserrat, St Kitts, Nevis, St Lucia, St Vincent)	LEV	Bulgarian Lev
BOB	Bolivian Bolivano			LFR	Luxembourg Franc
BRD	Brunei Dollar			LID	Liberian Dollar
BSD	Bahamian Dollar			LIT	Italian Lira
BTP	Botswanan Pula			LSL	Lesotho Maloti
BUR	Burman Kyat			MAL	Maltese Pound
BZD	Belize Dollar			MAR	Mauritian Rupee
CAD	Canadian Dollar	EGL	Egyptian Pound	MDH	Moroccan Dirham
CFA	CFA Franc (used in Benin, Burkina Faso, Cameroon, Central African Republic, Chad, Congo, Ivory Coast, Equatorial Guinea, Gabon, Mali, Niger, Senegal and Togo)	ETB	Ethiopian Birr	MEP	Mexican Peso
		FIB	Fijian Dollar	MOG	Mauritanian Ougiuya
		FIM	Finnish Markka		
		FFR	French Franc	MRK	East German Mark
		GAD	Gambian Dalasi	MVR	Maldives Rupee
		GHC	Ghanian Cedi	MWK	Malawi Kwacha
		GNF	Guinean Franc	MZM	Mozambican Metical
		GOU	Haitian Gourde	NER	Nepalese Rupee
		GUA	Paraguay Guarani	NGK	Papua New Guinea Kina
CFP	French Pacific Franc (used in New	GWE	Guinea-Bissau Peso	NGN	Nigerian Naira
		GYD	Guyanese Dollar	NIS	Israeli Shekel
		FMG	Madagascar Franc	NOK	Norwegian Krone

NTD	New Taiwan Dollar	SAT	Western Samoan Dollar	TTD	Trinidad and Tobago Dollar
NUP	New Uruguayan Peso				
NZD	New Zealand Dollar	SBD	Solomon Islands Dollar	TUD	Tunisian Dinar
PAR	Pakistani Rupee			TUG	Mongolian Tugrik
PEI	Peruvian Inti	SEK	Swedish Krona	TUL	Turkish Lira
PHP	Philippine Peso	SER	Seychelles Rupee	UGS	Ugandan Shilling
PTE	Portugese Escudo	SFL	Suriname Guilder	UKL	Pound Sterling
PTS	Spanish Peseta	SFR	Swiss Franc	USD	American Dollar
QUE	Guatemalan Quetzal	SID	Singapore Dollar	VBO	Venezuelan Bolivar
QRI	Qatari Ryal	SLE	Sierra Leone Leone	VUV	Vanuatu Vatu
REM	North Yemeni Riyal	SLR	Sri Lankan Rupee	WON	South Korean Won
RGT	Malaysian Ringgit	SOM	Somalian Shilling	YUD	Yugoslavian Dinar
RIO	Omani Rial	STD	Sao Tomean Dobra	ZAI	Zairan Zaire
RMB	Chinese Ren Min Bi	SUL	Sudanese Pound	ZAR	South African Rand
ROU	USSR Rouble	SYL	Syrian Pound	ZLO	Polish Zloty
RPA	Indonesian Rupiah	SZL	Swaziland Lilangeni	ZMK	Zambian Kwacha
SAC	El Salvador Colon	TAS	Tanzanian Shilling	ZWD	Zimbabwean Dollar

Appendix 5
True Cost of Travelling Checklist

Before you commit yourself to a holiday you need to work out its total cost to ensure you have taken into account all the extras which can easily force up the apparent price by hundreds of pounds. Below is a list of items you may have to pay for when you go abroad. Frequent travellers will already have many of them, in which case their costs are immediately reduced. First-time backpackers or skiers, however, may have to pay out more than they originally expected to equip themselves for their trip. Even package holidaymakers usually need some extras, like sun-tan cream, beach towels and adaptors for their hairdriers.

The list is aimed at the 'average' traveller, and does not take into account all the extra items long distance drivers, cyclists and motorcyclists need to take with them. Whether you buy new clothing for your holiday or not is very much a matter of personal preference, so the only items listed are those you may need to buy because of the different climate at your holiday destination. You might think things like shampoo superfluous, but in some parts of the world such luxuries are almost unobtainable so long-term travellers may need to stock up.

How to use the checklist

Place a tick against each item you will need to buy or pay for. Then write the actual or approximate cost in the space provided—the text should help you with prices for many things. Add it all together and you should have a realistic idea how much your dream journey is going to cost you.

Category of cost	Item	Cost
Before You Go	Passport	....
	Passport photos	....
	Visas	....
	Insurance	....
	Commission on currencies and travellers cheques	....
	ISIC or YIEE card	....
	Membership of clubs	....
	Language tuition	....
Vaccinations	Cholera	....
	Typhoid	....
	Polio	....
	Tetanus	....
	Yellow fever	....
	Gamma globulin	....
	Rabies	....

	Meningitis	....
	Others	....
Prescription Medication	Antibiotics	....
	Chloroquine tablets	....
	Lomotil or other stomach settlers	....
	Personal necessities	....
	Prepayment certificate	....
Non-prescription Medication	Paludrine tablets	....
	Antihistamine cream	....
	Insect repellent	....
	Antiseptic cream	....
	Iodine or other water purifiers	....
	Calamine lotion	....
	Painkillers	....
	Others	....
First aid	Plasters	....
	Bandages	....
	Sterile needles	....
	Eye drops	....
	Scissors	....
	Salt tablets	....
	Vitamin pills	....
Equipment	Suitcase	....
	Backpack	....
	Tent and mallet	....
	Camping stove	....
	Camping lamp	....
	Sleeping bag	....
	Sheet sleeping bag	....
	Foam or inflatable mattress	....
	Cooking utensils	....
	Others	....
Clothing (items you may need to buy especially)	Sandals	....
	Walking shoes or boots	....
	Thick socks	....
	Waterproofs	....
	Cotton clothing	....
	Hat	....
	Swimming costume	....
	Others	....
Skiers	Goggles	....
	Thermal underwear	....
	Gloves	....
	Salopettes	....
	Anorak	....

	Moon boots	....
	Skis and poles	....
	Ski boots	....
	Photos for lift pass	....
	Others	....
Photography	Camera body	....
	Zoom lens	....
	Wide angle lens	....
	Silica gel	....
	Filters	....
	Lead bag	....
	Camera case	....
	Films	....
	Developing and printing	....
Sundries	Toothpaste	....
	Soap	....
	Shampoo	....
	Multifit plug	....
	Razor	....
	Adaptor plug	....
	Tampax or other sanitary protection	....
	Sun-tan cream	....
	Sun glasses	....
	Lip salve	....
	Beach towel	....
	Condoms	....
	Toilet rolls	....
	Alarm clock	....
	Guidebook	....
	Map	....
	Phrasebook	....
	Dictionary	....
	Reading matter	....
	Note pad and pens	....
	Airmail paper and envelopes	....
	Calculator	....
	Personal stereo and cassettes	....
	Binoculars	....
	Washing kit	....
	Sewing kit	....
	Plastic bags	....
	Torch and batteries	....
	Penknife	....
	Knife, fork and spoon	....
	Mug and bowl	....
	Water bottle	....
	Water filter	....

	Malaria coils	....
	Mosquito net	....
	Matches	....
	Money belt or neck purse	....
	Padlock	....
	Small bag or daypack	....
	Compass	....
	International Driving Permit	....
	Small gift items	....
	Souvenirs	....
Package Holiday	Basic cost	....
	Room supplements	....
	Board supplements	....
	Flight supplements	....
	Tips	....
Transport	Rail and coach cards	....
	Transport to and from the port, airport or station	....
	Transport to and from destination	....
	Internal flights	....
	Internal train fares	....
	Internal bus fares	....
	Internal ferry fares	....
	Taxi fares	....
	Tips	....
	Hired transport	....
	Fuel	....
	Others	....
Accommodation	YHA Membership	....
	Cost per person, per night	....
	Single supplements	....
	Tips	....
	Others	....
Food and Drink	Average daily budget	....
	Tips	....
Taxes	Airport	....
	Port	....
	Trekking permits	....
	Other	....
On Your Return	Commission on resale of currency and travellers cheques	....
	Interest on loans	....

Author's Updates

Inevitably while this book was going to press changes have occurred which affect its contents. To keep you as up-to-date as possible, some of them are highlighted below:

- The staggering changes in **Eastern Europe** mean that more people will be contemplating a visit now. Of course the tourist infrastructure lags way behind that in the West and the shops are notoriously bereft of almost everything. Budget accommodation is also in short supply unless you're prepared to camp or stay with local families. You're often better off buying a package rather than trying to make your own arrangements. However, public transport is often a real bargain. The biggest gain for travellers is that the rules about changing fixed amounts of hard currency for every day of your stay are easing (see page 46). Sadly, the cost of visas remains high.

Cost of Eastern European Visas
Poland: £15 (or £20 if arranged more quickly through the tourist office).
East Germany: £5.
Hungary: £12.
Czechoslovakia: £20.
Bulgaria: £20.
Romania: £20.

The rules are likely to keep changing for some time. However, it's wise to arrange your visas as far ahead as you can and to double-check currency regulations before setting out. Don't leave anything to chance.

- The change of government in **Nicaragua** in April 1990 has put in doubt the continuation of the work brigades (see page 232). The Nicaraguan Solidarity Campaign will have the latest information.

- The situation in **Burma** (now renamed Myanmar) remains unsettled. However, some tour operators are now being allowed to run itineraries of up to two weeks instead of the traditional one.

- **Trailfinders** now has a second branch at 194 Kensington High Street, London W8 7RG (Tel: (01) 938 3939 or (01) 938 3232).

- Some branches of **Thomas Cook** now have 'Travel by Appointment' consultancy lounges which are staffed by people with long experience both in the travel business and of travel itself. They are aimed at people planning to spend more than £650 a head, which might not sound much like budget travel. However, many long-haul trips end up in that price range so you may qualify to book an appointment to discuss all aspects of your trip, including rail tickets and overseas hotels. Cook's reserves the right to charge £25 for consultancies that don't lead to bookings.

- A new company specialising in fares to **Central and South America** has opened. South American Experience Ltd offers very competitive prices and is at Garden Studios, 11-15 Betterton Street, Covent Garden, London WC2H 9BP. They prefer you to phone for an appointment before dropping in (Tel: (01) 379 0344).

- **Top Deck Travel** has opened a new Adventure Travel Centre at 131-5 Earls Court Road, London SW5 9RH (Tel: (01) 370 4555). This is an excellent place to go for advice on many of the long-haul overland tour operators. Top Deck also specialises in discounted worldwide air fares. Deckers, its travellers' club at the same premises, has an excellent noticeboard for collecting up-to-date information.

- **International Student Identity Cards** are now issued in virtually unforgeable plastic form (see page 195).

- Since the air disaster over Lockerbie in 1988 **airport security** has tightened. It is very doubtful whether you should either try and use the return portion of someone else's air ticket (see page 157-8) or ask anyone else to carry your excess baggage for you any more (see page 218).

- The London travel magazine *LAW* (see page 239) has ceased publication.

- **Travellers** has opened two 'one stop travel accessory shops' in Bristol. If they are successful other branches will probably appear countrywide. They bring together a wide range of suitcases and all those bits and bobs like luggage labels, mosquito nets and travel sickness pills that travellers need to buy. However, they aim for holidaymakers rather than long distance travellers, so don't expect to buy backpacks or sleeping bags there. The range of books and maps is also narrower than in specialist shops. Most of the smaller items come in sophisticated packaging which is pretty, but bumps up the price. You may be better off sticking with the usual outdoor/camping shops.

- **Waterstone's** bookshops now sell almost as many travel publications as the specialist shops.

- The **Travellers Bookshop** (see page 87) has an excellent noticeboard in its basement where travellers can exchange information or advertise for companions.

- **Yugoslavia** has recently revalued its currency. It is now difficult to buy dinars in the UK.

- **Guatemalan visas** are now issued free in the UK (see page 46).

- The UK has finally sorted out its differences with **Argentina**. Expect the London Embassy to reopen in the near future.

- British Airways has opened more **vaccination/medical advice centres** in Birmingham, Edinburgh, Glasgow, Harrow, Leicester, London (Heathrow Airport and Leicester Square), Manchester, Newport Pagnell, Nottingham, Purley, Reading and Stratford-upon-Avon. Telephone the Regent Street branch (see page 94) for addresses. In addition to the usual vaccinations British Airways also offers protection against **Japanese encephalitis**, a disease transmitted by mosquitos that have been in contact with pigs, and prevalent in rural areas of the Third World.

- Lloyds has introduced an annual **charge** for its Access cards. So far none of the other banks has followed suit but some may well do so. Watch out for differential charges; companies will soon be able to charge those paying by credit card more than those using cash or cheques.

- The clearing banks are now issuing **cheque guarantee cards** covering purchases of up to £100. Check whether you can get one; it's a distinct asset when buying travel services which often cost more than £50.

- If you think you may need to have emergency funds sent to you in the USA, Canada, Haiti, the Dominican Republic or The Netherlands try and find a local branch of an American company called **Western Union** which operates through four hundred UK newsagents and chemist's shops. A friend should take money to the local agent who will phone the details through to the London HQ. The overseas agent is then contacted and the money transmitted. The whole process can take as little as quarter of an hour. Charges start at £12 which is more expensive than an express telegraphic transfer which normally takes just a day to arrive. However, in a real emergency speed can be worth any amount of money. Western Union plans to expand its outlets both in the UK and Europe which would make it even more useful.

- Finally by the time you pick up this book all **London's telephone numbers** will have changed. Instead of prefacing numbers with 01 you will need to use 071 for Central London and 081 for Outer London. Sorry!

Index

Note that cities are indexed according to country, e.g. for Paris, read France.